The Occasional Affair

A Practical Plan for Life's Everyday Parties
by Maury Ankrum

Frederick Fell Publishers, Inc.
1403 Shoreline Way, Hollywood, Florida 33019
www.fellpub.com

First Printing 2014

ISBN 9780883912898

Library of Congress Cataloging-in-Publication Data
Ankrum, Maury,
The Occasional Affair: A Practical Plan for Life's Everyday Parties / by Maury Ankrum.
pages cm
Includes index.
ISBN 978-0-88391-289-8 (hardcover)
1. Parties--Planning. 2. Entertaining--Planning. I. Title.
GV1471.A65 2014
793.2--dc23

2014023375

Photography by Povy Kendal Atchison

Food styling and recipes by Eliza Cross

Book design by Maury Ankrum and Abbie Kozik Design, LLC

Matt – you are my anchor in this world, my buried treasure, my north star.
Love, friendship and loyalty.
My girls – you have transformed me in a thousand miraculous ways.
My parents – thank you for your inspiration and confidence.
To Povy, Eliza, Abbie and Anne thank you so much for your
brilliance, incredible talents and endless devotion.

Introduction

When I was a child, my mother never put the emphasis on Christmas gifts, in part because we didn't have a lot of money for them. Instead, she instilled something far more meaningful and intrinsic. During the holidays, my mother gifted us with time, allowing us to see and experience it in all its priceless beauty. She did this through celebration – hours and days spent together, planning, preparing, laughing, crafting, and in the end, savoring the fine form of a gathering of loved ones.

Today, I can't recall at all the gifts I unwrapped on my fifth or sixth Christmas, but I can recite verbatim the recipe for the handcrafted cookies we so diligently decorated for Santa. And these days, my mother's gift softly lingers. As I work closely with my own children, my mind wanders to vivid memories of family picnics, Thanksgiving Day talent shows, and birthday parties that were pageants of small-budget, but brilliantly creative décor and games. I smile, lost in nostalgia, even as I pass forward to my children the wonder of the moment.

My parents filled my childhood with ingenious celebrations and occasions, all the while teaching me that life's most precious gift is time spent with family and friends. With this book, I share my parents' lasting gift with you.

Table of Contents

Winter

Reflections of Christmas

Tiny footsteps, muffled whispers, the magic and nostalgia of Christmas is warmed with familiar faces and endless trays of hors d'oeuvres.

Pages 8 – 25

Arctic Freeze

The temperature just dropped another 10 degrees, but inside the fire is crackling, the mugs are steaming, the desserts are delectable and the laughter is contagious.

Pages 26 – 41

Send My Love

Intimate, secretive and seductive. A love story that started the day you met and continued through many houses, jobs, children and years. Reminisce with classic comfort food and fine wine.

Pages 42 – 57

Spring

Enchanted Easter Eve

The eggs have all been accounted for, the chocolate bunnies have been carefully unwrapped and sampled, the pristine white dresses spotted from a morning of curiosity and wonderment. Let the crisp and seasonal brunch be a continuation of giggles and memories.

Pages 58 – 71

Nesting

To build and protect, to cradle, nurture and love, is to nest. Welcome the newest branch on the family tree with a springtime lunch and tea among friends and family.

Pages 72 – 87

Portrait of A Lady

It's with unwavering grace and beauty that others see her… It's with unconditional love and compassion that you know her. A Mother's Day lunch that honors the most important woman in your life.

Pages 88 – 103

Summer

A Suitable Gentleman
He taught you how to live by showing you how.
Celebrate your father's undoubted love and devotion to
his family with a plentiful and bold coffee breakfast.   Pages 104 – 119

Chasing Stars
Childhood memories of dancing fireflies, and nights spent
watching for falling stars is the inspiration for friends and
family to come together for an Independence Day celebration.   Pages 120 – 135

A Night with the Stars
"This is the beginning of a beautiful friendship" and so it is...
with an outdoor movie, succulent food, and a box of Juju bees,
it's a night with the stars under the stars.   Pages 136 – 151

Autumn

Tasting in Tuscany
The sun sets against the Tuscan sky as the table comes alive
with a rustic Italian feast and a grape-stopping escapade.
This wine tasting dinner is sure to bring about a few laughs
and memories.   Pages 152 – 165

Formally Frightful
The moon laughs at the dark shadows, hollowing wind and
distant cackling. Tonight let the unsettlings of Halloween
be explored over the heartier flavors of autumn.   Pages 166 – 179

Birds of a Feather
The walls keep the blowing snow and cold out, the fire warms
our hands and hearts, the smell of hot apple muffins and
a homemade breakfast are just a few basic gifts on a day
dedicated to gratitude and appreciation.   Pages 180 - 195

Resources

Pages 197 - 216

Few occasions can match the joy, the wonder and the anticipation that is Christmas. It appeals to our senses and emotions: the scents of pine and cinnamon, the welcome of a warm fire, the serenity of watching the falling snow, and the precious laughter of loved ones blended with the soft strains of "Silent Night."

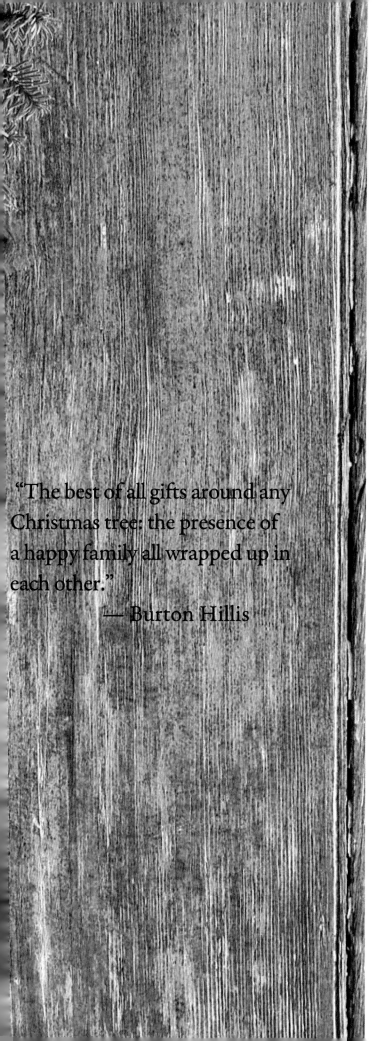

"The best of all gifts around any Christmas tree: the presence of a happy family all wrapped up in each other."

— Burton Hillis

AT A GLANCE

Theme:
Crystal Christmas

❧

Setting:
Home—formal dining room or living room

❧

Mood:
Elegant, sophisticated and classic
iridescent crystals, pale silks, unexpected lights
and a day rooted in traditions

❧

Colors:
Pale amethyst, polished silver and chandelier white

❧

Flowers:
Evergreen sprays and white winterberries (real and faux),
crystal floral sprays (in a variety of styles)

❧

Tastes:
Perfectly paired, globally influenced hors d'oeuvres. Small portions of warm
comfort food that enhances a celebratory mood and merry atmosphere.

❧

Sounds:
A custom playlist that features the much-loved holiday classics, from the
unparalleled pianist Michel Legrand's in Noel! Noel!! Noel!!! Or animate your
affair with *Michael Buble's Christmas*, a smooth, big-band approach to
some well-known favorites. Turn up *If On A Winter's Night* and let vocalist
Sting softly warm your winter night. Or alternate Faith Hill's strong vocals
in *Joy to the World. The Ultimate Relaxation Christmas Album* is perfect
orchestra background music for when you've had enough of
the typical holiday music.

❧

Experience:
A hired horse-drawn carriage (or several Pedi cabs) to guide your guests
on a neighborhood tour of festive lights.

Vary it: Implore your guests to gather up and bring several tree ornaments
they no longer need. As the evening winds down, invite them to bundle
up and be off with you to decorate a small pine at the neighborhood park.
Savor the moments with friends, fun and possibly even a few choruses of
your favorite carols. *Remember to remove the items right after the holiday.*

Simplify it: Serve up some hot buttered rum to sip while leading your
guests in a few renditions of those holiday tunes. Put your voice and
heart into it—carols always sound best when sung with friends.

"Until one feels the spirit of Christmas, there is no Christmas. All else is outward display—so much tinsel and decorations. For it isn't the holly, it isn't the snow. It isn't the tree, not the firelight's glow. It's the warmth that comes to the hearts when the Christmas spirit returns again."

– Anonymous

The festivities will begin at sunrise, first with the sound of tiny footsteps and muffled whispering. Their giggles wake us as they scurry down the stairs, anxious to see if their letters to Santa were answered. The glow of their tiny faces and twinkle in their eyes are the true magic of the season. But for now, the world is quiet and calm. Everyone sleeps as I shuffle around the house, tending to last-minute preparations for the day ahead. Our tradition is set, unchanged through the years: the kids wake early and open the first few gifts with reckless abandon. The rest we save for a more-civilized display when the grandparents arrive. Throughout the day, friends and family trickle in and out, enjoying a trademark drink and countless trays of appetizers. This is a joyous close to a year we've shared with the ones we treasure most in our worlds.

Through these traditions we find comfort and solace, for it is our loved ones who make the holidays so special.

'TIS THE SEASON

"Life is a series of moments. Each moment should be welcomed in joy and relinquished in joy."

– Deepak Chopra

The Invitation

Hand-letter the invitation on a large white or colored gift tag. Tie the tag to a small, but graceful piece of real mistletoe. (You can substitute with faux if needed.) The mistletoe message carries a sentiment of its own, and recipients can hang it in their homes. Gently place the mistletoe in a small, cardboard jewelry box, sealed with clear tape and proper postage for mailing (see Resources).

Vary it

Try tearing a page from an antique-looking book and glue it to a piece of card-stock paper. Attach a crystallized or beaded (sprig) of garland and raffia ribbon with a little glue (see Resources). Hand-letter party information on the back. Use stock paper for the envelope.

Simplify it

Grab a box of pre-made Christmas invitations in colors that correspond to your party's, or some with a crystal or snow motif. Hand-letter a personal note with time, date and your warm wish that the recipient will come.

A Seasonal Setting

Design your table's "look" with dishes of white, lavender or any
combination of the two.

Create your own placemats with old encyclopedias from your local antique
shop. Tear out the pages and tape them together vertically and horizontally,
so no two are alike.

Under a vertically folded napkin, tuck another torn book sheet with a listing
of the evening's hors d'oeuvres and a fresh stem of a small pine branch.

"What an enormous magnifier is tradition! How a thing
grows in the human memory and in the human imagination,
when love, worship, and all that lies in the human heart, are
there to encourage it."

—Thomas Carlyle

Trees

Why have one large tree when you can have several petite ones? This is a smart option if you have limited space or funds. These smaller trees are very affordable and easy to store (see Resources).

Dripping, dripping and dripping with crystals and lights— someone once said you can never over-decorate a Christmas tree. Subjective though that is, it fits in this case. Crystals bedazzle in proportion to their numbers, with lights and light spheres glittering and glinting and reflecting sheer radiance.

Try a bit of whimsy by adding a child's low-wattage chandelier, small vintage birdcages, and feathered white birds. Or make a sentimental montage of cages and nests enhanced with children's rattles, christening cups and silver baby spoons.

Crystal and Kids

Little hands at the holidays are for opening gifts and helping to make cookies, not for handling real crystal. The majority of our ideas entail faux-crystal plastic, available at any large retailer or craft store. None of the ornaments are too small nor breakable. So make those tykes feels special on this holiday, even as you reduce the chance of accidents. Let the adults toast the day away with real crystal, but give the kids plastic and enjoy.

Essential Elements of Entertaining

Calming Family Feuds

Ah, the joy of the holidays, a time when those you love most can gather for feasting and fun. Until the gauntlet is thrown, that is. Suddenly, the tension is tight, and words can grow hotter than your buffet burner. It's so true that holidays can be hard. Expectations peak, and bringing together friends and family, who might otherwise not mix, can bring on intense anxiety. Lower the pressure by planning ahead, preparing in advance, and understanding realistically what you can do—and want to do.

On the twelfth day of Christmas, my true love gave to me:

12 Fights a-Brewing;
11 Words Exchanging;
10 Zings-a-Leaping;
9 Grandpas Shouting;
8 Guests Embarrassed;
7 Aunts-a-Meddling;
6 Kids-a-Quarreling;
5 Drunken Songs;
4 Sisters Miffed;
3 Drinks Tossed;
2 In-laws Mad;
1 Drunken Uncle
And a Partridge in a Pear Tree

Why not make this the year you break the stress tradition? Here's how: Anticipate and act.

Identify the problem

Think back. What set off the previous clashes? Is it a person who misbehaved, or a sensitive subject that reared its ugly head? Is it, for example, Uncle Fred who drinks too much and stirs the pot? Or did Aunt Emma's estate leave more simmering tempers than heirs? Are these a pattern?

Tackle the problem ahead of time

Don't wait until words, or worse, hors d' oeuvres are flying—confront potential problems ahead of time. If it's always the same relative causing commotion, I recommend reaching out to that person. Try to meet in a neutral place. Remember—compliment-criticism-compliment. Gently explain that you love that person and enjoy having him at your gatherings. But this one behavior is hurtful to you. Ask what you can do to make the situation proceed differently. Together, try to devise a plan to catch the situation before it escalates and make gatherings easier on everyone, including him.

If it's a particular topic that continues to appear at every gathering, do the same. Talk it out ahead of time with those most likely to bring it up. If there are several people involved, consider writing a letter. No need to accuse or point fingers—simply state that all of you are aware of the situation and the emotions involved. Suggest that in the near future, everyone try to meet to work through the problem(s), but not now. Then tell them you'd like to enlist their help to keep peace at this time of year. Ask if they can shelve the topic for the holidays, if only to bring out what you all remember best about the family. Don't hesitate to remind them of the children involved, and that holidays are about those children. If anyone genuinely feels he cannot make it through an evening without raising the issue, ask if he would be more comfortable taking a rain check for the event.

Change the trigger

If alcohol helps escalate holiday tempers, consider limiting it and serving a homemade (non-alcohol) drink instead. This lets you control liquor tactfully. If the problem is location, consider a change in venue, particularly if reminders are at your home—for example, maybe seeing Aunt Emma's baby grand piano will overwhelm frayed nerves. Ask if someone else would like to host the dinner this year or look into a restaurant with a private room.

Change yourself

Accept responsibility for your role if you have one, and try to see the situation from others' perspectives. Vow to do everything possible to change the dynamics of this year's gathering, but at the same time, accept what you can and cannot control. Forgive.

All families are dysfunctional on some level, but they got you to where you are now. Only you can let that relationship continue to hurt or to help you. If nothing else, holiday disaster stories are usually funny after time has passed, and will provide for some great stories at your next dinner party.

The tablecloth is actually a king-size duvet cover in pale silk lavender. The color provides a strong contrast between the wood, crystal and dishware.

Bedeck your mantel with faux pine and crystal garland. Candlestick holders support an array of light spheres, while stocking holders fasten graceful rows of crystal garland and crystal-ball ornaments.

For this occasion, more is better—with an abundance of candles and crystals reflecting each other.

Set aside a petite table specifically for desserts. Often the most decorative parts of a meal, these sweet objets d' art deserve recognition of their own.

As a collector of old books, I'm always looking for ways to flaunt my vast collection. Nestled inside a glass dome, these books make a stunning display with a little pine, some painted nuts and a small strand of battery-operated lights (see Resources).

"There is no ideal Christmas; only the one Christmas you decide to make as a reflection of your values, desires, affections traditions." —Bill McKibben

GIFTS

A time-honored tradition, gift-wrapping builds on the surprise and anticipation of the present inside. It is part of the gift and as such, deserves the same effort you put into picking the perfect present. Your loved one will undoubtedly notice and appreciate such care.

Continue the party's theme and color scheme in your wrapping paper—particularly important if you set your gifts under the tree prior to Christmas Day.

To wrap these gifts, I carried over the theme of old, reclaimed encyclopedia pages (and lots of tape), as well as solid brown, white and silver paper for a sophisticated impact. I love using lots of ribbon, floral accents, beads, bulbs and ornaments—there is no end to the possibilities. And believe it or not, this will simplify your holiday and minimize waste (see Resources).

History of Saint Nicholas

How did a kindly old bishop, known for his work on behalf of the poor, transform over the years into a red-suited, fur-trimmed old elf with the "broad face and a round little belly" depicted in the beloved tale, "The Night Before Christmas."

Like many good stories, it's a small part fact, a large part fiction and a blend of numerous cultures, traditions and speculation.

The original St. Nicholas was born around 280 A.D., near Myra (now Turkey), according to History.com. Legend says he devoted much of his life to working with the sick and less fortunate, including donating his entire inherited wealth to the poor. One story has many differing details, but describes how St. Nicholas discovered a family so badly off that the three daughters faced being sold into slavery or prostitution. To help and to not embarrass the family with charity, St. Nick walked by the home one night and anonymously threw a bag of coins into an open window. They landed in the stockings the girls had hung to dry after washing—a happen-stance that would lead to the traditional Christmas stocking.

According to Catholic history websites, St. Nicholas became bishop of Myra, was imprisoned for his preaching, was released, and worked with the poor for the rest of his life before dying in 343 AD. He was canonized by the Catholic Church sometime in the fourth century, and became a patron saint of children, merchants, pawnbrokers, bakers, brides and grooms, and several other groups, depending upon whom you ask. Nicholas was one of the most popular saints throughout the centuries, with most sources noting his charity and generosity. Some say those qualities led to his connection as a gift-giving saint who comes on his feast day in December.

His popularity grew through the years, including during periods of religious persecution, and his reputation for generosity stayed especially strong in Holland. Thus the traditions that grew around St. Nick arrived in the New World with the Dutch in the late eighteenth century, History.com writes. The Dutch pronunciation of his name, *Sinter Klaas*, slowly evolved into the Santa Claus we know today in the United States.

Our American Christmas traditions likewise have a long and intricate history. In 1659, for example, the Massachusetts Bay Colony legislature banned Christmas celebrations, "For preventing disorders arising in several places within this jurisdiction, by reason of some still observing such festivals as were superstitiously kept in other country's, to the great dishonor of God & offence of others." Lawbreakers were hit with a five-shilling fine. It was repealed twenty-two years later, but Christmas' revelry continued to irk Puritans, who viewed it as papal idolatry or alternately, paganism, writes *American Heritage* magazine's website.

Still, Christmas celebrations began to take hold in the colonies. In the 1809 book, *A History of New York,* Washington Irving designated St. Nicholas as the patron saint of New York, encouraging the Sinter Klaas story, writes History.com. The 1820s saw the first retailers appealing to Christmas shoppers, and newspapers in 1841 began special Christmas advertising sections.

In 1822, Clement Clarke Moore wrote "An Account of a Visit from St. Nicholas" for his daughters, which later became "The Night Before Christmas." His depiction of Santa and flying reindeer took hold, and in 1881, Thomas Nast, a political cartoonist, turned Moore's words into the image we have today of Santa Claus. History.com adds that Nast also brought to us the ideas of a red-suited Santa at the North Pole with Mrs. Claus and working elves.

In 1890, department store entrepreneur James Edgar decided to dress up as Santa Claus in his Brockton, Mass., location, beginning the tradition of the department store Santa. "Within days trains from as far away as Boston and Providence brought families and their children to downtown Brockton to see Santa," according to the Plymouth County Registry of Deeds Notable Land Records Collection.

Finally, where would tradition—not to mention Santa—be without Rudolph the Red-Nose Reindeer? Robert L. May, a copywriter for Montgomery Ward, wrote the story of Rudolph for a 1939 advertisement as part of an effort to draw more traffic to the store during the Great Depression. The story sold more than 2.5 million copies that year. In 1949, May's friend, Johnny Marks, wrote a song about Rudolph that was recorded by singer Gene Autry, History.com says, and the rest, as they say, is history.

THE TRUEST GIFT OF GIVING

True to the generous spirit of St. Nicholas, try the gift of a charitable donation. For those loved ones fortunate enough to have no needs, consider donating in their name to a charity they support. This gift is dually meaningful— you have gifted someone less fortunate and helped a friend give to a cause he or she believes in. Usually, charities send you a gift card or certificate for your donation (but if they don't, ask for one). Box and wrap the card with the same care you would use on your other gifts. Often, I will try to find an ornament that corresponds with the charity selected. For example, if you choose a humane society, consider an animal ornament. If you gave to a children's charity, look for an ornament representing a toy or small child. This token will remind your loved one of the donation for years to come.

How to pick a charity

Most charities are set up to somehow better the world for a particular cause or group of people. They do this through donations from both public and private entities, the majority of which they promise to use toward their causes. But not all charities are as charitable or as fiscally responsible as you might wish. You can find several online watchdog sites, such as CharityNavigator.org or bbb.org/us/charity, that help explain what the charity does, who receives the help and how. These sites will also lay out the percentage of donations that are applied to administration— salaries, overhead, advertising—and how much goes directly to charitable works. A highly rated charity generally applies 80 percent or more toward its cause, with the remainder used for operations. Non profits with lower ratings generally invest half or more of donations in administration than in their respective causes. Most charities make their U.S. Internal Revenue Service Form 990s available on their websites. If they don't, ask for the past three years' forms. These valuable documents show how much the charity received in donations and government contributions, and how much it spent in salaries and overhead. And remember, smaller charities are sometimes just as generous and in many cases more so than their giant counterparts. They often work with more volunteers and have lower overhead costs.

Finally, if you're donating in a loved one's name, make sure it's a charity whose mission and values that person supports. A person's name is his reputation and cannot be donated lightly, even with the best of intentions.

Shopping List

- 1 small bunch fresh rosemary
- 4 medium, tart apples like Granny Smith
- 24 baby Yukon Gold potatoes, each about 2 inches across (2 to 3 pounds)
- 1 pound grape tomatoes
- 2 bunches fresh basil
- 1 bunch parsley
- 2 bunches green onions or 12 stalks celery
- 4 heads butter lettuce
- 2 large onions
- 1 head garlic
- 1 piece fresh ginger, about 4 inches long
- 1 small carrot
- 1 1/2 pounds large Medjool dates
- 1/2 pound candied pineapple
- 1/2 pound dried apricots
- 1/2 cup dried plums (prunes)
- 1/4 pound golden raisins
- 1/2 pound bacon
- 1/2 pound thinly sliced roast beef
- 2 pounds boneless, skinless chicken breast
- 2 pounds large shrimp
- 2 pound whole Brie cheese
- 1 pint heavy cream
- 1 8-ounce package cream cheese
- 1 pound butter
- 1 dozen eggs
- 4 ounces Parmigiano-Reggiano
- 4 ounces Colby cheese
- 6 ounces Gorgonzola cheese, crumbled
- 1 pound Ciliegine (small fresh Mozzarella balls)
- 1 loaf light rye bread
- 2 quarts pomegranate juice
- 6 750ml bottles Champagne
- 1 750ml bottle lemon-flavored vodka
- 1 small bottle bourbon or brandy
- 1 16-ounce can whole cranberry sauce
- 1 8-ounce jar orange marmalade
- 2 pounds roasted, unsalted cashews
- 1/2 pound chopped walnuts
- 1/2 pound pine nuts
- 1/4 cup blanched almonds
- 1 jar prepared horseradish
- 4 ounces Balsamic vinegar
- 1 quart clam-tomato juice, regular tomato juice or Bloody Mary mix
- 1 bottle tamari sauce or low-sodium soy sauce
- 1 bottle hoisin sauce
- 1 bottle rice wine vinegar
- 1 jar Asian chili sauce
- 2 8-ounce cans sliced water chestnuts
- 1 bottle sesame oil
- 1 jar chili paste
- 4 ounces unsweetened chocolate
- 1 small box sugar cubes
- 1 pound semisweet chocolate chips
- 1 jar small red candies
- 1 small bag green gumdrops or 1 small package green candied cherries
- 1 pound powdered sugar
- 2 sheets frozen puff pastry

The Essentials

- 24 Champagne glasses
- 24 wine glasses
- 24 low ball glasses for various drinks
- 24 coffee cups (for hot chocolate or coffee)
- 24 - 48 small plates for all the various appetizers
- 24 small plates for all the various desserts
- 24 shot glasses for shrimp shooters
- 24 place settings of cutlery, including dessert forks, knives and spoons
- 4 large serving trays for twice-baked potatoes, roast beef sandwiches, chicken lettuce wraps and baby apple strudels.
- 3 medium serving trays for gorgonzola-stuffed dates, caprese salad canapés and chocolate brownies.
- 2 cake stands or round platters for the baked brie and Christmas pudding
- 2 small bowls for rosemary cashews and chili dipping sauce
- 1 cheese knife
- Various serving cutlery for potatoes, sandwiches, dates, lettuce wraps, brownies, pudding and strudels.
- 24 napkins (have a few extra on hand)
- 1 tablecloth
- 24 napkin rings

Staples (replenish if needed)

- all-purpose flour
- granulated sugar
- dark brown sugar
- raw sugar
- cornstarch
- baking soda
- kosher salt
- regular salt
- freshly ground black pepper
- cayenne pepper
- ground nutmeg
- ground ginger
- ground cinnamon
- ground cloves
- celery salt
- milk
- extra virgin olive oil
- vanilla extract
- almond extract
- white vinegar
- Worcestershire sauce

MENU
For 24

Signature cocktail:
Pomegranate Champagne Sparklers

Appetizers:
Warm Baked Brie with Pomegranate-Cranberry
Compote and Walnuts

Twice-Baked Baby Yukon Gold Potatoes

Mini Open-Faced Roast Beef Sandwiches

Gorgonzola-Stuffed Dates with Balsamic Reduction

Caprese Salad Canapes

Shrimp Cocktail Shooters

Baby Chicken lettuce Wraps with
Sweet Chile Dipping Sauce

Desserts:
Chocolate Ganache-Frosted Brownies

Bite-sized Christmas Puddings with
Bourbon-Laced Hard Sauce

Baby Apple Strudels

The Recipes

Pomegranate Champagne Sparklers

1 sugar cube
1 ounce pomegranate juice
3 ounces Champagne

Place the sugar cube in the bottom of a champagne flute. Pour the pomegranate juice over it, then slowly add the Champagne.

Spicy Rosemary Cashews

2 pounds roasted unsalted cashews
4 tablespoons minced fresh rosemary leaves
2 tablespoon unsalted butter, melted
1 tablespoon plus 1 teaspoon dark brown sugar
1 tablespoon kosher salt, or to taste
1 teaspoon freshly ground black pepper
1 teaspoon cayenne pepper

Preheat the oven to 350 degrees F. Spread the cashews out on a large cookie sheet. Toast in the oven until warm, about 5 minutes. In a large bowl, combine the rosemary, butter, brown sugar, salt, black pepper and cayenne pepper. Thoroughly toss the warm cashews with the spiced butter and serve warm. 2 pounds.

Warm Baked Brie with Pomegranate-Cranberry Compote and Walnuts

1 16-ounce can whole cranberry sauce
1/4 cup sugar
1/4 cup pomegranate juice
1/4 teaspoon ground nutmeg
1/4 teaspoon ground ginger
1/2 teaspoon ground cinnamon
1/4 teaspoon ground cloves
2 medium tart apples like Granny Smith, peeled, cored and
  chopped
2 pound whole Brie cheese
1 cup chopped walnuts

To make compote, combine cranberry sauce, sugar, juice and spices In a large saucepan and bring to a boil over high heat, stirring once or twice. When cranberry sauce has dissolved, add the apples and reduce heat, cover and simmer 30 minutes until apples are tender. Cool briefly and use at once or refrigerate for up to three days.

To prepare the cheese, preheat the oven to 350 degrees F. Trim the rind off the top of the cheese and place it in a 10 to 11-inch round rimmed baking dish. Bake, uncovered, just until cheese begins to melt, about 15 to 20 minutes. To serve, spoon some of the warm compote over the top of the cheese and sprinkle with the chopped walnuts. 12 servings.

Twice-Baked Baby Yukon Gold Potatoes

24 baby Yukon Gold potatoes, each about 2 inches across
  (2 to 3 pounds)
2 tablespoons extra virgin olive oil
salt and freshly ground black pepper
1/2 cup sour cream
1/4 cup heavy cream
6 slices bacon, cooked until crispy and crumbled
1/2 cup coarsely grated Parmigiano-Reggiano
1/2 cup grated Colby cheese

Heat the oven to 400 degrees F. Put the potatoes on a large baking sheet and toss with the olive oil. Sprinkle with salt and pepper and bake the potatoes until they feel perfectly tender when pierced with a skewer, 20 to 25 minutes. Remove from the oven and let rest until cool enough to handle, about 10 minutes. Increase the oven temperature to 450 degrees F.

Cut the potatoes in half lengthwise and carefully hollow out each potato using a small spoon (a serrated grapefruit spoon works great!), transferring the potato mixture to a large bowl. Mash the potato with a masher or a fork, then combine it with the the crème fraîche or sour cream, cream, and salt and pepper to taste. Add the bacon and Parmigiano-Reggiano cheese and stir just until combined.

Using a small spoon, fill the hollowed potatoes with this mixture and sprinkle with the Colby cheese. Return the potatoes to the oven and bake until the filling heats through, 8 to 10 minutes. Serve warm. 48 appetizers.

Mini Open-Faced Roast Beef Sandwiches

9 slices light rye bread, toasted
1/2 cup sour cream
1 tablespoon prepared horseradish
salt and freshly ground black pepper to taste
1/2 pound thinly sliced roast beef
parsley for garnish

Preheat the oven to 350 degrees F. Cut the crusts from the bread and cut each bread slice into 4 squares, about 1-1/2 by 1-1/2 inches. Arrange the toast squares on a baking sheet and bake for 5 minutes, or until firm and dry. Cool on a wire rack.

Combine the sour cream, horseradish and salt and pepper. Cut the roast beef into 36 strips, each about 3 inches long by 1 inch wide. Fold each strip in half and arrange on a toast square. Top the roast beef with a small spoonful of the horseradish cream and garnish with fresh parsley. 36 appetizers.

Gorgonzola-Stuffed Dates with Balsamic Reduction

1/2 cup Balsamic vinegar
1 teaspoon sugar
6 ounces Gorgonzola cheese, crumbled
4 ounces cream cheese, room temperature
1 1/2 pounds large Medjool dates

In a small saucepan, combine the Balsamic vinegar and sugar and stir until the sugar is dissolved. Heat the mixture over medium-high heat and bring to a slow boil. Cook, stirring often, until the mixture is reduced by 1/3 and begins to get syrupy. Remove from heat and cool. (May be prepared up to three days ahead and refrigerated.)

In a small bowl, mash together the Gorgonzola and cream cheeses and stir until combined. Split the dates lengthwise just halfway through. Spoon some of the cheese filling in each date, arrange on a platter and serve with the Balsamic reduction on the side. Makes about 36 pieces.

Caprese Salad Canapes

1 pound Ciliegine (small fresh Mozzarella balls)
48 fresh basil leaves
1 pound grape tomatoes
extra virgin olive oil
salt and pepper

Use a toothpick to layer a Mozzarella ball, basil leaf and grape tomato. Arrange the canapés on a platter, drizzle lightly with olive oil and sprinkle with salt and pepper. Makes about 48 pieces.

Shrimp Cocktail Shooters

24 large shrimp (13 to 15 per pound), cooked and cooled
2 1/2 cups clam-tomato juice (or substitute regular tomato juice or your favorite Bloody Mary mix)
6 ounces (3/4 cup) lemon-flavored vodka
1 tablespoon horseradish (or more or less to suit your taste)
1 tablespoon Worcestershire sauce
1/2 teaspoon celery salt
1/2 teaspoon freshly ground black pepper
24 green onions or celery sticks for garnish

Peel and devein the shrimp, leaving the tails intact; reserve. Combine the tomato juice, vodka, horseradish, Worcestershire sauce, celery salt and pepper, and mix well. Divide the mixture among 24 shot glasses, filling each not quite half full. Arrange the shrimp in the glass and garnish with green onions or celery sticks. 24 servings.

Baby Lettuce Wraps with Sweet Chile Dipping Sauce

For the lettuce wraps:
2 heads butter lettuce, leaves separated
2 teaspoons extra virgin olive oil
1 pound boneless, skinless chicken breast, cut in 1/2 inch cubes
1 large onion, chopped
3 cloves garlic, minced
1 tablespoon tamari sauce (or substitute low-sodium soy sauce)
1/4 cup hoisin sauce
2 teaspoons peeled, minced fresh ginger
1 tablespoon rice wine vinegar
2 teaspoons Asian chili sauce
1 8-ounce can sliced water chestnuts, drained and chopped
1/2 cup pine nuts
2 teaspoons sesame oil

For the dipping sauce:
1 cup sugar
3/4 cup white vinegar
1/2 cup water
1 small carrot, peeled and fine grated
1 clove garlic, peeled and minced
1 tablespoon corn starch
1 tablespoon water
1 tablespoon chili paste
1/4 teaspoon salt

Heat the oil in a large skillet over medium heat, and cook the chicken, stirring occasionally to prevent sticking, until chicken is opaque. Add onion and cook for 2 minutes, stirring often. Add the garlic, tamari or soy sauce, hoisin sauce, ginger, vinegar and chili sauce. Continue cooking until chicken is browned and onion is translucent. Add water chestnuts and pine nuts and cook for 2 more minutes. Drizzle with sesame oil, stir and remove from heat. Cool for five minutes. (May be prepared up to one day ahead and refrigerated.)

To make the dipping sauce, combine the sugar, vinegar and water in a medium saucepan. Cook over medium high heat until the sugar dissolves and add the carrot and garlic. Bring to a boil and cook for 3 minutes. Combine the cornstarch and 1 tablespoon water in a small dish and whisk to combine. Slowly add to the sugar mixture and stir until combined. Add the chili paste and salt and boil for 3 minutes longer, or until mixture is shiny and thickened. Makes 2 cups. (May be prepared one day ahead and refrigerated.)

To serve, tear 12 large lettuce leaves in half and spoon a generous portion in the center of each. Gently roll up and arrange on a platter. 24 appetizers; double recipe for 48 pieces.

Chocolate Ganache-Frosted Brownies

2 (1-ounce) squares unsweetened chocolate
1/2 cup melted butter
1 1/4 cups sugar
2 eggs
2 teaspoons vanilla
pinch salt
1/2 cup flour
1/2 cup heavy cream
1 cup semisweet chocolate chips

Preheat oven to 325 degrees F and grease a 9- by 13-inch baking pan. Melt unsweetened chocolate in a large saucepan over medium heat and add melted butter. Remove from heat and stir in sugar until combined. Add eggs, vanilla and salt and beat well. Fold in flour and mix just until smooth. Spread the batter into prepared baking pan. Bake for 30-35 minutes or until a toothpick comes out clean.

To make ganache frosting, heat cream in a small pan over medium heat until simmering. Immediately remove from heat and add chocolate chips, whisking until melted and smooth. Drizzle the mixture on the brownies and smooth with a spatula. Cool and cut into squares; store in refrigerator. (Can be made one day ahead.) Makes 32 brownies.

Bite-Sized Christmas Puddings with Bourbon-Laced Hard Sauce

For the puddings
1/2 cup butter
1 cup firmly packed dark brown sugar
2 eggs
1/2 teaspoon salt
1/2 teaspoon baking soda
1/2 teaspoon almond extract
1 teaspoon vanilla
1/2 cup orange marmalade
1/2 pound candied pineapple, chopped
1/2 pound dried apricots, chopped
1/2 cup dried plums, chopped
1 3/4 cups flour
small red candies and green gumdrops or green candied
  cherries for garnish

For the hard sauce:
1 1/2 cups powdered sugar
1/2 cup butter, room temperature
2 tablespoons bourbon (or substitute brandy)

Preheat oven to 350 degrees F and grease mini muffin tins. In a large bowl, beat together butter and sugar and beat in eggs one at a time. Mix in salt, baking soda, almond extract, vanilla and marmalade.

Put pineapple, apricots and plums in a bowl and dredge in about half the flour. Add the mixture to the batter and fold in the rest of the flour. Pour batter into muffin tins and bake 10 minutes, or until puddings are lightly browned. Cool on a wire rack and remove from pan. (Can be prepared one day ahead and stored, tightly wrapped, at room temperature.)

To make the hard sauce, combine all ingredients in a small bowl and stir to blend well. (Can be made two days ahead and refrigerated.) To serve, top each pudding with a spoon of the hard sauce and decorate with red candies and green gumdrops or candied cherries cut to resemble holly leaves. Makes about 5 dozen.

Baby Apple Strudels

1/4 cup blanched almonds
1 teaspoon sugar
2 sheets puff pastry
2 tart baking apples like Granny Smith, peeled and finely sliced
2 tablespoons dark brown sugar
2 tablespoons golden raisins
1/2 teaspoon cinnamon
1/4 teaspoon nutmeg
1/3 cup milk
raw sugar, for garnish

Preheat oven to 400 degrees F. Sprinkle the almonds on a cookie sheet and bake for about 4 minutes, until lightly browned. Cool to room temperature and grind in a food processor with the sugar just until the mixture resembles coarse meal; reserve.

Line a baking tray with parchment paper. Lay 1 sheet of puff pastry on a cutting board and cut into 3 even strips. Repeat with other sheet. Cut each strip into 3 pieces to create mini squares. Lightly brush edges of pastry with milk.

Combine the apples, almond mixture, brown sugar, raisins, cinnamon and nutmeg in a bowl. Spread one-quarter of the apple mixture over 1 pastry square, allowing a 1/4 inch border at the edges. Place a square of pastry on top and crimp edges with a fork. (May be prepared ahead and refrigerated. Remove from refrigerator and hold at room temperature for 20 minutes prior to baking.) Slash tops of pastry and brush with milk and sprinkle with sugar. Repeat with remaining pastry and apple mixture. Bake for 15 to 20 minutes, or until pastry is crisp and golden. Cool to room temperature. 9 servings.

Party Timeline

6 weeks before the party:

- For holiday parties send invitations 4 to 6 weeks in advance.
- Make or purchase invitations
- Finalize guest list and mail invitations.

One Month before the party:

- Finalize the menu, including drinks (carefully selecting the food you wish to make and the food you will purchase).
- Create a look by selecting colors, mood, setting, and entertainment, if necessary.

3 weeks before the party:

- Order or gather the decorations and accessories.

2 weeks before the party:

- Make a shopping list for the food and liquor (see Shopping list).
- Order the food or any desert you do not wish to make.
- Order flowers, and consider having them delivered the day of the party.

1 week before the party:

- Assemble or purchase take-away gifts and wrap them.
- Purchase all nonperishable food and liquor (see Shopping list).
- Create a music play list or purchase CDs.

3 days before the party:

- Decorate.
- Prepare the bar with glasses and liquor.
- Assemble all the serving dishes and set up the buffet table, if using one.
- Make the Spicy Rosemary Cashews and store in a tightly covered container.

2 days before the party:

- Prepare the Pomegranate-Cranberry Compote and refrigerate.
- Prepare the Balsamic Reduction and refrigerate.
- Prepare the Hard Sauce and refrigerate.

The day before the party:

- Purchase perishable food (see Shopping list).
- Set the table.
- Pick up flowers or have them delivered.
- Prepare the filling for the Chicken Lettuce Wraps.
- Prepare the Sweet Chile Dipping Sauce.
- Prepare the Chocolate Ganache Frosted Brownies and refrigerate.
- Bake the Christmas Puddings and store tightly wrapped at room temperature.
- Prepare the Baby Apple Strudels and refrigerate.
- Make extra ice.
- Check that the bathroom is clean. Have fresh hand towels, soap and extra toilet paper on hand.

1 hour before of the party:

- Remove the Chocolate Ganache Frosted Brownies from the refrigerator and bring to room temperature.
- Bake the Baby Apple Strudels.

Prior to guests' arrival:

- Arrange food on platters.
- Turn on the music.
- Prepare the pomegranate champagne sparklers, including one for yourself!
- Light the candles.
- Enjoy!

TAKE AWAY GIFTS

The best gifts in life are the love and friendship
of those we hold close in our hearts.

A custom made CD of your favorite Christmas and holiday
songs. This is very simple by downloading songs from
I-tunes. Be sure to purchase the amount of licenses for
the amount of CD's you intend to burn.

Vary it

Think of warmth for a family who needs it. Buy four
hat-and-mitten sets (see Resources) for each guest to
donate to a local shelter.

Simplify it

Make a donation in your friends' names to the local
utility company to help with the heating bills of
those less fortunate.

"We make a living by what we get,
but we make a life by what we give."
— Winston Churchill

ARCTIC FREEZE

Each year the first fallen flakes of snow recreate the landscape, and reinvigorate the soul. The snow exposes the barren spirit and the quietness from within. Winter is a magical season, a true wonderland of sorts, a great time to reconnect sharing past memories and creating new ones.

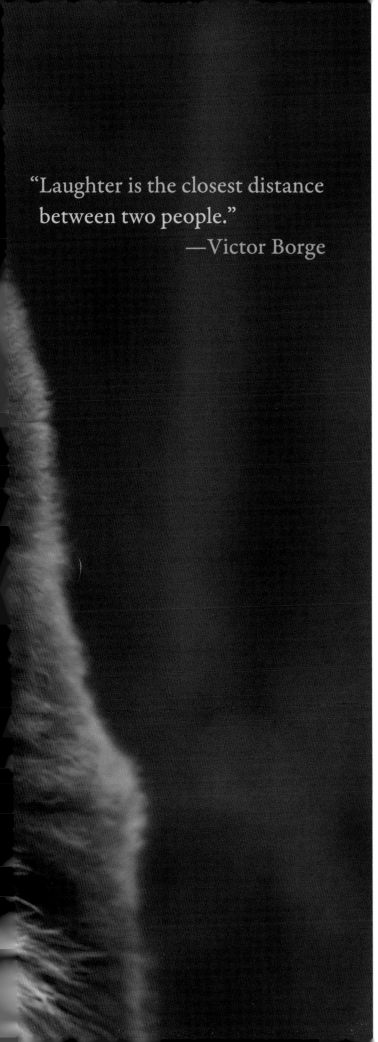

"Laughter is the closest distance between two people."
—Victor Borge

Theme:
Northern Lights

≈

Setting:
Chic, metropolitan high-rise.
Something unconventional- an unusual room in your home or
a rooftop deck (keep those faux furs on).

≈

Mood:
Sexy, Elemental, Cool, Cozy, and Sophisticated. Silky Satins and fluffy fur's,
clear crisp glassware and plenty of ice and snow looking textures.
Cold hands, warm hearts.

≈

Colors:
Ice Blue, shimmering white, twinkling silver and a spattering of Brown Furs

≈

Flowers:
White hydrangeas, white columbines, white asters and a variety of greenery

≈

Tastes:
Hot Drink and Cold Desserts. Course after course of dripping melted
chocolate, bursting sweet fruit and warm, crisp tarts and pies.

≈

Sounds:
A custom play list features a wide variety of comfortable favorites like
If On A Winter's Night by Sting. This album by world-renowned artist is a
haunting collection of carols and lullabies. Sarah McLachlan's albums
Solace or *Afterglow* are also great smooth bluesy type songs with hypnotic
lyrics. A personal favorite for almost any party is Matt Nathanson. *Some
Mad Hope* Has a romantic sound that is easy to listen to over and over.
For more traditional music, consider *"Winter Solstice* or *Hotel Café
Presents- Winter Songs*, both from various artists. Any of these are
sure to set the tone for the evening.

≈

Experience:
If you live in a location conducive – There is nothing like dog sledding.
It is an once-in-a-lifetime experience. Then meet back at your place for an
evening of desserts, laughter, and stories of a perfect day.

Vary it: Rent a snow making machine (prices are usually reduced after
Christmas). There is nothing like having a hot drink in hand while catching
snow-flakes on your tongue (even if its falsely created).
Encourage snow angles.

Simplify it: Create an outdoor bonfire. If the first two options feel a little
over the top or something you're not ready to take on, consider hosting a
unique experience with one of the many available fire pits.
Don't forget the marshmallows and hot toddies.

The temperature just dropped another 10 degrees; the wind is kicking up and blowing about a fresh dusting of new snow. I can think of little else than the piercing cold against my face as I race across the icy arctic tundra. The dogs are howling, anxious to get home to a well-deserved meal and warm bed. I too, eagerly await a night filled with overflowing mugs of hot cocoa and endless laughs among friends. So, the city is a far cry from the Alaskan terrain, but it's pretty easy to recreate the warmth and comfort that comes of steaming drinks, smell of burning pine, feel of fur (faux), glow from a crackling fire and love of friends and family. So whether your one of the luck few to stow away in a log cabin in Aspen or reside in a beautiful third floor apartment, bring the energy and invigoration from a cold arctic blizzard in with lots of candles, ice and icicle décor, a few touches of pale blue combined with rich browns and sexy silvers and a handful of furry little creatures any home can take on the cozy feel of an igloo during a blizzard.

Having your desserts laid out buffet style, optimizes the selection while adheres to the relaxed atmosphere and encourages mingling

Outside the weather
is frightful
But, inside it's
so delightful

JOIN US IN CELEBRATING OUR
ARCTIC FREEZE

DRINKS & DESSERTS
FRIDAY, JANUARY 12TH
6 TO 10 P.M.
MORGAN AND GARRET
2121 BLAKEFIELD AVE.

The Invitation

Shimmery pale blue card stock paper cut down to 5x5 sporadically stamped with one or more different snowflake stamps. Use a white or silver glitter stamp pad (found at any local craft store). Role the invitations and secure with a white ribbon. Insert invite into an empty icicle ornament (found at most craft stores and large retailers that carry Christmas ornaments-they are usually marked down after the holidays). Fill a clear plastic box half way with faux snow. Tape the top closed, attach an address label and correct postage directly to the plastic box (yes, they can be mailed as it).

Vary it

Buy a couple of clear plastic snowflake ornaments (left over from Christmas or purchased online). Attach a small card enclosure with invitation information to one of the snowflakes. Purchase a CD size mailing box or padded envelope, add a little faux snow, and mail with proper postage.

Simplify it

Purchase a pre-made holiday card featuring a winter scene or symbol (just be sure the inside is blank), write or print the pertinent information. Send with a light dusting of faux snow or white glitter. Mail with proper postage.

A SHIVERING START

So it's easier and faster to just send an e-vite, but there is a lost art in a personalized invitation. Everyone appreciates the time and thought that goes into it. Not only does it reflect your attention to detail, it shows your interest and commitment to the event. If nothing else, you can always fall back on beautiful stock invitations from your local papery. The intention is to build anticipation and intrigue.

Invite your friends to come in from the cold, take off their boots, get comfortable and settle in. These beautifully wrapped, inexpensive slippers will accomplish two things at once. Preserve your floors against the dirt and moisture as well as the infamous high heel dents. Second, is giving your friends a sense of comfort, relaxation and luxury. (You can substitute this with a fuzzy pair of socks). This little element will set the tone for the evening.

Essential Elements of Entertaining

Who makes the Cut? A guide to guest lists

A party is a great opportunity to expand your social network, by getting to know new people-as well as reconnecting with those near and dear to us. It is also a chance to create that capability among your fiends and family, by allowing them to get to know each other better.

Nothing may be as important to the outcome of a party as who you invite to it. No amount of decorations, enticing entertainment or appetizing food can or will save an event if your guests don't mesh, mingle or play nice with one another.

So here are a few tips to ensure you gather a diverse and intriguing grouping of friends and family for your next affair.

The occasion for the party largely stipulates the majority of the guests. Reunions, baby showers, and birthdays are just a few events in which you may have limited control over the attendees. However, you're not totally out of luck. My husband's birthday party is a great example; my in-laws have a hard time relating to most of our friends, so we have a dinner party with the family and later have a theme party with friends. This is also true of parties in which colleges or co-workers need to make up to majority of the guest list. Knowing that shoptalk is inevitable, I would spare certain friends the discomfort.

With that said, the remaining tips are for the events in which you have control over who does or does not come.

Select the size of function you are comfortable with. Over-extending your self is a near guarantee of undue stress and probable disappointment.

The original rule of thumb, is that one-forth of your guests will not be able to make it, so send out extra invitations in anticipation of this. In all my years of planning parties, I have never seen that rule play out. Who you invite, the type of parties you host and the time of year the party is planned for, are the largest determinations of attendance. My Halloween parties over the years have taken on a life of their own. Regardless of how many invitations I send out, it is rare to get even one decline. This is largely because there are very few adult Halloween events, and with school back in session, few people are traveling. The opposite is true of Christmas parties, where you are competing for a three-week window and travel plans.

My advice is to look at every event individually, taking these factors into consideration. Never invite more people than you could possibly handle. The type of people you include is the second most important consideration and often what causes the most stress.

First, do not invite people who all share the same career, background or set of beliefs. Bankers rarely want to talk to other bankers in their leisure time. Invite people who are lively and engaging, who will contribute to conversations. However, avoid inviting those who are so adversary they will cause problems or those who become obnoxious when they have had too much to drink. If that happens, see "Chasing Stars" chapter for suggestions of defusing confrontations. Realize that most of us, want to hear or be heard by those with different interests and perspective.

If possible try to include a lawyer or doctor everyone loves a little piece of free advice. Someone involved in restaurants or entertainment- everyone loves gossip or ideas on dinning out. Someone in investments as they often know a lot about the economy and a variety of industries. A realtor as they are often well versed in trends of different neighborhoods and changes to schools and government policies.

Entrepreneurs as they are risk takers and usually have grand ideas and ambitions. A stay-at home mom- they are often more knowledgeable in a variety of subjects then people give them credit for and usually have a couple great stories or anecdotes up their sleeve.

Second, don't invite those who clearly will be uncomfortable; your ninety-year old grandmother to your Indy 500 party, your only democratic friends to your republican candidates victory party, or anyone you feel would be so out of place that they are likely to have a miserable night and you are likely to continually try saving.

Third, don't waste much time worrying about the male to female ratio. Your not hosting a dating party and therefore don't need to match people up together.

Forth, don't worry about excluding people (this may not be the case for family get-togethers or smaller venues). I do not try to hide or excuse the fact that I do host functions that not all the same people are invited to. People don't expect to be included to a dinner party for you're new neighbors, your boss's retirement party, and your 8-year olds pool party.

Finally, have faith that your friends will play nice and get along. If you find redeeming qualities in them, trust that the will find them in each other. If they don't, make a mental note to reconsider them for the next time.

SHELTERED SETTING

To capture this cool and sophisticated look, I combined smooth and plush textures. The tablecloth is a simple snagged silk fabric, unfinished and cut to size. A faux fur is casually laid across a portion of the table (be sure to keep place setting either on or off the throw to avoid dishware from tipping). The dishware is a very unique etched glass that gives off the appearance of chipped ice. This pairs well with the modern, linear campaign glasses with carved bases. (See resources).

The décor is kept distinctive with clear glass trees partially filled with faux snow, bold flower arrangements that sit in wet floral foam placed on the top of the vases. Plastic ice cubes fill the bottom of the vases, while balloon light inserts make the vases come alive with light. (See resources) You can substitute the plastic ice for real ice, allowing it to transform into water within a few hours. As night begins to fall, these balloon lights provide all the light and feel of candles, but don't take up the space or pose as much danger with a faux fur on the table. Final touches are added with a faux snow and a few small foam snowballs. (See resources).

This chic, two bedroom high-rise is the ideal setting for an intimate gathering of a close group of friends. Share in the laughter and indulgences we rare allow ourselves to give into. So for one night bury the sensibility and relish in the company of loves ones.

Think snowballs are just for kids? Think again, over 25 million are sold each year. Created 60 years ago during WWII when sugar and flour were rationed. This is an indulgence everyone will love.

Desserts that are cool and icy, but dripping with warm sauces and decant toppings.

This beautiful igloo cake is made from a simple mold and surrounded by petite mints and chocolate drops (See Resources).

People buy more cakes, cookies and candy than any other food when a blizzard is in the forecast.

To make your own malts put the melted ice cream in a beverage decanter and added toppings in transformed spice racks.

Rock candy lollipops in a variety of blues are held up in a bowl of faux ice cubes to look like glaciers on a stick.

A warm apple tart and comfy couch is rivaled by the luxurious feel of faux fur, It is the quintessential part of winter lounging.

"Here's to cold nights, warm friends, and a good drink to give them."

–William Oldys

Your guests will love these whip cream dollop spoons with peppermint candy. You can make these up to 2 days in advance by freezing them. This is a small and effortless touches add something distinctive to a classic drink

Shopping List

1 bottle chocolate liqueur
1 bottle crème de cacao
1 bottle vodka
1 quart half-and-half
1 quart heavy cream
1 quart milk
1 pound butter
1 dozen eggs
1/3 cup cocoa powder
3 cups sweetened shredded
    coconut
2 cups sifted confectioners' sugar
1 bottle or tube blue food coloring
1/4 cup honey
1 cup salted cashews
1/3 cup pistachios
2/3 cup macadamia nuts
1/4 cup pecans
1/2 cup blanched almonds
1 19.5 ounce package chocolate
brownie mix
1/4 cup prepared chocolate or
    fudge frosting
36 lollipop sticks
3 cups semi-sweet chocolate chips
1/2 cup white chocolate chips

powdered sugar
6 ounces raspberries
2 8-ounce packages cream
    cheese, softened
1 box vanilla wafer cookies
2 pints fresh raspberries
1 pint fresh blackberries
1 lemon
1 24-ounce bottle chocolate
    syrup
2 gallons best-quality
    vanilla bean ice cream
1 13-ounce jar malted milk powder
2 cups peppermint pieces
3 cups milk chocolate sauce
3 cups dark chocolate sauce
3 cups premium caramel sauce
2 cups chocolate- covered
    almonds
3 cups marshmallow cream
1 cup crystallized blueberry
    sugar
2 cups strawberry sauce
1 cup cinnamon sticks
1 cup colored sprinkles
    coconut flakes
1 cup caramelized walnuts

MENU

For 12

Signature Drink:
Chocolate Martinis

Dessert Offerings:
White Coconut Snowballs

Frosted Mitten Cookies

Five Nut Caramel Tart

Brownie Pops

Mini Cheesecakes

Make Your Own Malts

Lemon and Fresh Fruit Tarts
(purchased from bakery)

Chocolate Mousse Igloo Cake
(purchased from specialty cake shop)

Staples (Replenish if needed)

granulated sugar
vanilla extract
almond extract
all-purpose flour

baking powder
baking soda
salt
cream of tartar
light corn syrup
vegetable oil

The Essentials

12 Champagne glasses
12 small low-ball glasses for
    costume malts
12 martini glasses
12 coffee cups (for hot chocolate
    or coffee)
12 – 24 small side plates for all
    the various deserts
12 small bowls (option if you are
    running short on dessert plates)
12 place settings of cutlery,
    including dessert forks, knives,
    spoons and small stir spoons
4 large serving trays for Igloo cake,
    brownie pops, five nut caramel

pie, and Individual
cheesecakes with fresh fruit
(A cake stand can be
substituted for one or
more tray)
3 medium serving trays for
    lemon and fruit tarts, frosted
    mitten cookies and chocolate
    moose cups
1 cylindrical server or bowl for
    rock candy suckers
12 napkins (have a few extra
    on hand)
1 tablecloth, 1 faux throw for
    the table
12 napkin rings

The Recipes

Chocolate Martini

1 1/2 shots chocolate liqueur
1 1/2 shots crème de cacao
1/2 shot vodka
2 1/2 shots half-and-half

Mix all ingredients in a shaker with ice, shake and pour into a chilled cocktail glass. 1 serving.

"The first fall of snow is not only an event, it's a magical event. You go to bed in one kind of world and wake up in another quite different, and if this is not enchantment then where is it to be found?" –J.B. Priestley

White Coconut Snowballs

For the chocolate cupcakes:

1/2 cup butter, room temperature
2 cups sugar
3 eggs
1 teaspoon vanilla
2 cups all purpose flour
2 teaspoon baking soda
1/2 teaspoon salt
1/3 cup cocoa powder
1 1/2 cups milk

For the filling and frosting:

6 large egg whites, room temperature
1 1/2 cups sugar
1 teaspoon cream of tartar
1/3 cup water
2 teaspoon vanilla
3 cups sweetened shredded coconut

Preheat the oven to 350 degrees F and lightly grease two 12-cup domed or regular muffin tins.

In a large bowl, cream together butter and sugar until light. Beat in eggs one at a time, followed by vanilla extract. In a small bowl, sift together flour, baking soda, salt and cocoa powder. Add half of flour mixture to the butter mixture, followed by the milk, then finished with the addition of the rest of the flour mix. Stir well between each addition and mix just until flour is incorporated. Pour batter into prepared baking cups. Bake for about 15 minutes, until a tester comes out clean. Cool pan on wire rack for five minutes, and remove cupcakes from pan to finish cooling.

Using a sharp paring knife, cut a cone shape out of each cake about 1 inch across and one inch deep. Trim off the pointy end of the cone, leaving a thin and flat circle of cake. Reserve the "plugs" of cake to seal the filled cakes later.

Put the egg whites in the bowl of an electric mixer or a large bowl with a hand mixer nearby.

Combine sugar, cream of tartar and water in a small saucepan fitted with a candy thermometer. Bring to a boil and cook until syrup reaches 242 degrees F. While syrup nears correct temperature, beat egg whites to soft peaks. Slowly stream in the hot sugar syrup, followed by the vanilla. Beat for about 10 minutes, until frosting becomes thick and creamy.

Process the coconut in a food processor until very fine. Pour into a shallow bowl and set aside. To finish the cupcakes, spoon about 1 cup of frosting into a piping bag and pipe the filling into each hollowed out cupcake. Top off with a flat circle of cake to plug the hole and keep the filling in place. Using a small spatula, frost the sides and top of each cupcake with a thick layer of the frosting. Holding the cupcake carefully, gently roll it in shredded coconut and set, unfrosted-side down, on a serving platter. Repeat for each cupcake. 24 cupcakes.

Frosted Mitten Cookies

For the cookies:
1 cup butter, softened
1 cup sugar
2 eggs
1/2 teaspoon vanilla
1/2 teaspoon almond extract
3 1/4 cups all-purpose flour
1/2 teaspoon baking soda
1/2 teaspoon baking powder
1/2 teaspoon salt

For the icing:
2 cups sifted confectioners' sugar
1 to 2 tablespoons milk
1 tablespoon light corn syrup
1/2 teaspoon vanilla
blue food coloring

To make the cookies, combine butter with sugar, eggs, vanilla and almond extract in a large bowl. Beat using an electric mixer on high speed until light and fluffy. In another bowl combine whisk together the flour with baking powder, baking soda and salt; gradually stir into the butter mixture until well blended. Cover and chill for 2 hours.

Preheat oven to 400 degrees F and cut parchment paper to fit two cookie sheets. Roll the dough directly on the parchment paper to about 1/4-inch thickness. Cut using mitten cookie cutters about 2 inches apart, and remove excess dough. Bake 4-6 minutes, or until lightly browned. Remove cookies to wire racks to cool completely before icing.

For the frosting, combine the confectioners' sugar with 1 tablespoon milk in a small bowl, gradually adding additional drops of milk if needed for spreading consistency. Beat in corn syrup and vanilla and stir until the icing is smooth and glossy. Spoon 1 cup of frosting in a decorating bag and pipe decorative trim on mitten cookies. Scoop unused frosting back into bowl, add 1 tiny drop of food color and stir. Add additional food color if necessary. Use a small spatula to decorate mittens and allow to set. Store at room temperature, carefully layered with waxed paper.

Five-Nut Caramel Tart

For the crust:
1 1/4 cup flour
3 tablespoons sugar
1/2 cup chilled butter
1 1/2 large egg yolks, blended with
1 1/2 tablespoons ice water

For the filling:
1/2 cup butter
1/2 cup packed brown sugar
1/4 cup honey
2 tablespoons sugar
1 cup salted cashews
1/3 cup pistachios
2/3 cup macadamia nuts
1/4 cup pecans
1/2 cup blanched almonds
2 tablespoons whipping cream
1 ounce white chocolate, melted
1 ounce dark chocolate, melted

For dough:
Mix flour and sugar. Add butter. Mix until mixture resembles coarse meal. Add yolk mixture and blend until dough begins to form. Gather dough into ball; flatten into disc and wrap in plastic wrap. Refrigerate at least 30 minutes.

Grease an 11-inch tart pan. Roll dough out on lightly floured surface to thickness of 1/8 inch. Fit dough into pan; trim edges. Refrigerate until well chilled, about 30 minutes. Preheat oven to 400 degrees F. Line tart shell with foil and fill with dried beans or pie weights. Bake 10 minutes. Remove foil and continue baking until golden brown, 10 minutes. Cool tart completely on rack.

For the filling:
Preheat oven to 350 degrees F. Place tart shell on baking sheet to prevent spill. Cook butter, brown sugar, honey and sugar in heavy saucepan over medium heat, stirring until sugars dissolve. Increase heat and whisk until mixture comes to boil. Boil until large bubbles form, about 1 minute. Remove pan from heat. Stir in all nuts and cream. Immediately pour filling into tart. Bake until filling bubbles, about 20 minutes. Completely cool tart in pan on a metal rack.

Dip fork into melted white chocolate. Wave fork quickly from side to side over tart, drizzling chocolate in lines across tart. Repeat with dark chocolate. Refrigerate until chocolate sets, about 3 minutes. Cut into wedges and serve. 12 servings.

Brownie Pops

1 19.5 ounce package chocolate brownie mix
1/2 cup vegetable oil
1/4 cup water
2 eggs
1/4 cup prepared chocolate or fudge frosting
36 lollipop sticks
3 cups semi-sweet chocolate chips
1/4 cup butter
1/2 cup white chocolate chips
powdered sugar for dusting

Heat oven to 350 degrees F and grease a 9- by 13-inch baking pan. Prepare brownie mix according to package directions using the oil, water and eggs. Bake as directed and cool on a wire rack to room temperature.

Line a baking sheet with a silicone mat, parchment or wax paper. Spoon frosting into large, microwave-safe bowl. Microwave on High for 15 seconds; stir until smooth. Trim overly-crisp edges from brownies if necessary. Coarsely crumble brownies over frosting. Mix gently into frosting. Roll into 1-inch balls. Place on prepared tray. Insert lollipop stick into center of each ball. Freeze for 30 minutes.

Put chocolate chips and butter in a medium, microwave-safe bowl. Microwave on High for 90 seconds and stir. If mixture is not completely melted, continue microwaving in 10-second intervals just until melted and smooth. Dip each frozen brownie pop into melted chocolate, coating completely and allowing excess chocolate to drip off. Return to freezer.

Put white chocolate chips in a small, microwave-safe bowl. Microwave on High for 45 seconds and stir. If chocolate is not completely melted, continue microwaving in 10-second intervals just until melted and smooth. Pour into a small, resealable plastic bag and snip the corner off. Drizzle each frozen brownie pop with a swirl of white chocolate, and sprinkle with a dusting of powdered sugar. Chill until serving time. 36 pops.

Miniature Cheesecakes

6 ounces raspberries
2 tablespoons sugar plus ¾ cup granulated sugar
2 8-ounce packages cream cheese, softened
2 eggs
1 tablespoon lemon juice
1 teaspoon vanilla
24 vanilla wafer cookies
Garnish: whipped cream, fresh raspberries and blackberries

Preheat the oven to 375 degrees F. Process raspberries in a food processor until smooth, about 30 seconds. Pass puree through a fine sieve into a small bowl; discard solids. Whisk in 2 tablespoons sugar, and set aside.

Using an electric mixer, beat the cream cheese, sugar, eggs, lemon juice and vanilla in a medium bowl until light and fluffy. Pour slightly less than half of the mixture in another bowl and stir in half of the raspberry mixture, reserving the rest. Line two 12-muffin pans with paper baking cups and put a vanilla wafer flat side down in each cup. Fill the cups of one pan about two-thirds full of the cream cheese mixture. Fill the cups of the other pan half-full of the raspberry mixture. Top with a spoonful of raspberry puree, dividing evenly among the 12 cups.

Bake the cheesecakes for 15 to 20 minutes or until the mixture is set. Cool on a wire rack and chill. Garnish with whipped cream and berries just before serving. Makes 24 cheesecakes.

Make Your Own Malts

2 tablespoons chocolate syrup
3 scoops vanilla ice cream
3/4 cup cold milk
1 heaping tablespoon malted milk powder
whipped cream, for garnish

Combine chocolate syrup, ice cream, milk and malted milk powder in blender and blend just until smooth. Pour in a chilled glass and top with whipped cream. 1 serving.

Toppings:

Peppermint pieces	Milk chocolate sauce
Premium caramel sauce	Chocolate covered almonds
Dark chocolate sauce	Marshmallow cream
Crystallized blueberry sugar	Strawberry sauce
Cinnamon sticks	Colored sprinkles
Cocoanut flakes	Caramelized walnuts

For the caramelized walnuts:
To make the caramelized walnuts, combine the brown sugar, corn syrup, butter and cinnamon in a non-stick skillet. Over medium-high heat, stir the mixture until it bubbles. Add the walnuts and continue cooking for 5 to 7 minutes, stirring constantly until nuts turn golden brown. Pour on a parchment-lined baking sheet, cool completely and crumble.

NORTHERN LIGHTS

Possibly one of the most spectacular natural phenomenon's is the Northern Lights also known as Aurora Borealis. This incredible light show is on display from September to March mainly in the Polar Regions. The technical explanation for this is electrically charged particles come from space and enter the earth's, magnetosphere. These particles accelerate along the Earth's magnetic fields with lines concentrated at the poles. Where they collide with gases that surround the earths surface. But, if like me, you're not a card caring molecular biologist, a more simplistic explanation is that it is a form of gases.

More important to me is the unbelievable beauty and grace at which there is no explanation adequate enough. The constant moving waves of light floating in endless streams vary in colors of red, purple, blue and green. Lasting from a few minutes to several hours, the Northern Lights have conjured up thousands of theories, myths and stories. Dating as far back as the 1621. Named after the Roman Goddess of Dawn, Aurora, and Borealis the Greek God of Wind, however, many cultures have adopted and changed the name to better suit their beliefs and way of life. Aurora can only clearly be seen within close proximity to the poles due to darkness and magnetic field.

Aurora borealis has intrigued and frighten people for years, in ancient times the fear was so great, that people felt direct harm could come to them if caught in their presents. Others thought it was a message from their Creator; that either he was angry or forewarning them of war, disasters of plagues. The Eskimos felt it was an attempt of dead relatives to communicate with those left behind, The Chinese believed the lights were fighting dragons, Native Americans believed the lights were imagines of large bon fires.

The perfect greeter, this miniature version of an igloo and friendly furry husky will encapsulate your entire icy theme. Pulling together all the elements of snow, ice and arctic creatures. (If you don't have a dog consider donating it to a local animal shelter after the festivities). The igloo is backlit with a grouping of LED branches (See Resources)

The History of the Snowman

One of the most recognizable symbols of winter is the infamous snowman. Created from three tapering size snowballs to represent the head, torso, and lower body. He's made his way onto everything from seasonal card to pajamas and everything in between. According to historic documents, these frozen friends have been a part of our culture dating back to the 15th century. Often taking on slightly different forms, the quintessential snowman has been entertaining us and borrowing our favorite cold weather apparel for as long as anyone can remember. Frequently adorn in scarves and hats with rocks or coal for eyes and the most common trait a carrot nose; snowmen have brought a lively face to the cold and dismal months of winter.

There are thirteen types of falling snow and twenty-four types of snow on the ground, and yet only a handful of these make for perfect snowman making snow. Powder is nearly impossible to pack and slush is too heavy and wet to mold into anything. So, I'm told that the best time to build a snowman is the warmest day following a good snowstorm. The world's largest snowman was created in Bethel, Maine standing 122 ft and tipping the scales at over 9,000,000 pounds. But, regardless of what shape or form Frosty takes on, he is the trademark of childhood memories, as pivotal as the first snowflakes captured on your tongue or first snow angel.

Party Timeline

One month before the party:

- Make or purchase invitations.
- Finalize guest list and mail invitations.

3 weeks before the party:

- Finalize the menu, including drinks (carefully selecting the desserts you wish to make and the desserts you will purchase).
- Create a look by selecting colors, mood, setting, and entertainment, if necessary.
- Order or gather the decorations.

2 weeks before the party:

- Make a shopping list for the food and liquor (see Shopping list).
- Order the igloo cake, lemon and fresh fruit tarts, and any dessert you do not wish to make.
- Order flowers, and consider having them delivered the day of the party.

1 week before the party:

- Assemble or purchase take-away gifts and wrap them.
- Purchase all nonperishable food and liquor (see Shopping list).
- Create a music play list or purchase CDs.

3 days ahead:

- Decorate.
- Prepare the bar with glasses and liquor.
- Assemble all the serving dishes and set up the buffet table, if using one.

2 days before the party:

- Prepare the ice cream toppings, including caramelized walnuts, and store in tightly lidded containers.
- Bake the mitten cookies and store in a tightly lidded container.
- Bake the miniature cheesecakes and refrigerate.
- Make the brownie pops and refrigerate.

The day before the party:

- Purchase perishable food (see Shopping list).
- Set the table and lay out the dishes.
- Pick up flowers or have them delivered.
- Bake the Five Nut Caramel Tart and White Coconut
- Snowballs.
- Frost the mitten cookies.
- Make extra ice.
- Check that the bathroom is clean. Have fresh hand towels, soap and extra toilet paper on hand.

2 hours before the party:

- Garnish the miniature cheesecakes.
- Arrange the cookies on plates.
- Set platters, flowers and decorations out on the table.

Prior to guests' arrival:

- Arrange food on platters.
- Turn on the music.
- Prepare the martinis, including one for yourself!
- Light the candles (if using).
- Enjoy!

"When we finally kiss goodnight
How I'll hate going out in the storm!
But if you'll really hold me tight
All the way home I'll be warm."

TAKE AWAY GIFTS

Keep the gratification going long after the night is over. Cleverly nestle several packs of world famous "serendipity Frozen Hot Chocolate" inside a pair of knitted gloves. It's unique, it's chicky and it's something most of us have never had the chance to experience. This is anything but ordinary cocoa. The gloves are always a useful essential come winter (if not needed, suggest they donate them).

Vary it

A gift certificate for a local ice creamery is sure to bring a smile to all your friends. It's a great way to extend the memories of a wonderful evening and sure to come in handy as the snow eventually melts and gives way to smoldering days.

Simplify it

Any token winter knickknack will work. A miniature snow glob, a fragrant winter candle or several sample sizes of liquor (airplane size) to add to there favorite winter drinks. Be sure to wrap with a beautiful bow and small plastic snowflake or pinecone.

The *Love* Letter

A romantic evening for two, designed to enhance memories of a life created and nurtured from one love and a thousand dreams.

"Love is composed
of a single soul
inhabiting two bodies."
— Aristotle

At A Glance

Theme:
Send My Love

❧

Setting:
Home – tucked away in a bedroom, living room or home office –
ideally, any place where "unconventional" and "comfortable" meet

❧

Mood:
Intimate, seductive, secretive, romantic, the room is
accented with inspiring antique books, time-honored
heirlooms, wax seals and lots of love letters.

❧

Colors:
Moss green, crisp white and scarlet red

❧

Flowers:
Red roses, white hydrangeas and
Queen Anne's Lace mixed with seasonal greenery

❧

Tastes:
Warm, hearty comfort food—classics with a twist

❧

Sounds:
Create a custom play list capturing a variety of romantic melodies:
Dinner for Two or *Book for Lovers*, an exquisite selection of classical
instrumentals. Consider one of the many hits from Nat King Cole,
a masterful vocalist with a velvet voice, or Harry Connick Jr.,
another artist with timeless appeal. Or set a more upbeat mood
with the soulful and romantic tunes of Celine Dion, Sting,
Toni Braxton or John Mayer.

❧

Experience:
Few of life's moments can equal those of fine food, soft music, and
slow dancing,then winding down with a candlelit, rose-petal bath.

Vary it: Re-create your first date or wedding night. Reminisce about
that moment you first met, disastrous vacations, triumphs in
parenting, experiences shared,memories created—a life started
and shaped out of one love and a thousand dreams.

Simplify it: Special-deliver a passionate invitation for cocktails at an
upscale hotel, followed by dinner and a spontaneous evening stay.

Aside from your own treasured anniversaries, Valentine's Day is the most romantic day of the year. Celebrate your life-long love and shared history with an intimate, unhurried dinner for two at home. Rich colors and soft fabrics are set against the eclectic backdrop of familiar furnishings arranged in a fresh way to create a cozy setting for rekindling romance and rediscovering why you fell in love in the first place. Recreate the seduction and intrigue of an 18th century library, with old books and love letters nearby to encourage the reading of a romantic poem or the shared sentiments from your courtship days.

Share a sumptuous meal paired with carefully chosen wines that complement each course, while candlelight illuminates a private table and soft music plays in the background. Savor your inspired setting as you gaze into each other's eyes and share a smile, the touch of a loving hand, warm laughter and engaging conversation. As the evening winds down, linger over a decadent chocolate dessert, before turning in for the evening—relaxed, content and more in love than ever.

Several stacks of books are casually piled in front of a freestanding table.

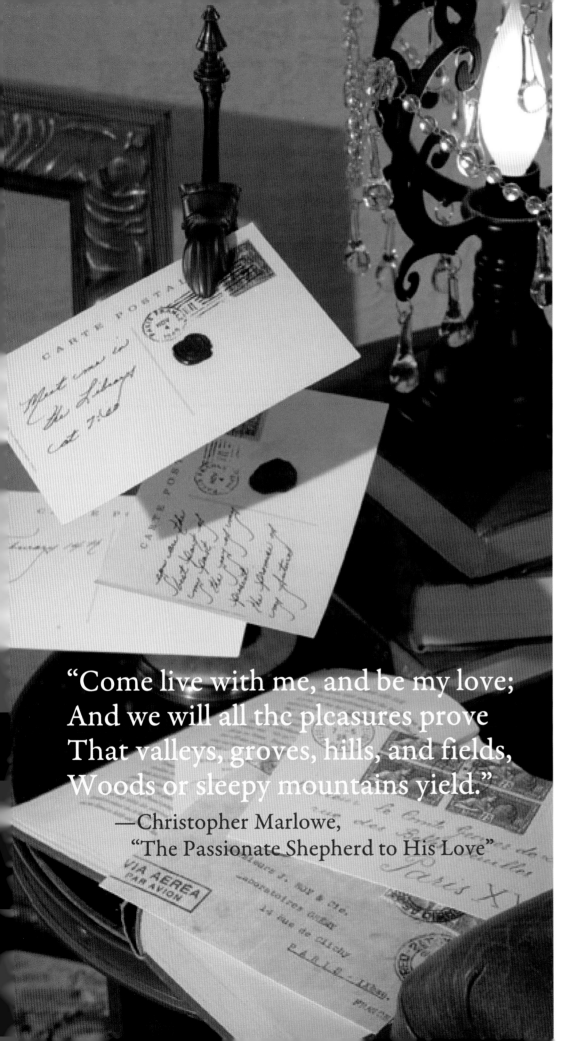

"Come live with me, and be my love;
And we will all the pleasures prove
That valleys, groves, hills, and fields,
Woods or sleepy mountains yield."

—Christopher Marlowe,
"The Passionate Shepherd to His Love"

Send My Love

Romance is an art form that takes constant attention and nurturing. It's so easy to get caught up in the rituals of day-to-day life and take each other for granted. Make the time and effort to show the one you love just how much you care.

The Invitation

Build the anticipation of the evening ahead by sending a series of love letters weeks before the night. For added effect, consider vintage-designed post cards. (see Resources)

Vary it

OK, so you don't have the time to sit down and script a chapter of love notes. Blend a potpourri of romantic quotes, wedding vows, song lyrics or phrases that are meaningful to the two of you.

Simplify it

Grab one of the many of elegant Valentine's Day cards—and write a brief and sexy note. Keep it simple with a heartfelt inscription, ending with an imprint of lips or a spritzing of your favorite perfume. No signature necessary.

Essential Elements of Entertaining Pairing Wine with Food

When food and wine are paired properly, the ordinary suddenly becomes extraordinary. Much like a good marriage, the mingling of flavor, smell and texture can create a powerful combination. But is there such a thing as the perfect pairing of wine and food? I would argue "no." In fact, countless books and magazines continually make and remake such lists. Clearly, selecting wines to enhance a meal is an art—not a science. Some basic guidelines will help you get started. Try to maintain balance, for example, pair lighter foods with lighter wines and heavier, heartier foods with more full-bodied wines. Ultimately, you can't go wrong by serving what you trust and love. Here are some general food-pairing ideas for each type of wine:

"Grow old with me,
the best is yet, to be."

—Robert Browning,
"Rabbi Ben Ezra"

A grouping of red roses, white hydrangeas and Queen Anne's Lace is mixed with seasonal greenery to add a touch of romance and warmth, without overdoing it. The flowers are arranged in wet floral foam and placed in individual baskets tied to the backs of chairs, keeping the table uncluttered.

White Wines (These typically pair well with Chinese, Japanese, Greek, Mexican, Indian and Thai cuisines).

Sparkling Whites Champagne and Prosecco pair well with:
- Salty snacks
- Caviar

Light-Bodied White Pinot Blanc, Riesling, Chablis, Sauvignon Blanc, Pinot Grigio, Pinot Gris and Frascati pair well with:
- Clams
- Oysters
- Sole
- Flounder
- Halibut
- Barbecue
- Pasta
- Seafood

Medium-Bodied White Montagny, Sauvignon Blanc, Chardonnay and Gewurztraminer pair well with:
- Soft Cheeses or Melted Cheeses
- Chicken
- Barbecue
- Shrimp
- Scallops
- Pasta—Red Sauce
- Pasta—White Sauce

Full-Bodied White Chardonnay pair well with:
- Salmon
- Tuna
- Lobster

- Duck
- Chicken
- Sirloin Steak

Red Wines (These traditionally pair well with French, Italian, Latin and German cuisines).

Light-Bodied Red Bardolino, Chianti, Burgundy, Bordeaux, Pinot Noir, Beaujolais, Valpolicella and Malbec pair well with:
- Salmon
- Tuna
- Duck
- Chicken
- Swordfish

Medium-Bodied Reds Burgundy, Bordeaux, Cabernet Sauvignon, Merlot, Zinfandel, Chianti Classico, Syrah/Shiraz, Pinot Noir, Malbec and Barolo pair well with:
- Hard Cheeses
- Game Birds
- Pork
- Barbecue
- Veal

Full-Bodied Reds Barolo, Bordeaux, Cabernet Sauvignon, Merlot, Zinfandel and Syrah/Shiraz pair well with:
- Lamb
- Beef/steaks
- Game Meats
- Pasta—Red Sauce

A Sultry Setting

This is one of the most important and intimate parties you'll ever throw. It takes a little more effort, but virtually no money for decorations. I wanted this special event to take place at home, in a room where we spend much of our time. But for effect, I also wanted to change its appearance. Redecorating with furniture and accessories from different areas in our house, I set out to create an Old World, romantic, eclectic backdrop. Using a variety of empty frames, old books, votive candles and an old wax stamp, I tried to capture the seduction and intrigue of an eighteenth century library. Absolutely nothing was purchased for this; instead, I rearranged a variety of objects and furnishings to surround us in things we already treasure.

The fireplace is quaint, cluttered and charming, covered with a garden statue; faux red berries; books; a charming, oversized, old Valentine's Day card; and an abundance of candles.

"I love you without knowing how, or when or from where,
I love you simply, without problems or pride;
I love you in this way because I don't know any other way
of loving but this, in which there is no I or you,
so intimate that your hand upon my chest is my hand,
so intimate that when I fall asleep it is your eyes that close."

—Pablo Neruda, "Love Sonnet XVII"

> *"Being deeply loved
> by someone gives
> you strength, while
> loving someone deeply
> gives you courage."*
> —Lao Tzu

To build on the ambience of inviting intimacy, the walls and tables are lined with elegant old frames, wedding pictures, and a selection of old and new love notes.

A savory dinner is served on a tabletop created from antique books and love notes.
(see Resources).

Candles and beloved valuables collected from around the home intensify the romance and comfort of the surroundings.

A glass box is entrusted with physical memories, such as the first movie ticket stub, the surprise invitation to Italy, and the hospital wristbands for all of your children.

St. Valentine's Legacy

To love and be loved may be life's greatest gift, and St. Valentine's Day is the one holiday that symbolizes and celebrates the ardent proclamation of one's love for another. For millennia, the need to express and proclaim the devotion shared between two people has compelled celebration, a need that survived war, famine and disease. The relatively more recent St. Valentine's Day is recognized around the world with the exchange of cards, candies, flowers and small tokens of love.

Its history retains a bit of mystery. Before the death of St. Valentine, the Romans celebrated the official beginning of spring in mid-February with the Lupercalia festival, a celebration of purification and fertility. At the heart of the festivities were naked men running through the streets and gently whipping the backsides of eligible women—who would deliberately stand in their way—and crops with blood-soaked hides, in hopes that both would prove to be fertile in the upcoming year. The festivities continued with the drawing of women's names by single men, pairing the two for the year and thus resulting in many marriages—albeit unconventional ones. The practice was later deemed sacrilegious by the church. In 496 AD, noting its superstitious foundation, Pope Gelasius I sought to do away with this pagan holiday.

Much uncertainty surrounds the history of Valentine's Day and the martyred saint honored for it. Indeed, there is much question as to which St. Valentine receives the honor. The Catholic Church has record of three Valentine's saints—the first, a priest in Rome; the second, a bishop in Terni; and the third, an unknown man residing in and killed in Africa, according to history.com. Ironically, all three were said to have been executed on February 14th.

Most historians believe the St. Valentine who inspired our current holiday was a priest in Rome who directly disobeyed the ruling of Roman Emperor Claudius II. With Rome in near ruins, the golden era crumbling, and in desperate need to rebuild and reinforce the Roman army, Claudius banished all marriages, stating that emotional entanglements fostered bad soldiers and weak men. St. Valentine deeply believed in the sacrament of matrimony, and defied this ruling by continuing to marry young lovers in secret. In time, Valentine was discovered and arrested. According to legend, Valentine was approached by Asterius, his jailor, while awaiting sentencing. Believing that Valentine

In keeping with the love-lettered theme, I embossed virtually everything with a wax stamp, from the invitation to glasses and napkins. The wax is easily removed from glass and porcelain, but I don't recommend trying this with heirloom pieces or crystal. The wax is not removable from napkins, so I used inexpensive cotton napkins just for this occasion.

held the saintly ability to heal, he asked Valentine to restore sight to his blind daughter. When Valentine was successful in healing her, a great friendship and possible love affair grew between the priest and the young woman. Claudius gave Valentine the opportunity to repent if he would reject the beliefs of Catholicism for that of the Roman Gods. Valentine not only refused, he made his final attempt to convert Claudius; with that, he was executed on February 14, 269 AD.

February continued to be revered as the month of love and romance through the Middle Ages in France and England, as it was believed to be the commencement of mating season among birds. In 1381, Chaucer composed a love poem honoring the engagement between England's Richard II and Anne of Bohemia. As was the poetic tradition, Chaucer associated the occasion with a feast day. In "The Parliament of Fowls," the royal engagement, the mating season of birds, and St. Valentine's Day are linked. Through the centuries, Valentine's Day has endured the unraveling of many customs and traditions, yet is still one of the most beloved holidays celebrated around the world.

Menu

For 2

Signature Drink:
Citrus Cooler

Appetizer:
An assortment of olives marinated in olive oil with
lemon zest and spices

Starter:
Tripe Cream Brie Soup with Thyme and Prosciutto
Crispy Pesto Baguettes
Wine suggestion: a full-bodied white wine

Salad:
Field-Green Salad with Radicchio, Walnuts, Pears and
Blue Cheese, Topped with Homemade Balsamic
Vinaigrette Dressing

Entrée:
Seared Filet-Mignon Steaks with a
Creamy Béarnaise Sauce and Fresh Tarragon
Wine Suggestion: a rich, deep-bodied Merlot

Accompaniments:
Roasted New Potatoes with
Arugula, Sauteed Cremini Mushrooms with Truffle Oil

Dessert:
Decadent Chocolate Torte with Gelato and
Fresh Strawberries

Shopping List

1 small head garlic
2 shallots
1 pound small, red new potatoes
1 ripe Comice pear
1 pint fresh strawberries
1 bunch fresh thyme sprigs
1 bunch fresh tarragon sprigs
1/4 pound mixed field greens
1 small head radicchio
1 small baguette
1 small chocolate torte*
1/3 cup heavy cream
1/2 cup heavy cream*
14-ounce wedge ripe Brie cheese
2 tablespoons grated
  Parmesan cheese

2 ounces crumbles blue cheese
1 pint gelato—flavor of
  your choice
1 pound, 6 ounces good-quality
  semisweet chocolate*
2 slices prosciutto
2 1 1/4-thick filet mignon steaks
1/2 cup good-quality
  white wine
1 cup chicken stock
1/3 cup walnut pieces
3 tablespoons balsamic vinegar
1 tablespoon prepared pesto
1/4 cup champagne vinegar

*If serving a purchased
  chocolate dessert, delete
  these items from list.

The Essentials

2 water glasses
6 wine glasses (2 for white wine,
  4 for red wine)
4 shot glasses
2 coffee cups (if desired)
1 small side plate for olives
2 soup bowls
2 bread plates

2 salad plates
2 dinner plates
2 place settings of cutlery,
  including soup spoons, salad
  forks, dinner forks, steak
  knives, dessert forks
2 napkins
1 tablecloth

Staples (Replenish if needed)
Salt
White and black peppercorns
Sugar
Olive oil
Butter

Cooking spray
All-purpose flour
Bay leaf
Dry mustard
Dried thyme
Dried oregano

Signature Drink: Citrus Cooler

This drink—served in a diminutive shot glass—will help cleanse the palate between courses.

2 scoops lemon sorbet
2 to 3 slices fresh lemon slices (rind removed)
4 slices cucumber (skin removed)

Combine the ingredients in a blender or food processor, and process until smooth. Pour into four chilled shot glasses and place at the table. Remove two glasses between the first and second course. Remove the second two glasses between the main course and dessert.

The Recipes

Triple Cream Brie Soup with Thyme and Prosciutto
2 slices prosciutto
12 slices prosciutto
1 tablespoon olive oil
2 tablespoons butter
1 finely diced leek (white part only)
3 tablespoons all-purpose flour
1/4 cup white wine
1 bay leaf
1 cup chicken stock
1/3 cup heavy cream
salt and freshly ground white pepper
1/2 cup diced ripe Brie cheese, rind removed
fresh thyme sprigs for garnish

Heat the oil in a skillet and fry the prosciutto until crispy. Drain on a paper towel and cut into strips; reserve for garnish. Heat the butter in a heavy saucepan over medium heat. Add the leeks and sauté until transparent. Stir in the flour and turn down heat slightly. Cook for 5 minutes. Whisk in the white wine, add the bay leaf and cook for 10 minutes. Add the chicken stock gradually and cook for another 30 minutes. Remove the bay leaf and add the cream; simmer for 15 minutes. Add the Brie to the soup and stir gently until the Brie is melted. Use a hand-held blender on high to blend the soup. Season with salt and pepper to taste, and pour into bowls. Garnish with prosciutto strips and thyme leaves.

Crispy Pesto Baguettes
cooking spray
1 small baguette
2 tablespoons butter, softened
2 tablespoons grated Parmesan cheese
1 small garlic clove, peeled and minced
1 tablespoon prepared pesto

Line a baking sheet with a piece of aluminum foil and spray with cooking spray. Preheat the oven to 400 degrees F. Carefully slice the baguette in half horizontally, and then cut each slice diagonally in the middle. Combine the butter, Parmesan cheese and garlic in a small bowl. Spread the mixture evenly on top of the four bread slices. Arrange the bread slices with the buttered side down on the prepared baking sheet. Bake in the oven for 4-7 minutes, or until the buttered side is crispy and brown. Remove from the oven, flip the bread slices over and cool on a wire rack. Spread two pieces with the pesto and leave two plain. Arrange the bread slices with the diagonal cuts facing to make two heart shapes.

Field Green Salad with Radicchio, Walnuts, Pears and Bleu Cheese
1/4 pound mixed field greens
2 leaves radicchio, washed and torn
1 ripe red Comice pear, cored and thinly sliced
1/3 cup toasted walnut pieces
6 tablespoons crumbled blue cheese
homemade balsamic vinaigrette (recipe follows)

Arrange the field greens and radicchio on two chilled plates. Fan the pears out on one side, sprinkle with the walnuts and bleu cheese, and drizzle some of the dressing on top.

Homemade Balsamic Vinaigrette Dressing
3 tablespoons balsamic vinegar
1/2 teaspoon sugar
1/4 teaspoon dry mustard
1/4 teaspoon dried thyme
1/4 teaspoon dried oregano
1/4 teaspoon salt
1/4 teaspoon freshly ground black pepper
1/2 cup extra virgin olive oil

Add the vinegar, sugar, mustard, thyme, oregano, salt and pepper to a blender or food processor and pulse to combine. With the motor running, slowly add the olive oil until the mixture is emulsified. Serve at once, storing any extra in a covered container in the refrigerator. Makes about 1/3 cup.

Seared Filet Mignon Steaks with Creamy Béarnaise Sauce and Fresh Tarragon
2 1 1/4inch-thick filet mignon steaks, about 1 to
  1 1/2 pounds total
coarsely ground black pepper
olive oil
sea salt

Classic Béarnaise Sauce (recipe follows)
2 tarragon sprigs

Season the filet mignon steaks generously with the pepper. In a heavy cast-iron skillet, heat the oil over medium-high heat. Arrange the filet mignon steaks in the pan and fry them for 4-5 minutes per side for medium-rare (the internal temperature should be 120 to 130 degrees F) or to the desired doneness. Remove from the pan and arrange on the plate, spooning some of the sauce on top and garnishing with tarragon sprigs. Serve additional sauce in a gravy boat on the side.

Classic Béarnaise Sauce
1/4 cup Champagne vinegar
1/4 cup good quality white wine
2 tablespoons minced shallots
3 tablespoons fresh chopped tarragon leaves, divided
1/4 teaspoon sea salt
1/4 teaspoon freshly ground white pepper
3 egg yolks
2 sticks unsalted butter, melted

Put the vinegar, white wine, shallots, 1 tablespoon of the chopped tarragon leaves, salt and pepper in a small saucepan over medium-high heat. Bring to a boil and simmer for about 5 minutes, until the mixture is reduced to a few tablespoons. Cool for 2 minutes. Place the cooled mixture with the egg yolks and 1 teaspoon of salt in the jar of a blender and blend for 30 seconds. With the blender on, slowly pour the hot butter through the opening in the lid. Add the remaining 2 tablespoons of chopped tarragon leaves and pulse just until combined. If sauce is too thick, add a few drops of boiling water until it thins to the desired consistency. Makes 1 cup.

Roasted New Potatoes with Arugula
1 pound small red new potatoes, halved
2 tablespoons extra virgin olive oil
1/2 teaspoon salt
1/2 teaspoon freshly ground black pepper
1 bunch arugula, washed and torn

Adjust oven rack to lowest position and heat oven to 450 degrees F. Toss potatoes with oil, salt and pepper. Arrange, cut side down, on a large, heavy baking sheet. Roast until tender and golden brown, about 25-30 minutes). Transfer potatoes to a bowl and toss with the arugula. Adjust seasonings and serve.

Sautéed Cremini Mushrooms with Truffle Oil
1 tablespoon butter
1/4 pound Cremini mushrooms (or substitute button
  mushrooms), cleaned and quartered
salt and freshly ground pepper to taste
1 1/2 teaspoons white truffle oil

Heat the butter a skillet over medium-high flame. As soon as the butter melts, add the mushrooms and toss to coat. Cook for 4 minutes, stirring occasionally, until mushrooms just start to brown. Remove from the heat, season with salt and pepper, drizzle with the white truffle oil and serve.

Decadent Chocolate Torte with Gelato and Fresh Strawberries
I purchased a chocolate torte from the bakery for our dinner, but if you'd like to make your own, this luscious chocolate torte is rich, delicious and easy to prepare ahead of time.

nonstick cooking spray
1nonstick cooking spray
1 cup water
3/4 cup sugar
9 tablespoons unsalted butter
1 pound high-quality semisweet chocolate, finely chopped
6 eggs
boiling water
Chocolate Ganache (recipe follows)
1 cup gelato ice cream
1 cup fresh sliced strawberries

Preheat the oven to 350 degrees F. Spray a 10-inch spring-form pan with cooking spray and line the bottom with a round of parchment paper; spray the parchment. Wrap 3 layers of heavy-duty foil around the outside of pan; bring the foil up to the rim.

In a small saucepan, combine the water and sugar. Bring to boil over medium heat, stirring until the sugar dissolves. Simmer 5 minutes; remove from the heat. In a large saucepan over low heat, melt the butter or margarine and chocolate. Whisk sugar mixture into chocolate mixture. Set aside to cool slightly.

Whisk in the eggs until well blended. Pour the batter into the pan. Place the pan in a roasting pan. Add enough hot water to the roasting pan to come halfway up the sides of the cake pan. Bake the cake for 50 minutes or until the center no longer jiggles when the baking pan is shaken gently. Lift the pan from the water; transfer to a rack to cool the cake completely in the pan. Frost the cake as directed below and refrigerate until 15 minutes before serving time. To serve, run a knife around the sides of the pan to loosen the cake and unlatch the spring. Cut the cake into wedges and serve with gelato and sliced strawberries. 8 servings.

Chocolate Ganache
3/4 cup heavy whipping cream
4 tablespoons butter
6 ounces semisweet chocolate, chopped

In a medium saucepan over medium heat, combine the cream and butter. Bring to a simmer and remove from the heat. Add the chocolate and whisk until smooth. While the cake is still in the pan, pour the ganache over the top. Without spreading it, gently shake the pan to distribute the ganache evenly. Refrigerate the cake in the pan for at least 2 hours or as long as overnight, or until the ganache sets.

Keep Old World Traditional

Sealing a letter with a wax seal pays tribute to a tradition rich with historical relevance and significance. Dating as far back as the Old Testament, the wax seal created a bond of privacy and served as an unquestionable mark of authenticity. In a day and age when distance and illiteracy dramatically hindered communication, the custom-designed seal served two primary functions. The first ensured privacy, and the second—equally important—was to authenticate documents, much like a signature does today.

Royalty, courts, social peers and governments often created several seals, with a variety of meanings and approvals—for example, the "Great Seal of the United States." Wax seals ensured that love letters remained personal, and such documents as wills and last wishes were upheld and not tampered with. For thousands of years, a simple dripping of candle wax and stamping determined the way documents were handled.

This mark of legitimacy is what most likely led to the popularity of the signet ring, a personalized stamp that remained only in the bearer's hands. The stamp size and design often expressed the wearer's status, interests and ego. It was traditional to destroy personal seals upon the death of the bearer; therefore, there are very few originals in circulation today. Official seals of royalty and courts were passed down to successors in formal, drawn-out rituals, very much reflecting the important positions they represented. The traditions and importance of wax seals were continued in America, when Benjamin Franklin, John Adams and Thomas Jefferson were tasked, immediately following the reading of the Declaration of Independence on July 4th, 1776, with creating a Great Seal. The result, finally designed by Charles Thomson in 1782, can be seen today on the reverse of the one-dollar bill.

A Love Letter

The love letter is the foundation of any great romance. The clearly expressed confession of feelings and intentions, felt with every breath and every beat of the heart, is what makes great love stories so very great.

There is some question as to whether the first Valentine was actually sent by St. Valentine himself to his jailer's daughter. Legend says that the daughter of Asterius (Valentine's jailer) and Valentine formed a strong relationship after he restored her eyesight. Upon learning of Valentine's upcoming execution she was overcome with grief, and in an attempt to bring comfort, Valentine wrote a farewell letter signed, "From your Valentine." The phrase remains popular today. However, because there is no proof of this letter, historians cite the first written valentine as, according to The History Channel (www.history.com), "a love poem written by Charles, Duke of Orleans, to his wife, while imprisoned in the tower at the Battle of Agincourt. The greeting, which was written in 1415, is part of a manuscript collection of the British Museum in London, England." Years later, King Henry V wrote a love letter to Catherine of Valois; it is believed, however, that the letter was written and composed by a hired writer.

Valentine's Day saw continued popularity throughout Europe, growing commercially in the nineteenth century. It was introduced to America sometime during the seventeenth century, but didn't catch on until the Revolutionary War. In the late 1840s, Esther A. Howland, a student at Massachusetts' Mount Holyoke college, crafted a valentine using lace, colored paper, velvet and ribbons and sold it in her father's store. Their popularity grew, and Howland is credited with starting the American Valentine's Day industry. Her designs included hearts, cupids and birds to symbolize love, particularly during a time of emotional discouragement.

Today Valentine's Day continues to enjoy exceptional popularity, flourishing well beyond lovers to include celebrations of affection between children, parents and friends. According to the Greeting Card Association, it is the second-most-popular holiday in the United States, after Christmas. Not a bad result from the efforts of a holy man, who believed so deeply in the power of love that he sacrificed his life to help seal the vows of those who wished to live happily ever after.

Party Timeline

One month before the dinner:

- Make or purchase letters or postcards and begin sending them.

3 weeks before the dinner:

- Finalize the menu, including drinks (carefully select the items you wish to make and those you wish to purchase).
- Create a "look" by selecting colors, mood, setting, and if necessary, entertainment.
- Order or gather the decorations and accessories.

2 weeks before the dinner:

- Make a shopping list for the food, wine and liquor (see Shopping list).
- Order the food or any desert you do not wish to make.
- Order flowers, and consider having them delivered the day of the dinner.

1 week before the dinner:

- Assemble or purchase take-away gifts and wrap them.
- Purchase all nonperishable food and liquor (see Shopping list).
- Put together a selection of music or create a custom CD.

3 days before the dinner:

- Decorate.
- Assemble all the serving dishes and set up the buffet table, if using one.

2 days before the dinner:

- Make the marinated olives and butter spread for the baguettes.

The day before the dinner:

- Purchase perishable food (see Shopping list).
- Pick up flowers or have them delivered.
- Set the table and lay out the dishes.
- Make the chocolate torte or pick up the prepared dessert.
- Make extra ice.
- Check that the bathroom is clean. Have fresh hand towels, soap and extra toilet paper on hand.

The morning of the dinner:

- Finish preparing the food.

Prior to your special guest's arrival:

- Start the music.
- Mix the citrus cooler, including one for yourself!
- Open bottle of wine so it can breathe.
- Light the candles.
- Enjoy!

(Opposite page) A basket of bath essentials includes salts, sea sponges, a book of love poems, romantic music and the makings of a perfect cup of tea.

Take Away Gifts

Night falls, giving way to a calm quiet and familiarity of a soft hand, a warm body, a whispered wish, an unspoken look. Commemorate, behold, entrust and celebrate your world together by falling asleep on a romantic poem or love letter written with a fabric-safe marker on a fitted bed sheet.

Vary it

Writing your favorite memories from past years in a special notebook. Tuck it away, and create an annual tradition of adding to it throughout the years.

Simplify it

If creativity is harder to come by, consider making a list of all the attributes you love the most in him— leaving room for him to do the same.

An Enchanted Easter Evening

Little explorers have unearthed each hidden egg, sampled those chocolate bunnies, and after a morning's delight, ensured that Easter dresses will never see pristine white again. Extend and enhance this festive celebration of spring with a colorful family affair. Crisp, seasonal fare and décor let you and your loved ones savor fine food, fond memories and a sense of annual renewal.

"You give but little when you give of your possessions. It is when you give of yourself that you truly give."

—Kahlil Gibran

At A Glance

Theme:
Play it by Ear

Setting:
An outdoor enclosure in a resplendent garden.

Mood:
Charming, cheerful and crisp. The lowering midday sun signals
the unexpected magic of an outdoor room of enchantment.

Colors:
Grass green, jelly-bean pink and orange, with touches of whisker black.

Flowers:
Light-pink eustoma lisianthus, dark-pink petite roses and green spider mums

Tastes:
Inspiration from holiday classics and the garden's early-spring offerings.

Sounds:
A custom play list blends the fretless bass instrumentals of the
fresh indie group El Ten Eleven or similarly *Explosions in the Sky* for
background music. Or if you seek something with more strength, try
What It All Means by Chantal Kreviazuk, whose poetic songs suit most
casual gatherings. For something more light, try Paul McCartney's
All The Best or Frank Sinatra's classic *Nothing But The Best.*

Experience:
A classic, Easter egg hunt, has delighted children and entertained
parents for generations. This year mix it up a bit with color-coded plastic
eggs, denoting a specific color for each child or adult. This customizes
the hunt for varied ages and skill levels. Be creative, instead of candy,
enclose puzzle pieces, fortunes or love notes, small toys, barrettes, and
movie or lottery tickets in the eggs.

Vary it: A week or so prior to Easter, package and pass out ten pennies
(or other collections of things) to each guest. Attach a note explaining that
each item represents a good deed toward another person, all of which must
be done prior to the event. Following Easter dinner, hold a brief ceremony
that lets each person share his or her good deeds.

Simplify it: : Consider a flowering bulb or rose bush exchange.

As the world slowly emerges from its winter slumber, with unfolding buds, bursting seeds and muffled chirps of baby birds, one's spirit rebounds with a joyful renewal. With the gray days of late winter finally past, the eye and soul rejoice in tentative colors and reliable nature. The earth continually astounds us with its ability to renew, to breathe new life into old things, to regenerate and refresh itself year after year. Easter is spring's invitation to celebrate the wonders of the earth's rebirth.

Create small lamps, with battery-operated candlesticks supporting petite chandelier shades that are transformed by the effects of sheet moss and a little green wire.

Unwrap the Season

Pay tribute to the support, love and laughter that your friends and family bring into your life. Return the joy they give to you by giving the best of your culinary talent to them. Make this dinner your gift to them.

Using spring as your inspiration, create a fun, colorful and light-hearted invitation. Save formality for another event.

The Invitation

An egg-straordinary invite comes in a hollow plastic egg, filled with a touch of grass, a couple of jellybeans and a petite scrolled request for the honor of their presence. A simple time and place will suffice (family should know where you live). Gently deliver the egg in person, or wrap it carefully and place it into a small square box. Seal it with clear tape and proper postage (see Resources).

Vary it

Purchase simple card stock in any size, shape or color. Print pertinent information on the top 2/3 of the paper. Attach plastic grasses and little flowers with transparent glue, and mail in a narrow box or a padded envelope with proper postage (see Resources).

Simplify it

Skip the ordinary invitation section at your local retailer and opt for individual Easter cards. This way you can customize the card for the recipient—while sending an Easter greeting, you're also sending an invitation. Be sure to include time and place.

> "Life is a great big canvas, and you should throw all the paint on it you can." —Danny Kaye

Easter Eve

The eggs have been accounted for, the chocolate bunnies carefully unwrapped, and the Easter dresses are no longer white so join us, as we gather together to continue the giggles and memories.

Keri and John Owens
1782 East Willow Drive
4:30 p.m.

Stylish Setting

Alfresco-style dining starts with a cozy outdoor room, created from a striped Gazebo with full-length curtains. Decorate the interior with berry-like garlands and an empty silver picture frame and three suspended flower vases. Add an easy sophistication by moving your indoor furniture outside and minimizing the typical Easter décor. Drape your table with an inexpensive fuchsia duvet, topped with a white tablecloth. Try placemats that are cut-open (straw pot liners). Use simple clear-glass dinner plates, topped by subtly textured, green melamine salad plates. Tie the unadorned grass-green napkins with simple kitchen twine. The delicately etched, highball-style water glasses are paired with elaborate green- and clear-glass wine goblets. The glass pillar candlesticks are fitted with battery-operated candles under moss-covered mini lamp shades (see Resources).

A cone-shaped wire basket, stuffed with Bibb lettuce and simple carrots, is secured with orange and pink ribbons, and attached to the back of each chair. This adds a touch whimsy and is a low-cost alternative to extra flowers.

Essential Elements of Entertaining
Planning the perfect menu for any occasion

Whether a simple Sunday get-together or an elaborate Thanksgiving Day feast, planning a perfect menu has more to do with strategy than it does with food. These nine steps will help you organize and present a meal that allows the food to stand out and you to enjoy your guests.

1. Determine the event or occasion.
2. Set the time of day and place.
3. Decide on the number of guests (including children, as their cuisine needs may be different.)
4. Establish any food allergies.
5. Choose a seating style—sit down or buffet.

Once you've decided on these key points, you are ready to embark upon the menu.

First and foremost, a caveat: It has been said again and again, and with good reason—don't try new dishes for dinner parties. Experimenting at this time with new recipes adds tremendous and unnecessary stress to your event. Practice ahead of time or stick with your tried-and-true favorites.

6. Start with the main course—all else is designed around it. Most main courses entail meat, chicken or seafood, but pasta is perfectly acceptable.

Craft your menu with seasonal foods—once out of season, an item will be hard to find; won't hold its flavor, texture or nutrition; and rest assured, will stand out for all the wrong reasons.

7. Select one or two side dishes—typically one starch and one vegetable. (A salad is often considered a side dish.)
8. Plan your appetizers. Stick to one or two types, and plan three to four pieces per person. Limit them to a single theme, for example, don't serve chips and salsa before an Italian dinner.
9. Finally, choose your dessert. It's perfectly acceptable to cheat and purchase this—in fact, I highly recommend doing so. But if you choose to create your own, find one with no last-minute preparation.

Once you finalize the menu, build a thorough list of ingredients and double-check your pantry. If you already own it, is there enough of it left? Is it fresh? Divide the remaining list into items to purchase early and those you must pick up the day before, or the day of, the event.

On this note, ensure the best possible outcome (meaning no surprises with ingredients, timing or tools) by reading each recipe completely. Select recipes that you assemble in advance—this is the key determinant of how much time you spend with your guests versus in the kitchen.

Finally, embrace cheating. I often purchase a side dish or dessert from my favorite restaurant, asking them to box all dressings and toppings separately. I can add them myself later. I also make sure to get reheating instructions.

On this note, it's important to recognize your limits. If you're stressed, your guests inevitably will notice. Therefore, as your budget allows, consider hiring a personal chef or friend to help in the kitchen. I often pay a young girl to help take coats, serve drinks and clear plates. She charges less than the babysitter, and I end up having a much more enjoyable evening.

"The great gift of family life is to be intimately acquainted with people you might never even introduce yourself to, had life not done it for you."

—Kendall Hailey

Small details make all the difference— straw pot liners cut open, petite flower vases and miniature garden tools set in the water glasses give this table an elegant, English-garden feel.

> "The Easter Bunny came by today, and left surprises along the way."
> —Easter verse

Is it any wonder that the symbols of Easter conjure feelings of renewal, rebirth and transformation? The holiday heralds spring and the anticipation of longer, warmer days. Easter speaks of color, budding leaves, the promise of flowers and baby animals.

Rabbits, for example, are considered one of the most fertile of all animals, giving birth to several litters a year and capable of carrying two completely separate litters at one time. Birds, too, are symbolic of the season, laying a large clutch of eggs in the spring.

The Easter rabbit first appeared in America in the 1700s, according to History.com, likely through German immigrants who settled in Pennsylvania. Children crafted nests to hold the anticipated delivery of Easter eggs.

The Easter egg is connected to pagan traditions, History.com adds. "The egg, an ancient symbol of new life, has been associated with pagan festivals celebrating spring. From a Christian perspective, Easter eggs are said to represent Jesus' emergence from the tomb and resurrection."

Celebrants have decorated eggs since at least the thirteenth century, possibly because eggs were forbidden during Lent. Coloring eggs marked Easter and the end of Lent—and a renewed enjoyment of eggs.

For its part, Easter candy traditions vary. Chocolate eggs were popular in nineteenth century Europe, History.com notes, while Easter and jelly beans connected in the 1930s— "although the jelly bean's origins reportedly date all the way back to a Biblical-era concoction called a Turkish Delight."

Individually hung wire baskets are tied with pink and orange ribbons, and stuffed with Bibb lettuce and carrots.

An empty picture frame and three hanging vases are suspended with heavy fishing line from one of the tent poles.

65

Shopping List

1 fully cooked ham, about 6 to 8 pounds

2 750ml bottles Prosecco

3 8 or 9 inch white layer cakes, purchased or prepared

3 large bunches fresh watercress

3 medium beets

2 lemons

1 orange

1 bunch celery

1 bunch chives or 1 container alfalfa sprouts

1 small onion

1 large onion

1 medium leek

1 pound green asparagus

1 pound white asparagus

1 1/2 cup fresh shelled green peas or thawed, frozen peas

1/2 pound baby carrots

2 cup finely grated Parmesan cheese, finely grated

3 cups Arborio rice

10 cups chicken broth or stock

1 jar colored sugar

1/2 pound coconut flakes

1 quart mango nectar

1 package mini toasts or small Melba toast crackers

1/2 dozen large eggs

1 pound butter

3 cups heavy cream

2 8-ounce packages cream cheese

1 jar Dijon or gourmet mustard, your favorite

The Essentials

10 water glasses

10 juice glasses

10 wine glasses

1 pitcher – Prosecco mango mimosas

10 small plates—mini egg salad toasts (optional)

10 salad plates—watercress salad

10 dinner plates

10 place settings of cutlery, including salad forks, dinner forks, knives and dessert forks

10 napkins (have a few extra on hand)

1 or 2 tablecloths in different colors (one necessary and the second optional layering)

2 small serving trays—egg salad toasts and steamed asparagus

1 large serving tray—baked ham

2 medium serving bowls—salad and vegetable risotto

1 small bowl—mustard glaze

1 cake stand Coconut cake

Staples (replenish if needed)

salt

black pepper

all-purpose flour

white sugar

light brown sugar

cinnamon

curry powder

cider vinegar

dark corn syrup

vanilla extract

extra-virgin olive oil

red wine vinegar

Worcestershire sauce

mayonnaise

"You've touched people and known it.

You've touched people and never may know it.

Either way, you have something to give.
It is in giving to one another that each of
our lives becomes meaningful."

—Laura Schlessinger

Menu
For 10

Signature Drink:
Prosecco Mango Mimosas

Appetizer:
Mini Egg Salad Toasts

Salad:
Watercress Salad with Roasted Beets
and Parmesan Crisps

Entrée:
Baked Ham with A Brown Sugar
and Mustard Glaze

Accompaniments:
Steamed Green and White Asparagus
with Citrus Butter
Spring Vegetable Risotto
Mini pita breads, stone-ground mustard

Dessert:
Toasted Coconut Cake with
Spring Strawberries

The Recipes

Prosecco Mango Mimosas

1 fresh lemon
1 cup colored sugar
2 750ml bottles Prosecco, chilled
1 quart mango nectar

Cut the lemon in quarters and pour the sugar in a shallow saucer. Run the cut side of the lemon around the edge of a glass and quickly dip the glass in the sugar, creating a sugar rim. Repeat with remaining glasses and allow the sugar to set for 30 minutes. Combine the Prosecco and mango nectar in a pitcher and stir gently. Carefully pour the mixture in the prepared glasses, being careful not to disturb the sugar rims.

Mini Egg Salad Toasts

24 mini toasts or small Melba toast crackers
1/4 cup mayonnaise
1/2 teaspoon salt
1/4 teaspoon curry powder
1/4 teaspoon freshly ground black pepper
6 large eggs, peeled and finely chopped
2 stalks celery, finely chopped
chopped chives or alfalfa sprouts for garnish

In a medium bowl, combine the mayonnaise, salt, curry powder and black pepper and stir until combined. Add the eggs and celery and stir gently. Top each toast square with a generous spoonful of egg salad and garnish with chives or sprouts.

Baked Ham with Brown Sugar Mustard Glaze

1 fully cooked ham, about 6 to 8 pounds
1 cup light brown sugar, packed
1/4 teaspoon cinnamon
2 tablespoons flour
1 tablespoon prepared Dijon or gourmet mustard,
  your favorite
1 tablespoon cider vinegar
2 tablespoons dark corn syrup
2 tablespoons water

Heat oven to 325 degrees F. Line a roasting pan with foil. Wrap the ham in foil, keeping the ham fat side up; place it in the baking pan. Bake for 18 to 20 minutes per pound, or until a meat thermometer or temperature probe registers about 145 degrees F.

Meanwhile make the glaze. In a medium saucepan, combine brown sugar, cinnamon, flour, mustard, vinegar and corn syrup. Stir over medium-low heat until smooth. Add water and bring to a simmer. Simmer, stirring, for 1 minute.

Remove the foil from the ham and remove excess fat. Score the ham all over the surface, creating a diamond pattern. Brush the glaze all over the ham and return to the oven. Continue baking until meat reaches a temperature of 155 to 160 degrees F, basting with the glaze mixture frequently.

Watercress Salad with Roasted Beets and Parmesan Crisps

For the dressing:
2/3 cup extra-virgin olive oil
1/4 cup red wine vinegar
1 tablespoon Worcestershire sauce
1 teaspoon salt
1 tablespoon minced onion
2 tablespoons sugar

For the salad:
1 cup finely grated Parmesan cheese
3 medium beets, scrubbed and trimmed
3 tablespoons extra virgin olive oil
salt and freshly ground black pepper
3 large bunches fresh watercress, thin stems and
  leaves only (10 to 12 cups)

To make the dressing, whisk all the ingredients together in a bowl and refrigerate for at least one hour before serving; can be made up to 2 days in advance. Makes about 1 cup.

To make the Parmesan crisps, preheat the oven to 325 degrees F. Line a cookie sheet with parchment paper or a nonstick silicone baking pad. Drop level tablespoons of parmesan cheese on the baking sheet, and pat the cheese into a thin circle about 3 inches across in size. Bake five minutes, or until golden and crisp. Crisps can be made 1 day in advance and stored layered with waxed paper in an airtight container.

To roast the beets, preheat oven to 375 degrees F. In a medium bowl, toss the beets with the oil. Sprinkle with salt and pepper and wrap them in foil. Arrange on a baking sheet and roast in the oven until tender, 45 to 60 minutes. Remove from the oven, let cool for 10 minutes, and then peel and slice into 1/4-inch thick slices.

To finish the salad, transfer the watercress to a large bowl and drizzle with some of the salad dressing, tossing gently to coat. Divide salad among chilled plates and top with roasted beet slices and Parmesan crisps.

Steamed Green and White Asparagus with Citrus Butter

4 tablespoons butter at room temperature
1 teaspoon fresh squeezed lemon juice
1 tablespoon fresh squeezed orange juice
1 teaspoon finely minced orange zest
1 teaspoon finely minced lemon zest
1 pound green asparagus, rinsed and trimmed
1 pound white asparagus, rinsed and trimmed

Steam the asparagus in a steamer basket set over boiling water, just until tender.

While the asparagus is cooking, heat the butter over low heat in a small saucepan, just until melted. Remove from heat and add the lemon and orange juices; whisk to combine.

Arrange the asparagus spears in a serving dish. If you wish, arrange the white spears on one side and the green spears on the other. Drizzle with the citrus butter and garnish the white asparagus with the orange zest and the green asparagus with the lemon zest.

Spring Vegetable Risotto

6 tablespoons butter
1 large onion, finely diced
1 medium leek, white and pale green section only, diced
3 cups Arborio rice
10 cups chicken stock or broth
1 1/2 cups fresh, shelled green peas or thawed, frozen peas
18 baby carrots, trimmed and sliced on a diagonal
salt and pepper, to taste
1 cup freshly grated Parmesan cheese, plus extra for garnish

In a flameproof casserole, melt 3 tablespoons butter. Add the onion and leek and cook over medium heat for 10 minutes, stirring often. Add the rice and cook over medium heat, stirring, for 2 minutes. In a large saucepan, heat the chicken stock until it comes to a boil; reduce heat and simmer. Add 3 cups of the hot stock and cook the rice, stirring constantly, until almost all of the stock has been absorbed. Add 4 more cups of the stock, 1 cup at a time, and cook, stirring constantly, until it is absorbed. Remove the pan from the heat. Spread the risotto on a rimmed baking sheet. Cool, cover with plastic wrap, and refrigerate. Refrigerate the remaining stock.

Just before serving, return the risotto to the casserole. Reheat the remaining stock. Set the casserole over medium heat. Add the peas and carrots. Slowly add 2 cups of the remaining stock, 1/4 cup at a time, and cook, stirring constantly, until the rice absorbs the liquid. Add the remaining 1 cup of stock a little at a time, only enough to make a risotto that is cooked through and creamy. You may not need all of the remaining stock or you may need a little extra.

Stir in the salt and pepper, the remaining butter, and the Parmesan cheese. Immediately spoon the rice into a serving dish, sprinkle with extra Parmesan, and serve at once.

Toasted Coconut Cake

1/2 pound coconut flakes
3 8 or 9 inch white layer cakes, purchased or prepared
12 ounces (1 1/2 8-ounce packages) cream cheese, softened
3/4 cup sugar
1 1/2 teaspoons vanilla
3 cups heavy cream

To toast the coconut flakes, preheat the oven to 350 degrees F. Spread the coconut flakes on a cookie sheet or metal baking pan. Bake for 3 to 5 minutes or until golden brown. Cool to room temperature.

To make the frosting, combine the cream cheese, sugar and vanilla in a large mixing bowl or the bowl of a stand mixer. Fit the mixer with the whisk attachment and mix on medium speed until smooth. While the mixture is still whipping, slowly pour in the heavy cream. Continue whipping until the cream can hold a stiff peak.

Fill and frost the cake and cover it with the toasted coconut. Garnish with fresh strawberries.

Party Timeline

One month before the lunch:

- Make or purchase the invitations.
- Finalize the guest list and mail invitations.

3 weeks before the lunch:

- Finalize the menu, including drinks (carefully selecting the items you wish to make and the items you will purchase).
- Create a look by selecting colors, mood, setting and entertainment, if necessary.
- Order or gather the decorations and accessories.
- Purchase straw pot liners and cut them open.
- Purchase Easter eggs and treats to go inside.

2 weeks before the lunch:

- Make a shopping list for the food and liquor (see Shopping list).
- Order the food or any desert you do not wish to make.
- Order the ham.
- Order flowers, and consider having them delivered the day of the lunch.
- Assemble the Easter eggs.

1 week before the lunch:

- Assemble or purchase take-away gifts and wrap them.
- Purchase all nonperishable food and liquor (see Shopping list).
- Create a music playlist or purchase CDs.

3 days before the lunch:

- Decorate (if the lunch is indoors).
- Prepare the bar with glasses and liquor (if the lunch is indoors).
- Assemble all the serving dishes and set up the buffet table, if using one.

2 days before the lunch:

- Set up the outdoor gazebo if good weather is predicted.
- Attach garland and frame to posts.
- Move indoor furniture outside.
- Prepare the salad dressing and chill, covered.

The day before lunch:

- Purchase remaining perishable food (see Shopping list).
- Trim the watercress and chill in damp paper towels in a resealable bag.
- Prepare the egg salad and chill in a covered container.
- Prepare the Parmesan crisps for the salad and store, tightly covered, at room temperature.
- Prepare the risotto through the first step and refrigerate.
- Pick up flowers or have them delivered.
- Make extra ice.
- Check that the bathroom is clean. Have fresh hand towels, soap and extra toilet paper on hand.

The morning of the lunch:

- Set the table and lay out serving dishes (if the lunch is outside).
- Prepare the bar with glasses and liquor (if the lunch is outside).
- Make lettuce and carrot baskets to hang on the backs of the chair.
- Hide the Easter eggs.
- Start the ham about 1½ hours before guests are due to arrive. Prepare the asparagus and finish cooking the risotto.
- Remove the cake from the refrigerator and garnish the cake with fresh strawberries.

Prior to guests' arrival:

- Arrange food on platters.
- Brew a pot of coffee.
- Start the music.
- Prepare the Prosecco mango mimosas, including one for yourself!
- Light the candles.
- Enjoy!

Take Away Gifts

Finish the evening as beautifully as it started with a tangible thank you. These gifts not only show your appreciation of their company, but also eliminate the need to follow up with your guests in the days after the event.

Among my all-time favorite take-away (or hostess gifts) is the "next morning" breakfast basket. Simply stuff any small to medium size basket or gift box with a half-dozen of fresh pastries and half-pound of fresh ground coffee. Enclose a simple card that reads, simply, "thank you." You'll find this one of the most well-received (and used) gifts ever.

Vary it:

Leave a lasting impression on your guests with these unique cocktail jelly beans. These adult-only beans come beautifully packaged in petite, individual tins. Choose among several flavors, such as Cosmopolitan, Mojoito, Bellini and Lemon Drop. Secure two or three tins together with a thin ribbon a small feather (see Resources).

Simplify it:

A Stylish frame is always going to find a home among your guests. Consider tearing out a pretty picture from a magazine to fill it until you can print and send pictures from the day. Gift wrap the frames with simple paper, and faux grass and flowers. (I used zinc plant markers to identify the recipient (see Resources).

"Life is to be interpreted not simply in terms of things but in terms of ideals."

—Charles M. Crowe

71

Nesting

Surrounded by those most dear, join the mother-to-be in the instinctual ritual of bustling, readying and preparing for life's greatest gift. Embrace this final opportunity to bring together family and friends and share advice, wisdom, laughter and tears over a cup of tea and classic accompaniments.

"From this day forward,
you shall not walk alone.
My heart will be your shelter,
And my arms will be your home."
—Unknown

At a Glance

Theme:
A New Little Bird is on His Way

Setting:
A large backyard or private courtyard

Mood:
Elegant, traditional, nurturing, warm and instinctual

Colors:
Robin's egg blue, picket fence white

Flowers:
French, 'Endless Summer' hydrangeas in pale blue,
white lilacs, mixed greens and blueberries

Tastes:
The menu features a crisp, lighter presentation of springtime offerings,
starting with cherry tomatoes stuffed with a delicate crab filling, chilled
blueberry-Meyer Lemon bisque and crunchy cashew citrus chicken salad.
A lemon raspberry 'nest' cake and an assortment of light and
dark chocolate cupcakes are served for dessert.

Sounds:
A custom play list features a variety of beautiful music from the CDs
On a Starry Night, *The Modern Baby Shower Collection* (Vitamin String
Quartet), A Collection, *Rockabye Baby*, renditions from U2, Dave Matthews,
Led Zeppelin and Coldplay (many others available). Rock songs that have
been transformed into beautiful instrumental lullabies, these soothing
sounds are great for background music and double as a wonderful gift for
the mom-to-be after the shower to help lull her baby into a sweet slumber.

Experience:
Enlist the help of an experienced knitter. You will be asking your
guests to each knit a very simple 8- by 10-inch pocket. These will later be
made into a baby blanket composed of 12 pockets. This blanket will no
doubt become a treasured heirloom for the mother and child, holding the
most precious of keepsakes for years to come.

Vary it: Have your guests write a brief wish for the baby on a heavy piece
of cloth with a permanent fabric marker. Later have the patches sewn
onto a high quality baby blanket.

Simplify it: Attach beautiful note cards with wishes using old-fashioned
diaper pins to a high quality baby blanket.

Gather together loved and
cherished family and
friends on a brisk spring
afternoon to celebrate the upcoming
new branch on the family tree.
Nesting is an instinct as
strong as a mother and
child bond:
an irresistible urge to clean,
gather, to build and protect;
to cradle, to nurture and to love;
to hold your children's hopes and
harness their dreams;
to create a home both
physically and emotionally;
to have and hold;
to love more than one
thought possible;
to weather out the bright, warm days
and the dark, cold nights...
this is what it means to nest.
A little bundle of joy arrives, one whose very
existence makes you a better,
stronger, more perfect person
just by being in your life.
It is what motherhood does to you:
it makes you believe in miracles,
laugh out loud,
chase fireflies and make mud pies,
and realize above all,
that life doesn't come
wrapped in a pretty package
tied with a bow,
but the opportunity to nurture a child
is the single greatest
gift in life.
A baby shower is just the beginning of
countless memories.

"The tiny bundle by her side stirred a little, and though it was scarcely more
        then the ruffling of a feather,
She awoke; for the mother-ear is
        so close to the heart that it can hear
        the faintest whisper of a child."

—Kate Douglas Wiggin

A Whimsical Welcome

For the most miraculous celebration in life, there is no better way to share it than with a handmade invitation announcing an afternoon of nibbling, knitting and connecting.

The Invitation

A rectangle of robin's egg blue card stock frames a piece of vertically striped paper on which the party details have been printed in a classic script font. Staple the papers together and cover the staple with a natural raffia ribbon bow topped with miniature nests, birds, and petite eggs. (These can be found at any local craft or floral store.) A thin 8- by 8-inch box filled with natural grass paper cradles and nests this sweet and simple invitation and protects it during mailing.

Vary it

Glue a small, marble-sized ball of yarn to the top of a rectangle of robin's egg blue card stock paper. Insert two crossed and shortened toothpicks to look like knitting needles. Send in the box described above.

Simplify it

Purchase very simple and elegant pre-made baby shower invitations, and enclose several downy white feathers inside the envelope.

A New Little Bird Is On His Way
Let's Celebrate With A Shower Before The Big Day!
Please join us in honoring
Morgan Middlefield
Saturday, May 12th 11:30

284 Crest View Lane
R.S.V.P.
303-333-1001

The Connection Between the Stork and Childbirth

Millions of children from nearly every culture have grown up believing that a stork casually wrapped them up in an appropriately colored blanket and dropped them at the doorstep. For obvious reasons this tale handily deflected a rather uncomfortable conversation regarding sex and childbirth, but clearly there's more to it than that.

The link between the stork and the birth of a child is deeply rooted within both Eastern and Western cultures; the Greeks, Egyptians, Chinese, Europeans and Americans have all spun tales that tie the two together. The Greeks believed it started with a scandal between two women, a curse, an abduction and of course, a war. The Egyptians felt that the stork represented one's soul before and after death. The Chinese considered these mystical birds to be sacred creatures that also delivered people to heaven. The connection and underlying coincidence is that historically, storks have been associated with luck, happiness and prosperity.

The Hebrew meaning of the English word 'stork' is "kind mother" – appropriate qualities for these large, waddling birds with exaggerated bills. The species are committed to establishing and staying with both their mate and their nest, thus fitting the attributes of ideal parents. Contributing to the lore's prevalence is the stork's statue and size – some are almost six feet in length, giving some credence to the image of them carrying around an infant swaddled in a sling. It is this folklore that led to the nickname "Storks Bite," a common pinkish spotting found on infants' foreheads, upper lip and nape of the neck. That's a nice touch; these enormous birds swoop down, drop you off to an unsuspecting family and send you off with a farewell bite – what a great image to give young children!

Essential Elements of Entertaining
Budgeting

Planning a party can be as much fun as throwing one; nonetheless, it's easy to get so caught up in all the particulars that one of the most important details gets pushed aside: the budget. Without one, costs can quickly get out of hand, or worse, you could run out of money before addressing some of the most important and essential elements. Parties can quickly go from wonderful to stressful when expenses are not focused on and held to. Your budget needs to cover all the expenses and therefore, it is important to understand what the potential costs are, how to allocate the money you've set aside, and when to reassess the funds, if necessary.

Timing is Everything
The better you plan, the better the payoff. The longer you have before a party the more time you have to shop around for the best values; it also gives you the ability to call for more estimates in which you can compare prices and services.

Start by determining a budget amount you are comfortable with. Next, prioritize what aspects of the party are most important and work from there. For some it is the food; for others, the location, the drinks, or the décor are high on the priority list. There is no right or wrong answer, only what is best for you.

Next, think about the type of affair you feel would best fit the occasion: a friend's baby shower, your husband's 40th birthday bash, a Mother's Day celebration, a Fourth of July picnic, a meal on Christmas Day – or 'just because,' which is as good a reason as any.

Once you've determined the type of party you'd like to host, consider how you'll serve the food:

Sit-down Meal
The sit-down, plated meal is usually reserved for a smaller gathering of friends and family and is typically more intimate and personal than a buffet or cocktail party. While the common perception is that these are the most expensive parties, that is not always the case as the number of guests is usually limited.

Buffet
The buffet meal is a good alternative when you want to have a less restrictive guest list and accommodate a larger group for a full meal. Buffets are sometimes more casual affairs, but they can easily come with high price tag as they often include more food and a wider variety of options.

Cocktail Party

The cocktail party is an excellent option when you want to invite lots of people yet maintain a more limited budget. In lieu of a full meal, you can serve several hors d' oeuvres or appetizers that are typically smaller and fewer. The liquor cost can be high if you have an open bar, but you can control costs by serving wine, beer and a few pre-made signature drinks.

Guest List

The number of guest can largely impact the cost of any party adding to the food, liquor, take-away gifts expense. However, there are fixed costs with many events, such as entertainment, flowers, invitations (usually a minimal impact), décor, and some hired help. It is just as easy to spend the same amount for a sophisticated sit-down dinner for 20 as it is for casual cocktails for 100, so make a budget and stick to it. Keep in mind that typically 20 to 25 percent of your guests will not be able to attend, so plan accordingly or keep a back-up list of people you can invite if needed as your RSVP's start coming in.

Hidden Talents

One of the best ways to save money is to figure out what you can do yourself, and outsource what you can't. Decorating, arranging flowers, and preparing food represent some of the more substantial expenditures for most parties, so if you are talented in these areas you can minimize costs. A word of caution, however; if cooking is really something you don't have a knack for, preparing the food for a party is probably is not the best time to try to learn. Instead, hire a caterer or a good friend who loves to cook and spare yourself the stress and worry that can dampen the atmosphere and your overall enjoyment of the festivities.

Décor

When it comes to decorating for a party, you don't need to spend a lot of money if you plan carefully and think creatively. Once you've settled on a theme, do some brainstorming and make a list of all the associated elements you can think of. For example, if you are planning a seaside escape (but live in a land-locked state) you might consider covering the tables with sand and adding pots of tall grasses. Stick with basic white colored plates and serving pieces; these are usually very inexpensive to buy or rent. You might consider live goldfish in bowls as takeaway gifts, or baskets filled with a variety of the famous gold fish crackers. For every great idea, there is usually a cheaper option if given a little thought.

Budgeting is an art, not a science, so use your common sense and practicality and remember that most people will never notice the details that can get you in financial trouble. Make a budget, stick to it, and enjoy the celebration!

(See Resources at the back of the book for more extensive budgeting tools.)

Location:	$_____
Invitations:	$_____
Décor:	$_____
Flowers:	$_____
Music:	$_____
Drinks:	$_____
Food:	$_____
Gifts:	$_____
Miscellaneous Costs:	$_____

Shopping List

Fresh lavender (can be found at specialty markets or spice shops)
1 bottle Monin Lavender Syrup
X bottles Perrier
3 pounds fresh red cherry tomatoes
1 pound fresh or frozen shredded crabmeat
12 ounces soft herbed cheese, such as Boursin
8 cups fresh blueberries (or substitute frozen)
4 cups fresh pineapple juice
4 cups sour cream
1 pint lime sherbet
1 bunch fresh tarragon
1 bunch mint leaves
4 pounds boneless, skinless chicken breast poached
12 large sticks celery
2 heads romaine lettuce
4 large ripe avocados
16 green onions
2 to 4 cups salted cashew halves
4 oranges
2 -3 large bunches of fresh cilantro
2 -3 large bunches of fresh parsley
Red wine vinegar
Dijon mustard
Tabasco sauce
8 ounces fresh orange or orange pineapple juice
Springs of rosemary
Assorted tea bags
Coffee
Prepared cake and cupcakes

The Essentials

12 water glasses
12 chic glasses
12 coffee cups
12 small side plates for stuffed peppers
12 soup bowls
12 dinner plates for salad
12 place settings of cutlery, including soup spoons, salad forks, knives, and dessert forks or spoons
1 serving tray for lemonade glasses
1 large pitcher for lemonade
1 or 2 cake stands or serving trays for desserts
12 napkins (have a few extra on hand)
3 tablecloths

The Staples
(Replenish if needed)

Salt
Fresh ground pepper
White sugar
Vegetable oil
Tabasco
Raw brown sugar
Milk

The Menu
For 12

Signature Drink:
French Lavender Lemonade

❧

Appetizer:
Cherry Red Tomatoes stuffed with
Crab and Herbed Cheese

❧

Starter:
Chilled Blueberry Bisque with Meyer Lemon

❧

Entrée:
Cashew Citrus Chicken Salad

❧

Dessert:
Light and Dark Chocolate Nesting Cupcakes
Lemon and Raspberry filled Knit Cake

French Lavender Lemonade

Served with Lavender Syrup and a splash of Sparkling Water

Cherry Red Tomatoes Stuffed with Crab and Herbed Cheese

3 pounds fresh red cherry or grape tomatoes
1 pound fresh or thawed frozen shredded crab meat
12 ounces soft herbed cheese such as Boursin, room
  temperature

Slice tomatoes in half and remove the seeds; drain them cut side down on paper towels. Use a fork to gently combine the cheese with the crabmeat in a medium bowl. Scoop a generous spoonful of the mixture into each tomato half and chill, covered, for two hours.

Chilled Blueberry Bisque with Meyer Lemon

8 cups fresh blueberries (frozen if fresh are not available)
4 cups fresh pineapple juice
3 Meyer lemons, juiced
½ cup sugar
4 cups sour cream
1 pint lime sherbet
Chopped fresh tarragon
Mint leaves for garnish

Process blueberries in a food processor until smooth. Add pineapple juice, lemon juice, sugar and sour cream. Process to blend. Transfer mixture to a saucepan and bring to a boil. Gently boil for 15 minutes. Cool slightly. Chill for 8 to 10 hours. Mix sherbet with tarragon and freeze to set. When ready to serve, pour bisque into bowls and garnish with a dollop of sherbet and a couple of mint leaves.

Cashew Citrus Chicken Salad

For the dressing:
2 cups fresh cilantro
1 cup fresh parsley
1 cup vegetable oil
1 cup fresh orange juice or orange pineapple juice
2 tablespoons red wine vinegar
2 tablespoons Dijon mustard
4 teaspoons salt
8 teaspoons Tabasco sauce
freshly ground black pepper

For the salad:
4 pounds boneless, skinless chicken breasts, poached
12 large sticks celery, sliced
2 heads romaine lettuce, gently torn
4 large avocados, peeled, pitted and cut in slices
16 green onions, cleaned and sliced
2 to 4 cups salted cashew halves
4 oranges, peel and white pith removed, sliced
1 bunch fresh cilantro or parsley for garnish
12 small rosemary springs

To make the dressing, process the cilantro, parsley, oil, orange juice, vinegar, mustard, salt, sugar, and Tabasco sauce in a food processor. Season with pepper. Set aside.

Slice chicken into 1/4-inch pieces. Place in a large bowl. Add celery, romaine, avocados, green onions, and cashews. Toss with dressing. Serve on a platter or on individual plates garnished with orange slices and cilantro or parsley and a spring of rosemary.

Serene Settings
Accents and Accessories Create a Nurturing Atmosphere

In a large backyard or private park, custom-made table-cloths and a covered umbrella convey the baby bird theme from which everything else is built on. The petite bird and nest design is continued in the dishware and tea service along with heirloom napkins and mismatched silverware. The chairs are each adorned with a personal bouquet of flowers identified by the individual initial of each guest. (These tags are antique hotel key chains – see resources for more details.)

The antique mahogany buffet is constantly changing throughout the afternoon, beginning with the signature lavender lemonade served with a side of lavender syrup and raw sugar with lavender buds. The buffet later bears the much-anticipated lemon and raspberry cake decorated to resemble a knit blanket with a bird and nest

residing atop. The milk and dark chocolate cupcakes look like nests cradling several small eggs and are served from an antique birdbath. A gorgeous bronze statue is covered with hydrangeas, evoking images of childhood innocence and fragility.

Some of the gifts are carefully wrapped in vintage sewing patterns, giving a truly delicate and unique presentation. The other gifts are wrapped in various patterns of blue stripes or birds and bee paper. These one-of-a-kind gifts are tied with old and new blue ribbon, some with glued little nests, birds, feathers or twigs. A few have antique sterling teaspoons attached– these make great baby spoons and can be found rather inexpensively at most antique stores or online.

"A mother holds her child's hand for a short while and their heart forever."

—Author unknown

The flowers are kept simple and effortless with large groupings of French 'Endless Summer' hydrangeas in pale blue and white lilacs to add contrast and their amazing fragrance; the blossoms are accented with greenery and blueberries. I embellished virtually everything with these flowers, allowing them to serve as a primary decoration. The flowers function as the centerpieces, in the individually baskets hung behind each chair, on the buffet table, around specific gifts and surrounding the desserts. If bought in bulk, these flowers can be purchased inexpensively.

In keeping with surroundings of beloved heirlooms, a 200-year-old crib plays double duty holding the gifts for the little boy on his way.

A Timely Debut

The baby shower is often considered a rite of passage, a celebration in anticipation of a new person. To be part of a shower is a great honor and gift. Throughout all the years baby showers still serve to rejoice in a new life, support the expectant parents and help in providing some material necessities.

Dating as far back as Roman times, baby showers have been popular for many centuries. Until modern times, most of these celebrations were typically held after the baby was born. The shower was an occasion to 'present' the baby, and the baptism was often conducted at the same time.

Only women attended these afternoon parties, dressed in their finest and carrying parasols; in fact umbrellas have long been a celebratory symbol and may have even inspired the term "baby shower." Guests typically brought handmade gifts of food, clothing and blankets. Many women did not often appear in public during their pregnancies and were confined to the home for a month or more after their babies were born. Showers were often one of the few ways for a new mother to socialize after the birth of her baby while also getting advice and support from friends and family.

Mortality rates have shrunk and technology has advanced, so today's showers are commonly held a month or two before the baby's birth – and now we often know the baby's gender and predicted due date. Some modern celebrations include the men in the baby's life as well as the women. Gifts these days are still largely practical, but can also range from fun to eccentric.

Suggested Themes for Gifts

The Clothes Line
Suggest that each guest bring an outfit in a different size (double up if it's a large gathering). Keep the gifts unwrapped and attach the outfits with clothespins on the line in order of size. Attach the cards to each outfit and pile the grouping into a large laundry basket. For a dramatic effect, slowing pull the rope out, exposing a wardrobe that will outfit the wee one for a year or more.

Nursery Shower
Gifts are simply based on the theme and colors that the parents have selected for the baby's nursery.

Mom's Shower
For the mom who is already prepared for the baby's arrival, bring gifts just for her; fill a large basket with items like beautifully scented candles, soft slippers, a gift certificate for a perfect pedicure and theatre tickets.

Baby's Firsts
Have each guest bring a gift that will make each milestone memorable: bath supplies for a baby's first bath, cutlery and dishware for the baby's first meal, shoes for the first steps, and so on.

Baby's Day
Perfect for smaller showers, each guest brings gifts appropriate for a particular time of day: items for wake up, meal-time, playtime, bath time and bedtime.

Regardless of the type of shower you throw, make sure that above all the mother-to-be's wishes are met and honored. This is a blessed event that she will always remember.

Shower Considerations

Who should host?
Anyone except the mother-to-be; other than that, it is perfectly acceptable and appropriate for mothers, mother-in-laws, sisters, co-workers, friends–and in many cases, a group of friends and family–to throw the shower, thus spreading out the responsibility and expense. While showers are often held at the home of the host, the event could also be held at a restaurant (many have private rooms), a quaint coffee house or even a small local park. The host commonly picks up the bill, so plan ahead and devise a budget.

Who should be included?

In many cases, you may be close enough to the recipient to know most of the guests she will want included. However, I always recommend playing it safe and asking the mother-to-be about the guest list as she may have a new friend or neighbor she would like to include. This is one reason why I am not an enthusiast of surprise showers. I think parenthood throws enough surprises at you, so let the guest of honor be excited and prepared for this momentous event.

Should men be included?

This depends on the type of shower, the theme, and the feelings of the mother-to-be. Personally, I haven't known many men who want to be included in a baby shower, but that is a completely personal decision.

What about inviting friends who have miscarried or faced infertility?

This can be a sensitive issue, so never make assumptions either way with invitations. I have always thought it best for someone very close to call and talk to anyone on the guest list who may have suffered a loss or disappointment before the invitations are sent. The caller can make assurances that the guest's presence at the shower would be welcome and also convey that everyone would understand if this is too painful for her, accepting whatever her reply may be with compassion and grace.

Is a baby shower appropriate for an adoption?

Absolutely! Every child needs an extraordinary welcome into this world. However, due to the possibility of unforeseen complications, it's best to talk with the mom-to-be about timing. Adoption showers are often held after the baby or child has joined the family or once the adoption becomes legal. You may want to consider altering the wish list or theme of the shower to fit the age of the child.

What about single mothers?

I can't think of anyone who needs it more. Single moms will need all the extra support and love out there. Some of the best gifts could be in help with cleaning, meal preparation or baby-sitting.

Are baby showers typically held for the second or third babies and beyond?

Traditionally, a party was only given for the first baby, with the idea that the gifts would be handed down. But any more this school of thought is changing. I personally think every baby is special and needs its own recognition. Showers for sequential children don't need to necessarily include gifts or be as elaborate. But in cases where the mother is having a different gender baby than the one or ones she has, or a long period of time has lapsed between her children, you might consider a clothing or toy shower. Showers after the baby's birth that do not incorporate gifts were traditionally called a 'Sip and See' (see the baby, sip some tea).

Are games appropriate for a baby shower?

Games played at baby showers became popular in America after WWII when showers became more common, but this is something you're either on one side of the fence or the other. Some love them; others won't go to showers in fear of them. Personally, I don't really think "Guess the Gerber" (baby food tasting) or "Guess the Girth" of the mother-to-be (like any pregnant woman pregnant wants people focusing on how wide her bum has become) is fun for anyone. Some games are better than others; just always be conscious of the mother's wishes, the average age of guests, and the type of party you want to achieve. I have always fallen back on two rules in regards to games at any party. Ask yourself , "Will this embarrass the guest of honor or other guests"? If the answer is yes, rethink it. Second, are you using games to break up monotony? There are much better ways; with careful planning and helpful introductions, most guests will get along great. Instead, of playing games you may want to consider an activity or experience such as I suggested in "At A Glance." at the beginning of the chapter.

'My Wish For You' Blanket

Inspired by the wonderful book "The Twelve Gifts of Birth" by Charlene Costanzo A book that "through a tender and inspiring tale reveals the birthright inheritance that all children receive at this moment." Using "messages that help form a strong foundation of self-respect and values. With this as your inspiration, make 12 small cards adorn with a small feather, each titled with the suggested twelve gifts. Ask your guests to each return one of the small note cards with the finished pocket, filled out with an example, wish, or piece of advice regarding the "gift" the have selected. When the blanket is assembled (usually by the host of the shower or a knitting shop will usually provide this service) the wishes will be enclosed in the 12 pockets.

These note cards can be removed as the momentous keepsakes such as the first lock of hair, rattle, first tooth are achieved.

The Gift of Faith
The Gift of Courage
The Gift of Joy
The Gift of Talent
The Gift of Love
The Gift of Compassion
The Gift of Hope
The Gift of Beauty
The Gift of Reverence
The Gift of Strength
The Gift of Imagination
The Gift of Wisdom

Knitting Instructions for Twelve Pocket Heirloom Blanket

Measurements of each Pocket:
Approximately 8 X 10 inches
(2 inches folds over to make top of the pocket).

Measurement of completed blanket:
Approximately 32 inches across X 42 inches long

Materials
Approximately 36 3 oz. balls chunky merino (super soft)
  yarn (3 balls per pocket)
Approximately 8-10 3 oz. balls for borders

A collection of knitted baby gifts for the mother-to-be is draped from a clothes line. This cozy resting spot is created to invite the guests to circle around and knit following their light lunch.

Size 6.5 knitting needles (1 for each knitter)
12 pearlized buttons (1 for each pocket)

To Make Pockets
Cast on 26 stitches 1st row (right side) Knit all stitches
2nd row (wrong side) Purl all stitches
Repeat this pattern until work measures approximately
 10 inches or 48 rows down
Bind off all stitches on a Knit row (right side).

Finishing
Sew sides together to form an envelope leaving 2 inches for the fold over of the pocket. Sew button centered and close to the top of under flap (cast on edge).

To Make Blanket
Cast on 6 stitches (2 inches). Purl stitch approximately 192 rows. Repeat this pattern 4 times. This will be your vertical border along the two edges and between the 3 pockets (approximately 42 inches). Bind off

Cast on 64 stitches. Purl stitch 10 rows. Repeat this pattern 5 times. This will be your horizontal border along two edges and between 4 pockets (approximately 32 inches across). Bind off.

Finish
Sew together the horizontal borders and pockets with the two outer pockets against the edges of the border. Equally space the inner two pockets with 2 inches between each. Sew together the vertical borders with 2 inches between each pocket.

This is just one of many types of blankets that can be assembled. All measurements are approximate – gauge of yarn, knitting needle size will alter measurements.

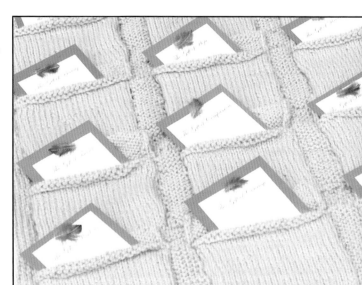

Party Timeline

One month before the shower:

- Make or purchase invitations.
- Finalize the guest list and mail the invitations.

3 weeks before the shower:

- Finalize the menu, including drinks (carefully selecting the items you wish to make and the items you wish to purchase).
- Create a look by selecting colors, mood and setting.
- Order or gather the decorations and accessories.

2 weeks before the shower:

- Make a shopping list for the food and liquor (see Shopping list).
- Order the food or any desert you do not wish to make.
- Order flowers, and consider having them delivered the day of the shower.

1 week before the shower:

- Assemble or purchase take-away gifts and wrap them.
- Purchase all nonperishable food and liquor. (see Shopping list).
- Put together music or create a custom CD.

3 days before the shower:

- Decorate (if shower is inside).
- Prepare the bar with glasses and liquor (if the shower is inside).
- Assemble all the serving dishes and set up the buffet table (if the shower is inside).

2 days before the shower:

- Prepare the blueberry bisque and chicken for the salad, cover tightly and refrigerate.

The day before the shower:

- Purchase perishable food (see Shopping list).
- Set the table and lay out the serving dishes.
- Pick up flowers or have them delivered.
- Make extra ice.
- Check that the bathroom is clean. Have fresh hand towels, soap and extra toilet paper on hand.

The morning of the shower:

- Decorate (if the shower is outside).
- Finish preparing the food.

Prior to guests' arrival:

- Arrange the food on platters.
- Brew a pot of coffee.
- Start the music.
- Prepare the French lavender lemonade.
- Light the candles.
- Enjoy!

Take Away Gifts

Your guests have showered and pampered the mother-to-be with gifts created from love, time, and generosity. Show them how much their support and devotion means to you.

A Season of Flower or Herb Seeds
Your friends will love months of beautiful blooming flowers or delectable herbs from their own miniature garden. Buy a pre-made kit (see Resources) or assemble your own with three to five small planting pots filled ¾ with soil and three to five seed packets (all available at a local garden store). Stack the pots and enclose the seeds in a clear "treat bag" (available at any large retailer that carries party supplies). Secure with a lovely blue ribbon and a small white feather.

Vary it
Indulge your friends and family with a petite spa basket containing a collection of comforting and tranquil gifts. Nestled in little basket is a small bottle of milk bath, birds egg soaps, a scented candle and lavender tea bags (see Resources). These can be trial-sized items that make a huge impact while keeping with the nesting theme.

Simplify it
Remove the attached flower baskets from behind each chair to present to your guests. Each woven, cone-shaped basket holds a breathtaking arrangement of Baby Blue Hydrangeas adorned with a vintage hotel key (or substitute another unique accent piece) and tied off with thin velvet ribbon.

Pearls of Wisdom

It's with unwavering grace and poise that others see her...
It's with unconditional love and compassion that you know her.
She embodies hope, elegance, enduring strength and dignified beauty –
So with heartfelt gratitude, honor the woman – or women
most important in your life to a Mother's Day brunch.

"My mother is my root, my foundation. She planted the seed that I base my life on, and that is the belief that the ability to achieve starts in your mind."

—Michael Jordan

Theme:
The Picture of a Lady

Setting:
A well-loved, cherished family home

Mood:
Sentimental, tender, loving, and unforgettable. Sun-faded fabrics, heirloom china, and polished silver create a gracious ambience fit for royalty. Delicate jewels, lovely peonies and an indulgent pedicure ensure a perfect morning for a woman of great nobility.

Colors:
Petal pink, pearl white and accents of tourmaline pink

Flowers:
Peonies in a variety of colors, lamb's ear and small boxwoods

Tastes:
An elegant brunch created with time-honored recipes handed down through generations

Sounds:
A custom play list soothes to the instrumentals in Spa Lounge, *Sounds of Spa: Tranquility* or *Sounds of Spa: Serenity*—all collections of various artists. If you seek something a bit more classic, consider Nat King Cole's *Best of Instrumental* or one of the many jazz/classical CDs from renowned trumpeter Chris Botti.

Experience:
What better way to enhance existing bonds and build new memories than a morning of pampering and well-earned indulgence? Gift your mom, your guests and yourself with the soothing spell of a spa treatment. Tap the services of a pro to help transform your own home into a spa, complete with facials, manicures and pedicures.

Vary it: Treat mom to an elegant English tea on the patio, rounded out with proper teacups and saucers, and of course, accompanied by a raspberry mousse and almond cake.

Simplify it: Surprise your mom with a trip for all to a local day spa for manicures and pedicures. Check to see if you can bring your own mimosas and cake.

Pearls, diamonds, gold, silver and wisdom are things of deep, unbreakable substance, the kind achievable only through time, occasional fire, and infinite patience. Mothers are like that, too—graceful, finely honed, wise without judgment, multifaceted and steely, and exquisite. Of all the precious jewels in our worlds, mothers are our most priceless.

Today, take a moment to appreciate this gem, this single-most-influential person in your life. Your mother, who rocked you to sleep, bandaged your knees and mended your broken heart. A woman who put all of your hopes, dreams and aspirations ahead of hers. A person whose single greatest desire was to see you grow, learn, love and find a place in this world. A mother that chose to forget your terrible twos, threes and sometimes fours, your unruly and awkward adolescence, your insolent and impertinent teens. A woman who still believes in her heart of heart that you can be the president, an astrophysicist, or a noble prize recipient. She believes in fairy tales and happy endings because that is what she wants for you. She has given up a part of her life for yours, she's bestowed upon you the qualities for love and greatness, and in return, your life gave hers significance beyond measure.

"I looked on childrearing not only as a work of love and duty but as a profession that was fully as interesting and challenging as any honorable profession in the world, and one that demanded the best I could bring to it."

—Rose Kennedy

A Treasured Heirloom

Didn't your mother teach you better than that? In the midst of our families, we tend to take short cuts. Secure, comfortable, fun-loving and informal, we grant each other leeway, a determined overlooking of mistakes and shortcomings. This camaraderie makes it easy to forgo what seems small— for example, the traditional invitation. Instead, we settle for a phone call, or even worse, an e-vite. This time, set the tone for a different affair, one of elegance, appreciation and honor. Build anticipation with a handcrafted invitation to a morning meal and personalized pampering.

The Invitation

Embellish a pale pink, square sheet of card stock paper with several half-round pearl adhesives (found at any local craft store). Place them off-center and lined up to look like a double-strand pearl necklace. Print party details on the left-hand side of the card before adhering the pearl stickers. If mailing, add a few pieces of tissue paper or foam packing around the invitation to help protect the pearls. Write "Hand-Cancel" on the outside of the envelope and adhere proper postage.

Vary it

On a square sheet of card stock paper, glue a small piece of lace trim. Bunch the lace together to look like a collar of a Victorian blouse. Pin a costume brooch or cameo to the lace. Print party details on the lower half of the paper prior to affixing the lace and brooch. If mailing, insert the invitation in a thin, cardboard jewelry box (found at any craft or container store). Seal with clear tape and proper postage.

Simplify it

Purchase one of the many pre-made party invitations. Look for some with flowers or other feminine motifs. Enclose several loose pearls (found at any craft store in the bead section). Send in a padded envelope with proper postage.

Revitalize an overgrown gazebo with sheer drapes, candlelight and a flower-filled chandelier.

An antique tea service, cake and cutlery sit tidily on a table, awaiting the festive guests. Outdoor benches offer cozy extra seating under the watchful eyes of two Roman sculptures.

Portrait of a Lady

Mother's Day Brunch

Sunday May 12th
at 11:00 am
Cambridge Hill House
2808 Ivy Crest Lane

Please join us in the gardens to share
stories, champagne, and pearls of wisdom

"It is not until you become a mother that your judgment slowly turns to compassion and understanding".

—Erma Bombeck

Charmingly mismatched silver was acquired over time to replace missing and damaged pieces.

For an elegant touch, roll napkins and secure with a child's strand of pearls, then attach a costume cameo.

Essential Elements of Entertaining
A Hospitable Host

Does anything at all bring you the satisfaction of a successful soiree? Only the hostess will know the orchestrated effort that went into it. Guests will feel reluctant to leave and eager to return. They remember the hostess not as the gifted practitioner of party planning, but someone who emanated confidence and graciousness, who seemed prepared and thus relaxed.

If you take just one piece of advice on proper party planning, let it be this: your clothing, your cuisine, your cleanliness and your decor will matter not at all if your guests do not enjoy themselves. And that single aspect depends upon you.

Special needs

Carefully consider whom you invite to what, and any special needs of your individual guests—before developing the guest list. Small children at adult affairs pose challenges, as will your great aunt's presence at the water-park party for your 5-year-old's birthday. And always ask ahead of time about any dietary restrictions.

Be prepared

The college-dorm ambience of your younger years allowed the spontaneity of beer kegs and pizza. No longer. Today's galas call for planning and preparation—the more you complete in advance, the more you'll relax and enjoy your guests. Establish a timeline that schedules cleaning, decorating and pre-crafted cuisine. You'll want to be dressed and ready at least twenty minutes before guests arrive.

Introductions

An old saw says that "to be a successful hostess, when guests arrive, say 'at last!' When they leave, say, 'so soon!'" On that note, stay close to the door to welcome your friends, make introductions and take coats. Quickly provide drinks. If you can't slip away to do that, direct your guests to the bar area (set up in advance with glasses, ice, open bottles and a signature drink).

Awkward Silences

No one wants to stand awkwardly, gazing around the room for familiar faces. Quickly and briefly establish common ground between guests you're introducing, starting the conversation. As host, your job entails initiating the chat, then allowing guests to continue. Beforehand, catch up on national and local news (including sports and entertainment), which lets you jump in with a comment if talk starts to dwindle.

Early and late arrivals

When guests arrive early, get them drinks and invite them into the kitchen while you finish preparing. If you need to go change, give them simple tasks to do—lighting the candles or starting the music. Ensure they feel comfortable and helpful.

Children and Elderly Guests

Pay special attention to younger and older guests. They bring us gifts that no one else can, and their comfort and wellbeing is essential. Stock up on coloring books, movies or easy-to-clean craft tools for children and their entertainment quests.

For older guests, small things spell comfort, from food to seating arrangements. Mention the location of restrooms, check room temperatures, and offer to refill their beverage or get seconds to minimize their need to get up. Think safety first, ahead of time, and check stairs, rugs, electric cords or other home aspects that may pose concerns.

Pets

As much as you may love your furry companion, realize and respect that others may not. And as for those endearing and unique habits of theirs—understand that your guests may not like little Fido licking the lotion off their legs nor Kitty's constant rubbing on them. If your pet companion gets anxious around others or has quirky habits, consider finding a pet sitter. This also applies if any of your guests have allergies.

Phone calls

Years ago, taking a non-emergency phone call during a party ranked as an irreparable faux pas. Your conversation would make you the topic of conversation for a long time to come. In these days of indispensable phones, it's still considered rude. The difference: more people do it anyway. Set an example as host. Turn off the ringer on your house phone and switch your cell to vibrate. If you must take a call, politely and briefly excuse yourself. If guests receive calls, assure them you do not mind (even if you do) and offer a room with more privacy.

Drinking

Liquor arguably enhances a party, but when guests overindulge, grace and tact must prevail. Discreetly insist on calling your guest a cab, and when it arrives, walk your guest to the taxi. Graciously thank him for coming, even as you slip the driver the guest's address—plus fare and a little extra to ensure he sees your guest safely into the house.

Breaks and Spills

Three things in life are certain: death, taxes and, if you entertain, accidents. Carefully consider your party paraphernalia and location. If damage to either will upset you beyond all measure, DO NOT USE IT!

Use tact. When—not if—something breaks or spills, attend to it quickly, assure your guest it is no big deal, quickly hand him a replacement glass or plate, and divert the attention back to the party. If you're upset, hide it. Chances are your guest feels horrible enough.

Offers for help

Kind offers of assistance depend upon you, the event and your relationship with the person doing the offering. I typically don't mind letting a few people help clear the dishes, but I never let friends help wash or dry. In fact, I leave the dishes until guests leave. Doing them implies you want the evening to be over or that you've grown bored with their company.

Good byes

Most guests leave within thirty minutes or so of the first departure. If guests continue to linger, though, start with subtle clues. Offer coffee, turn up the lights, blow out candles, turn off the music. If that doesn't work, ask them to help you clean the kitchen.

A Sophisticated Setting

Few occasions will so properly call for your fine china, your antique silver or your great-grandmother's cutlery. Pull them out of storage—hold nothing back. Dishware needn't match and can range from understated to elaborate. Capture the look and feel of refined elegance by combining multiple shades of pink fabric with soft and delicate motifs.

Collect as many costume-pearl necklaces and cameos that you can find (see Resources).

Simplify flower arrangements with peonies, lamb's ear and boxwoods, and prepare the spa stations so you can enjoy the treatments along with your guests. And finally, tap your creative side when it comes to gift wrap—nothing is too feminine or delicate.

A vase of peonies and outdoor statuary draped with extra flowers offset a buffet table and its sumptuous display.

The dishware offers an eclectic mix of old and new, simple and elaborate, lending a refined and understated feel.

The almond cake with fresh raspberry filling embodies culinary art. Marzipan pearls edge the top and bottom and gracefully drape the sides. The top combines a solid piece of icing with airbrushed art to emulate the face of a cameo.

Dress a bare Roman bust with peony buds and generous amounts of pearl necklaces for a touch of elegance.

For a whimsical touch, give each place setting its own miniature urn, with a single peony and lamb's ear, and casually draped pearls across the front.

The first draft of a letter I wrote to my mother years ago, kept safe in an old journal.

Embellishing the back of each chair is a dried boxwood wreath (see Resources), bedecked with costume-pearl necklaces and an old-fashioned cameo.

A decorative bowl contains a collection of cameos and jeweled trinkets.

"I thought my mom's whole purpose was to be my mom. That's how she made me feel."

—Natasha Gregson Wagner

Pearls of Significance

Considered the "Queen of Gems" throughout history, Pearls are among the oldest and most loved of all known gems. Their origins date back thousands of years, across countless countries and integrated in hundreds of religious, spiritual and mythological beliefs.

Virtually every culture has had a hand in propelling pearls' continued popularity and significance. Researchers trace pearls to an ancient fish-tribe along India's coast. Legend claims, Krishna, the Hindu god, gave a pearl from the sea to his daughter on her wedding day; Egyptian use of pearls dates to the fifth century Persian conquest; and Roman women even upholstered their sofas with the gems. The Greeks believed pearls brought undying love and marital bliss. The Koran depicts the pearl as "one of the greatest treasures in Paradise." Lore has it that Cleopatra bet Marc Anthony that she could consume the wealth of an entire nation in one meal. She removed a single pearl earring, valued at thousands of pounds of gold, and dropped it into a glass of acidic wine. Upon drinking the dissolved pearl, she won the wager and his heart.

The discovery of the New World revealed a new abundance of pearls in the fresh-water river beds. Upon depleting that resource, explorers were quick to take pearls from Native Americans and export remaining supplies back to Europe. By the late nineteenth century, pearls were all but gone from North, Central and South America. Supplies had also dried up in other parts of the world because of over-fishing and industrialization.

Pearls returned in the early twentieth century with the refinement and newfound techniques of oyster farms. Kokichi Mikimoto, a Japanese businessman, developed a process for planting and harvesting pearls from oysters, making them affordable and accessible to most of the world.

Today the pearl remains a treasured and coveted gem, cherished not only for its rare beauty and exceptional iridescence, but for the belief that pearls symbolize class, purity, femininity and love.

Shopping List

1 small bottle raspberry-flavored liqueur like Chambord
1 750 ml. bottle chilled champagne
4 cups fresh raspberries
1 cup fresh blackberries
1 pint fresh strawberries
1 cantaloupe
1 honeydew melon
1 bunch fresh mint
1 lemon
1 onion
1 head garlic
1 1/2 pounds asparagus
1 1/4 pounds (5 sticks) butter
1 1/2 dozen eggs
6 ounces buttermilk
1 pint heavy whipping cream
1 10-ounce package frozen chopped spinach
1 9-ounce package frozen artichoke hearts
2 10-ounce packages frozen raspberries
4 ounces shredded sharp cheddar cheese
1 ounce grated Parmesan cheese
12 thin slices prosciutto
2 envelopes unflavored gelatin
1 package natural amber sugar crystals
1 jar currant jelly
6 3-inch chocolate dessert cups
 (available at specialty stores)
18 candied violets (available at specialty stores)
4 ounces almond paste (available at specialty stores)
1 bottle almond extract

Staples (replenish if needed)

flour	paprika
sugar	cornstarch
powdered sugar	vanilla
salt	milk
black pepper	olive oil
baking powder	mayonnaise
cinnamon	

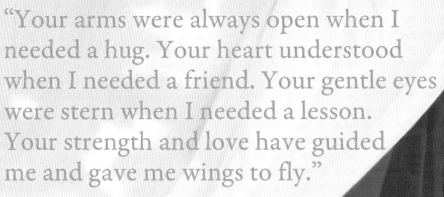

"Your arms were always open when I needed a hug. Your heart understood when I needed a friend. Your gentle eyes were stern when I needed a lesson. Your strength and love have guided me and gave me wings to fly."

—Author Unknown

The Essentials

6 water glasses
6 champagne glasses
6 coffee or tea cups
6 small side plates for scones
6 deep glasses or bowls for fruit compote
6 side plates or shallow bowls for the vanilla raspberry mousse
6 dinner plates
6 place settings of cutlery, including spoons, salad forks, knives, desert forks
6 napkins
1 tablecloth

Menu

For 6

Signature Drink:
Raspberry Champagne Cocktails

Appetizer:
Raspberry Cinnamon Scones with Lemon Butter

Starter:
Fresh Fruit Salad
Drizzled with Red Currant Dressing

Entrée:
Warm Spinach and Artichoke Soufflés

Accompaniments:
Prosciutto wrapped Asparagus Bundles

Dessert:
Vanilla Raspberry Crème Mousse
Nestled in Chocolate Cups Crowned
with Candied Violets
Purchased Cameo Cake or
Almond Cake with Fresh Raspberry Filling

The Recipes

Raspberry Champagne Cocktails

1 1/2 tablespoons raspberry-flavored liqueur
  such as Chambord
1 750 ml. bottle chilled champagne
6 large raspberries

Pour 3/4 teaspoon Chambord in the bottom of six champagne flutes. Carefully fill each glass with champagne, pouring along the side of the glass. Add a raspberry and serve.

Raspberry Cinnamon Scones

2 1/2 cups flour
1/4 cup sugar
2 teaspoons baking powder
1 teaspoon cinnamon
1/2 cup (1 stick) butter, well-chilled
1 cup fresh raspberries
1 egg
2/3 cup buttermilk
2 teaspoons natural amber sugar crystals

Preheat oven to 400 degrees F. Line a baking sheet with parchment. In a large bowl, mix flour, sugar, baking powder and cinnamon together until well-blended. Cut in butter with a fork or pastry blender and gently stir in raspberries.

Break egg in a measuring cup and add buttermilk until mixture measures 3/4 cup. Blend into flour mixture, until evenly moistened, forming a soft dough; do not over-mix.

Transfer dough to a lightly floured surface and pat into an 8-inch circle about 3/4-inch thick. Sprinkle evenly with sugar crystals. Use a sharp knife to cut into 8 triangles and transfer to parchment-lined baking sheet, about 1 inch apart. Bake until golden, about 15 to 20 minutes. Cool for 5 minutes and serve warm or at room temperature. 8 scones.

Lemon Butter

1/2 cup butter or margarine, softened
3 tablespoons powdered sugar
2 tablespoons lemon zest, grated

Blend butter, powdered sugar and grated orange zest together until smooth. Serve with warm scones.

Fresh Fruit Salad Drizzled with Red Currant Dressing

1 cantaloupe, peeled and cut in 1-inch chunks
1 honeydew melon, peeled and cut in 1-inch chunks
1 cup fresh raspberries
1 cup fresh blackberries
1 pint strawberries, hulled and halved
1/2 cup currant jelly
1/4 cup mayonnaise
1/4 cup whipping cream, whipped
fresh mint leaves for garnish

In a small saucepan, heat currant jelly over medium flame until melted. Cool to room temperature and transfer to a small bowl. Whisk in mayonnaise until combined and gently fold in whipped cream. Combine the cantaloupe, honeydew, raspberries, blackberries and strawberries in a large bowl and stir gently to combine. Serve accompanied with red currant dressing.

Spinach and Artichoke Soufflés

1 10-ounce package frozen chopped spinach, cooked
  and drained
1 9-ounce package frozen artichoke hearts, cooked,
  drained and chopped
1/4 cup (1/2 stick) butter
1/4 cup flour
1 1/4 cups milk
2/3 cup shredded sharp cheddar cheese
5 eggs, separated
1/2 cup chopped onion
1 1/2 teaspoons salt
1 small garlic clove, minced
1 teaspoon paprika
1 tablespoon grated Parmesan cheese

Preheat oven to 400 degrees F and butter eight individual soufflé dishes. Melt butter in a saucepan. Add flour, and whisk until smooth. Still whisking, gradually add milk. Cook until thickened and bubbly. Add cheese, stirring until it melts. Remove from heat.

Beat egg yolks on medium with an electric mixer until thick and pale. Add onion, cooked spinach and artichoke hearts, salt and garlic, and stir to blend. Gradually add the hot cheese mixture, stirring mixture constantly.

Beat egg whites on high until stiff. Gradually fold egg whites into spinach mixture. Pour into prepared dishes and sprinkle with paprika and Parmesan cheese. Bake for 10 minutes and reduce heat to 350 degrees F; bake 8 to 10 additional minutes, or until puffed and golden. Serve immediately.

Prosciutto Wrapped Asparagus Bundles

1 1/2 pounds asparagus, trimmed to six-inch lengths
salt and freshly ground black pepper
12 thin slices prosciutto
2 tablespoons extra-virgin olive oil

Preheat the oven to 400 degrees F and grease a 9- by
13-inch baking dish. Bring a large pot of water to boiling and
cook the asparagus for 3 minutes; drain and season with
salt and pepper. Divide asparagus into six bundles and wrap
each bundle with two slices of prosciutto. Arrange in baking
dish and drizzle evenly with olive oil. (Dish may be covered
and refrigerated at this point. Remove from refrigerator
20 minutes before baking.) Bake for 10 minutes, or until
asparagus is tender and prosciutto is lightly browned.

Vanilla Raspberry Crème Mousse Nestled in Chocolate Cups Crowned with Candied Violets

2 10-ounce packages frozen raspberries, thawed
2 envelopes unflavored gelatin
1/2 cup sugar, divided
1 teaspoon fresh lemon juice
1 teaspoon vanilla
1/4 teaspoon salt
4 egg whites, room temperature
1 1/2 cups heavy cream
6 3-inch chocolate dessert cups (available at
  specialty stores)
18 candied violets (available at specialty stores)

In a food processor or blender, puree raspberries until
smooth; strain and discard seeds. Transfer to a medium
saucepan and sprinkle gelatin evenly over liquid; cook over
low heat, stirring until dissolved. Remove from heat; stir in
1/4 cup sugar, lemon juice, vanilla and salt. Chill, stirring
occasionally, until mixture begins to thicken, about
20 minutes. In large bowl with mixer at high speed, beat egg
whites until soft peaks form. Slowly add 1/4 cup sugar and
beat until whites form stiff peaks. Gently fold in raspberry
mixture. In a separate bowl, beat heavy cream until soft
peaks form. Fold whipped cream into raspberry mixture.
Refrigerate. To serve, spoon the raspberry mousse into the
chocolate cups (reserve any extra for another use) and
garnish with additional whipped cream and candied violets.

Almond Cake with Fresh Raspberry Filling

1 1/3 cups sugar
4 ounces (3/4 cup) almond paste (available at
  specialty stores)
1 1/4 cups (2 1/2 sticks) unsalted butter, softened
7 eggs, room temperature
1 teaspoon vanilla
1/2 teaspoon almond extract
1 cup all-purpose flour
1 teaspoon baking powder
1/2 teaspoon salt

For the filling:
1 tablespoon cold water
1 teaspoon cornstarch
2 cups fresh raspberries
1/4 cup sugar

Pre-heat the oven to 325 degrees F and line the bottom of
a 9-inch cake pan with a round of parchment paper. With
an electric mixer, beat together the sugar and almond paste
until the paste is finely broken up. Add the butter and beat
for a few minutes until light and fluffy. In a separate bowl,
beat the eggs with the vanilla and almond extract. Continue
beating the almond mixture and slowly add the egg mixture.

In a separate bowl, whisk together the flour, baking
powder and salt. Stir into the almond mixture just
incorporated. Spoon the batter into the prepared pan and
bake on the middle rack for about 1 hour, or until a pick
inserted in the cake comes out clean. Cool on a wire rack.

To prepare the filling, combine the cold water and
cornstarch in a small bowl and whisk to blend; reserve.
Combine the berries and sugar in a medium saucepan and
cook over medium heat for 10 minutes. Increase the heat
to medium high and add the cornstarch mixture, stirring
quickly, for 1 minute. Remove from heat, strain through a
sieve, discard seeds and cool completely.

To assemble, split the cake in half and arrange one half, cut
side up, on a serving plate. Spread the raspberry filling over
the cake and top with the second layer.

The Relevance of Cameos

Cameos are one of the rarest combinations of art and jewelry, although they were never intended to be either. Described as messages in stone, cameos were originally cherished for telling stories and depicting historical events, customs and significant people.

Cameos were collected and gifted to families of prominence and noble class. These collections were considered status symbols that were typically only worn by men and used to decorate helmets, breastplates and swords. Proudly displaying them proved loyalty and often secured safety for those serving in the military. Ruling monarchs often created their own custom cameo, displaying it on pewter dishware, ships, clothing and jewelry, much like a monogram.

Legend claims, Pope Paul II, a passionate collector of cameo rings, wore several on every finger. His refusal to cover his hands in cold weather led to frostbite and his eventual death. Napoleon was commonly seen adorned with them, wearing several on his wedding day. His admiration for the art was so profound he headed up a cameo carving school in Paris.

In the 15th and 16th centuries, Queen Victoria of England took such as liking to these miniature pieces of art that she commonly wore several at a time-incorporating them in her clothing, crowns, belts and jewelry. She popularized the softer look, pastel colors and women's profiles. From that point forward, Cameos took on a more feminine look. Carvers turned to shell in place of agate and other hard stones allowing for increased production and distribution. The advent of the Industrial Revolution brought cameos into mass production, and styles that are still popular today.

Wrap spa boxes in a pale pink napkin, and embellish with flowers and petite pearls.

How to Host A Home Spa

Who wouldn't savor the luxury, the tranquility, the soothing elements of a spa? Truly the ultimate in pampering, the calm, peace and release of a spa day caters to your mother and delights your guests. Customize the experience with a handful of treatments designed to leave behind your tensions and stresses and for a few precious moments, to relax and enjoy.

First, decide the type of spa day you'd like:
Spa at Home
Hire Professionals
Do it Yourself
Spa at a Day Spa

***Combining the home party with professional help?* Decide next what you'll do:**
Massage   Manicure
Body Scrub   Pedicure
Facial

Start by determining what's available. Call a local day spa to see if they offer in-home services. If not, look for one of the national chains that offer mobile spas. Find some of these online. Ask about their services and whether they offer group discounts—be clear about what is included and what you need to provide. Find out how far in advance you must schedule appointments and what the cancellation policy is.

Will you choose to attend a day spa? If you opt for a day spa, ask ahead of time what type of services your group would like, and then start calling your favorite local spas.

Many spas offer a spa-party package that can include discounted rates, as well as refreshments. Find out how far in advance you must schedule appointments and what the cancellation policy is.

If you decided to host a "Do It Yourself" spa party, again, consider the treatments you'd like, but keep the choices small. I recommend limiting choices (and your costs) to manicures, pedicures and facials.

1. To start, stock the proper supplies:

For Massages:
Bath Robes (or ask your guests to bring their own)
Towels
Body Lotion
Sheet

For Facials:
Headbands / rubber bands   Cotton balls
High-quality astringent   High-quality facial cleanser
High-quality facial masks   High-quality facial lotion
Eye gel mask or cucumber slices Towels

For Manicures or Pedicures:
Foot tubs
  (or large plastic cleaning buckets)
Rose petals or lavender buds
  (to add to the foot and hand-soak bowls)
Inexpensive flip flops
  (or ask your guests to bring their own)
Pumice stones   Small bowls for finger-soaking
Nail files   Cottons balls
A selection of nail polish   Towels
High-quality hand scrub   Nail polish remover
High-quality hand lotion   Cuticle remover
Cuticle pushers/cutters

2. Schedule Treatments. Anticipate approximately thirty minutes for each treatment (massages may be longer). Keep to two treatments per person.

Post a printed schedule so everyone knows what she is supposed to be doing and when.

3. Create the Mood. Ensure the surroundings match the soothing treatments. Decorate the spa room with flowers and mildly scented candles. Set soothing music to play softly in the background. If you don't own one of the CDs we mentioned (commonly found at most large retailers), play classical music.

Have lots of extra towels and pillows on hand.

4. Remember the Extras Around the spa area, put out pitchers of fruit-infused ice water, with extra glasses and small bowls of cut fruit and nuts.

Party Timeline

One month before the brunch:

- Make or purchase the invitations.
- Finalize the guest list and mail invitations.

3 weeks before the brunch:

- Finalize the menu, including drinks (carefully selecting the items you wish to make and those you wish to purchase).
- Create a look by selecting colors, mood, setting and, if necessary, entertainment. Organize spa arrangements either at home or at a local spa.
- Order or gather the decorations and accessories.

2 weeks before the brunch:

- Make a shopping list for the food and liquor (see Shopping list).
- Order the food or any desert you do not wish to make.
- Order flowers, and consider having them delivered the day before the brunch

1 week before the brunch:

- Assemble or purchase take-away gifts and wrap them.
- Purchase all nonperishable food and liquor (see Shopping list).
- Create a music play list or purchase CDs.

2 days before the brunch:

- Decorate (if the brunch is indoors).
- Prepare the bar with glasses and liquor.
- Assemble the serving dishes and set up the buffet table, if using one.
- Prepare the Vanilla Raspberry Crème Mousse, cover tightly and refrigerate.

- Prepare the Spinach and Artichoke Soufflé, cover tightly and refrigerate.

The day before:

- Purchase remaining perishable food (see Shopping List).
- Pick up flowers or have them delivered.
- Set the table and lay out serving dishes (if the brunch is indoors.
- Chill the champagne.
- Prepare the Lemon Butter and Red Currant Dressing.
- Prepare the cake if you aren't purchasing from the bakery.
- Prepare the Prosciutto Wrapped Asparagus Bundles and refrigerate.
- Make extra ice.
- Check that the bathroom is clean. Have fresh hand towels, soap and extra toilet paper on hand.

The morning of the brunch:

- Decorate (if the brunch in outdoors).
- Set the table (if the brunch in outdoors).
- Cut fresh fruit, cover and refrigerate.

Prior to guests' arrival:

- Brew a pot of coffee.
- Start the music.
- Prepare the Raspberry Champagne Cocktails, including one for yourself!
- Light the candles.
- Enjoy!

Cover an old chair with faux moss (see Resources) and set it out to hold gifts.

Take Away Gifts

Conclude the celebration with a gift to remind your mother of her day of rest and repose. You filled your day with love and laughter, reminiscence and memory-making—and a dose of good health. These take-away's will recreate the day when used at home. Craft a "Spa Box" filled with everything needed to create a spa moment at home. Include a mixture of bath salts, a scented small candle, a lavender eye pillow and foot lotion, or anything else that personalizes the package for your guests. Wrap the box with a vintage napkin (a novel way to reuse napkins that are no longer a complete set), and secure it with a beautiful ribbon. You can also use a rubber band concealed with a grouping of pearls. Add a fresh flower for accent.

Vary it:

Grab one of the many spa CDs, a small note pad and a pencil, and wrap them together on top of a small, faux-silver tray. Secure with a beautiful ribbon or raffia. I have found many of these Spa CDs for a couple dollars each at large retail stores.

Simplify it:

You can never go wrong with a stunning pair of slippers (and you rarely need exact foot sizes). Wrap in a gorgeous box or roll in vintage cloth and tie with a ribbon. Embellish with pearls or a costume brooch (a gift within a gift).

"The greatest thing I'd learned over the years is that there's no way to be a perfect mother, but a million ways to be a great one."
—Author Unknown

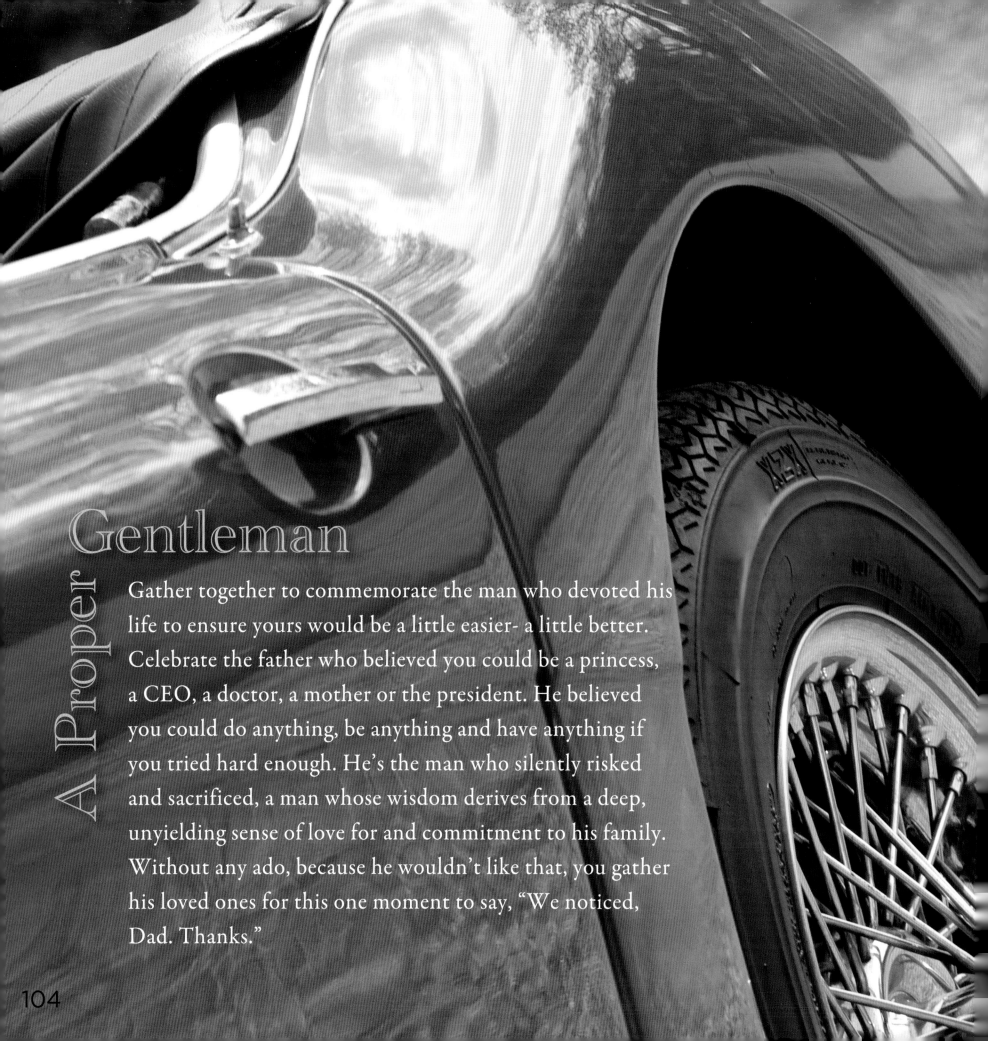

A Proper Gentleman

Gather together to commemorate the man who devoted his life to ensure yours would be a little easier- a little better. Celebrate the father who believed you could be a princess, a CEO, a doctor, a mother or the president. He believed you could do anything, be anything and have anything if you tried hard enough. He's the man who silently risked and sacrificed, a man whose wisdom derives from a deep, unyielding sense of love for and commitment to his family. Without any ado, because he wouldn't like that, you gather his loved ones for this one moment to say, "We noticed, Dad. Thanks."

"It's only when you grow up, and step back from him, or leave him for your own career and your own home—it's only then that you can measure his greatness and fully appreciate it. Pride reinforces love."

—Margaret Truman

At A Glance

Theme:
Finely Fashioned

Setting:
Your childhood home, if possible, or current family residence

Mood:
Nostalgic, profound, grateful, familiar, reflective, enduring, and most of all, loving

Colors:
Classic men's suiting: houndstooth checks, chalk strips, and herringbone weave. Carmel brown, claret red and smoky black.

Flowers:
Burgundy roses, red oriental or stargazer lilies, and hypericum berries

Tastes:
The menu features a wholesome interpretation of a timeless Sunday brunch.

Sounds:
A play list of your father's favorites, or if in doubt, consider such jazz classics as Sinatra, Armstrong or Davis, or newer favorites like Michael Buble, Daina Krall or Harry Connick Jr. For country music, try Willie Nelson, George Strait or Garth Brooks. Or tune in some classic rock—Neil Young, The Beatles or Tom Petty. If you find yourself stuck, ask your mom, or check his car or iPod for clues.

Experience:
Dads rarely favor a big "do," and instead lean toward personal. Keep it simple, but profound. My father has always loved classic sports cars like the 1963 Mercedes Benz. I rented a similar vehicle so my dad and I could go for a mountain drive.

Vary it: Rally your siblings for a few hours of whatever hobby Dad enjoys— golf, fishing, hiking. Skill level and age are irrelevant. Remember all those childhood talks on applying more effort? Put that wise counsel to work now: Effort matters. Try something Dad wanted, but never got around to doing. Skydiving, anyone?

Simplify it: Sometimes active or family events simply won't work. Try ordering a DVD of his favorite sports team—maybe a season or highlight reel. Throw some popcorn in the microwave, and join him for a day of cheering or jeering the home team.

The gray hair and not-so-fine lines gave away the stress and worry he carried for years. Never letting on the pain he felt when you shed your first tear, skinned your first knee, lost your first friend, failed to score your first goal or got dumped by your first boyfriend. The sleepless nights as he contemplated whether your future would include "paging Dr. (you)" or "would you like fries with that?" Or the days filled with unadulterated pride as you took your first step, received your spelling bee ribbons, passed your driver's test, tossed your graduation cap or walked down the aisle. He earned every wrinkle and lost hair; he stood by, sometime silent, sometimes with pursed lips, sometimes smiling, but he stood by noticing, loving, praying, hoping, worrying. He stood by always.

Fathers often get passed over for all their paternal efforts. They are often the quiet partner who had a harder time with expressions of love and concern. But without their support and influence, most of us wouldn't be the person we are today. On this day, show him that you noticed.

Back at you, Dad.

A Debonair Debut

Indeed, how daunting to craft a one-of-a-kind invitation, one that issues delight along with data. But nothing can match the anticipation and fun that come from a creative request for one's honored presence. Sure it's easier to just call your dad and confirm the plans, just as you always do. But an invitation shows his success. You have put forth that long-sought effort. And through that, you will take the time to honor this man who so greatly and genuinely deserves it.

The Invitation

Simple and masculine, but elegant—purchase inexpensive handkerchiefs from any large clothing retailer (see Resources). Spell out the party details, and scan or type into a computer. Print to iron-on sheets, found at any craft store (see Resources). **Remember to use editing software to mirror the image before you print!** Play it safe and print your design to a piece of paper first. Then in turn, iron the message onto the handkerchief. Enclose the handkerchief in a brown-paper envelope.

Vary it

Find some classic, masculine-patterned—stripes, plaids or houndstooth designs—card-stock paper at your local craft store. Print party details on the paper or glue to the paper, allowing the card stock to frame the invite. Insert the invitation into the front page of a newspaper or favorite magazine. Securely roll or bag the paper, and deliver it to Dad.

Simplify it

Hand-deliver (or mail) a printed invitation on card-stock paper attached to a bag of his favorite coffee beans. It will generate a smile, while setting the tone for the upcoming event.

A WELL SUITED BRUNCH

Father's Day
June 15th
11:00 am

> "A truly rich man is one whose children run into his arms when his hands are empty."
> —Unknown

Fashion a distinguished table with "suit"-able houndstooth fabric, buttoned-up napkins and individual espresso cups.

"He who is taught to live upon little owes more to his father's wisdom than he who has a great deal left him does to his father's care."

—William Penn

A Striking Setting

A quick goodbye kiss on your forehead, the lingering scent of aftershave, a half-empty cup of coffee and a tie slightly askew—will you ever forget your father's daily departure routine? For a few precious moments, return to the security of those days. Adorn your table in this gentleman's suiting material, finely placed to conjure memories and reminiscing.

What gives Dad a dignified thank you more than a sophisticated coffee brunch? To enhance the theme, dress your table in a classic houndstooth fabric. Fashion napkins from a rough-cut herringbone, with leather suit buttons sewn down one side. Complement the effect with casually draped ties across each chair. The family china and silver complete a masculine but elegant ambience. At each place setting, put an individual espresso cup (filled with coffee beans) and a personal bouquet set in a children's tea set (see Resources). Keep flowers simple and low to allow conversation.

Set this clever arrangement in an inexpensive plastic flower box with floral foam. Conceal the foam with an old coffee bag (see Resources).

A side table holds the silver heirloom tea set. Ensure convenience for you and guests—fill the pots with extra coffee, sugar and cream.

Add ambience without cost by raiding the closets of the men in your life for accessories. Look for shoe forms, ties, sport coats, cuff links, hats—those things that clearly depict your theme. Old family photographs, strategically lining the table and placed casually through the house focus on your dad's many achievements at home.

I wrapped some of the small gifts in old shirts, ties and belts, all reclaimed from the donation bag. It makes for a beautiful presentation and gives a second life to items no longer used.

Essential Elements of Entertaining

Deciphering the Dress Code

The dress code—sometimes you want a fashion cryptologist to decipher it for you. Matching your wardrobe with our culture's intricate and varied social codes can leave you looking like a disco star at a church banquet. Dressing for your boss' barbeque, for example, dictates a far different look than would dressing for friend's event.

What you wear evolves with the occasion, too. Does that to-die-for outfit work equally as well at holiday parties, weddings, dinner parties, charity events, receptions, showers, theater events and meals at discerning restaurants? In a word, no.

And finally, your outfit must adhere to logistics. Consider:
- Time of day
- Location—country club or a friend's backyard?
- Place—indoors or outdoors.
- Climate—warmer climates lean casual, while colder ones are dressier.
- The West Coast is more casual than the East Coast.
- Your relationship with the host. Know your audience!

If you feel as confused as an outfit of mismatched stripes and plaids, take heart. I offer the basics below.

Formal Casual

White Tie	Black Tie
Black Tie Invited/Optional	Cocktail Attire
Formal	Semi-Formal
Jacket Required	Jacket Preferred
Business Casual/Dress Casual	California Casual
Casual	Informal
Anything Goes	Theme (costumes)

White Tie

Represents the highest level of formality, generally reserved for the opera, charity balls or political events.

Men are expected to wear, without exception, a tail coat; white pique vest; single-cuffed and winged white shirt; white bow tie; black tuxedo pants (satin seams on the outside leg); and black, polished, laced-up shoes.

Women must wear a full-skirted, ankle-length gown; heels high enough to match the gown; her finest jewelry (avoid watches and jewelry with religious affiliation); and a clutch-style handbag. She can wear dress gloves, but should remove them when dining.

Black Tie

This depicts the second tier of formality, generally reserved for weddings, charity events, theater events and political parties.

Men are expected to wear a black tuxedo, with no exceptions. This includes a black jacket (sometimes excepted in warmer climates, but check with hostess); a stiff-collared, white shirt (no variation); a black vest (or to match jacket); a black tie (with matching cummerbund, if preferred, over a vest); black tuxedo pants (satin seams on the outside leg); and black, laced-up shoes (other colors accepted for nonblack tuxedos).

Black-Tie Invited/Optional: "Invited" means the host would prefer that you wear a tuxedo, but won't turn you away for wearing a suit. Optional means the host does not have a preference between a tuxedo or a black (or dark-colored) suit. In either situation, only a black or dark-colored suit would be acceptable.

Women may wear anything from a cocktail dress to a ball gown. This includes dresses (not above the knee or too showy); shoes coordinated with the dress; accessories, such as gloves (to be removed during dining); her finest jewelry (avoid watches and

> "Do not ask that your kids live up to your expectations. Let your kids be who they are, and your expectations will be in breathless pursuit.
>
> —Robert Brault

jewelry with religious affiliation); hats, if appropriate (usually for weddings and outdoor events); and a clutch or small handbag.

Semi-Formal

This is the third tier of formality, generally reserved for weddings, dinner parties, charity events, receptions, the theater and some restaurants.

For Him: A dark-colored suit with a tie and dark laced-up shoes.

For Her: A long or cocktail dress (avoid anything too revealing), coordinating shoes, tasteful jewelry, and a clutch or small handbag.

Cocktail Attire/Semi-Formal

This represents the final tier in formality, generally reserved for weddings, dinner parties, receptions, showers, some theater events, some restaurants and some social gatherings.

For Him: A suit and tie, or a coat and tie; a pressed shirt and nice dress pants; and a tailored pair of lace-up shoes or loafers.

For Her: Here, women have the most leeway in dressy attire—a dress of any tasteful length and fabric is appropriate. Dress styles can be a little less conservative. Add coordinating shoes, and tasteful jewelry and handbag.

Jacket Required/Preferred: Means exactly that. Some restaurants with these requirements will keep loaners for gentlemen to borrow. If you suspect this to be the case, call ahead to make provisions.

Business Casual/Dress Casual

The first tier in casual attire, generally reserved for some weddings, some dinner parties, some holiday parties, after-hours business meetings, and most restaurants and social gatherings.

For Him: Optional sports coat; a pressed, button-down shirt; pressed pants or khakis; and a suitable pair of laced-up or loafer-type shoes. Jeans, T-shirts, shorts and sandals are not appropriate.

For Her: Anything that is appropriate in a business environment. Pressed slacks and shirt; a simple dress; a blouse or fitted sweater; coordinating shoes; tasteful, minimal jewelry; and a handbag or purse. Keep with a conservative style. No jeans, T-shits, tank tops or shorts.

California Casual/Casual/Informal

The second tier in casual attire, generally reserved for outdoor parties or gatherings, barbecues, some showers and a smaller grouping of restaurants.

For Him: Comfortable, but still appropriate: button-down shirts, polo shirts, or T-shirts (avoid slogans and logos); casual pants, including khakis, clean jeans (no holes) or shorts that fit slightly above the knee; and loafers, sandals or trendy sneakers.

For Her: Comfortable, but appropriate: tasteful dresses, skirts, pants, jeans or shorts will all work (be sure the length is appropriate). Most shirts, T-shirts or tank tops are acceptable (avoid slogans and logos). Choose sandals or coordinating shoes.

Anything Goes means just that, but use good judgment.

Theme or Costume

This is the trickiest of all specified attire. Call ahead if you don't know the host well, and ask how elaborate the costumes should be. But as a general rule, the more decorative the costume, the better. These lighthearted events allow more leeway. But remember children who might be present, or people whose opinions count (such as co-workers, bosses and some family members). It is safer to be slightly overdressed than under dressed.

You will never go wrong with creative and well-thought-out costumes.

The Perfect Cup
Coffee Tastes and Differences

Who first savored the flavor of the ubiquitous coffee bean? Legends credit goats. Long ago—the year remains uncertain—an Ethiopian goatherd, Kaldi, noticed that his goats would eat berries from a certain tree and grow so spirited, they would not sleep at night, says the National Coffee Association. Local monks turned it into a drink, whereupon word of its energizing effects began to grow. During the next centuries, coffee and its trade spread through the Arabian Peninsula and "by the sixteenth century it was known in Persia, Egypt, Syria and Turkey," and then throughout the world, NCA reports. "By the end of the 18th century, coffee had become one of the world's most profitable export crops." Indeed, insurer Lloyds of London came from the dealings that went on in Edward Lloyd's Coffee House, circa 1688. Today, more than 75 percent of Americans drink coffee and most of those do so daily.

To meet that demand, growers have developed more than 65 types of coffee trees, of which two are most popular commercially:

Arabica: Descended from the original tree in Ethiopia, Coffee Arabica trees "produce a fine, mild, aromatic coffee and represent approximately 70 percent of the world's coffee production," according to the National Coffee Association. Grown in mild climates between 2,000 and 6,000 feet above sea level, these beans are hard to cultivate. This coffee commands the highest prices on the world market.

Robusta:
Coffea Canefora, a.k.a. Robusta, represents 30 percent of the world market, the NCA reports. It resists disease and parasites better than Arabica, making it more cost-effective to grow. It does best in warmer temperatures, thus lower altitudes, and its distinctive taste is used mostly in blends and instant coffees. On an arguably positive note, it contains about 50 percent to 60 percent more caffeine than Arabica.

Overall, factors that affect coffee's flavor and texture include the location of the harvest—including climate, soil, temperature, moisture, altitude and farming methods—and the processing and packaging practices.

More easily controlled, but still affecting flavor and texture, are freshness, temperature, type of storage, ratio of water to ground, brewing temperature and cleanliness of the brewer.

Sources: Italiancook.ca/orgins-coffee and the National Coffee Association, www.ncausa.org

An extraordinary espresso maker highlights the coffee-tasting theme with a varied display of samples and their origins. Don't own one of these magnificent pieces of art? Achieve the same effect with an array of beautiful coffee pots. They needn't match. Attach an empty frame to black poster board. Using a piece of chalk, write out the different coffees for simple, but effective and authentic café objet d'art.

Distinctive Coffee's

Hawaii: Above average Kona coffee rich, aromatic, mild- to medium-bodied.
Mexico: Above average. Has a depth of flavor with noticeable sharpness. Light-bodied.
Haiti: Above average sweet, mellow. Fair-bodied
Jamaica: Excellent well-balanced, rich, full-bodied.
Puerto Rico: Excellent deeper acidity, fruity aroma. Balanced-bodied.

Central America
Guatemala: Excellent rich, spicy, or smoky flavor. Medium- to full-bodied.
El Salvador: Average mild acidity. Medium-bodied.
Costa Rica: Excellent hearty, rich, with sharp acidity. Medium-bodied.

South America
Venezuela: Average to above sweet, delicate, low acidity. Average balanced-bodied.
Colombia: Good to excellent solid flavored, sweet with slight acidity. Full-bodied.
Peru: Inconsistent to average. Aromatic, good flavor with mild acidity. Medium-bodied.
Brazil: Average sweet and fruity with low acidity. Medium-bodied.

Africa & Middle East
Ethiopia: Inconsistent sweet with floral aroma. Bold and full-flavored. Full-bodied.
Kenya: Excellent sharp, rich flavor with hints of black currant. Full-bodied
Uganda: Above average rich deep flavor. Medium-bodied.
Tanzania: Average sharp, winey, and acidic. Medium- to full-bodied.
Zimbabwe: Above average. A distinctive spicy flavor. To excellent Mild-bodied.
Yemen: Excellent winey, smooth deep flavor. Full-bodied.

Asia
Vietnam: Average light acidity with good balance. Mild-bodied.
Sumatra: Above average. Very rich, distinctive and acidic. Full bodied.
Java: Average spicy or slightly smoky with a strong flavor. Full-bodied.

Types of Roasts
New England Roast Beans are very lightly roasted
American Roast not as dark as a European roast. Also known as Medium Roast
Viennese Roast is roasted longer than American roast
City Roast darker than standard American roast. Some roasters make as dark as French roast
Full City Roast is darker than City roast
Continental Roast slightly lighter than French roast
French Roast roasted for a long time at high temperatures. Also known as Dark Roast. Often used to make espresso and
Italian Roast. The darkest roast. Beans roasted to a very dark brown. Also used for espresso, and also known as Heavy roast

Sources: Italiancook.ca/orgins-coffee and the National Coffee Association, www.ncausa.org

Shopping List

1 small bottle dark rum
1/4 pound premium dark roast
ground coffee
1 cup walnuts
1 fresh lemon
1 fresh orange
6 croissants
12 slices thinly sliced
  Black Forest ham
6 pounds baby red potatoes,
  each 1 1/2-2 inches in diameter
1 bunch fresh thyme
3 large ripe tomatoes
1/2 cup fresh bread crumbs
1 clove garlic
1 bunch fresh parsley
1 pound butter
8 ounces sour cream
1 dozen eggs
1 box coarsely ground sea salt

Staples (replenish if needed)

granulated sugar
brown sugar
ground cinnamon
all-purpose flour
baking powder
baking soda
grated nutmeg
salt
black pepper
white pepper
cayenne pepper
dried oregano
olive oil
grated Parmesan cheese

The Essentials

6 water glasses
6 juice glasses
6 to 24 small coffee mugs
  for sampling the different
  coffee blends (cups can be
  rinsed between tasting)
Small plates—coffee cake
6 dinner plates
6 place settings or cutlery
  including soup spoons, salad
  forks, knives, and dessert forks
6 dessert plates
6 napkins (have a few extra
  on hand)
1 tablecloth
2 serving trays or cake stands
  coffee cake and pocket-
  watch cakes
1 serving bowl—new potatoes
1 coffee pot for the featured blend
  (4 to 5 more coffee pots to keep
  the other coffee blends warmed)
6-8 small shot glasses for the
  buttered rum

Menu
For 6

Signature Drink:
Premium Dark Roast Coffee with
a Warmed Shot of Buttered Rum

Appetizer:
Classic Caramel Cinnamon Walnut Coffee Cake

Starter:
Roasted Sugar Butter New Potatoes and
a Baked Tomato Topped with
Breaded Bacon and Parsley

Main Course:
Croissant Ham Benedict Served with a
Poached Egg and Citrus Hollandaise Sauce

Dessert:
Individual Chocolate Mocha
Pocket Watch Cakes

The Recipes

Premium Dark Roast Coffee with Hot Buttered Rum

3 tablespoons butter, softened
3 tablespoons firmly packed brown sugar
1 teaspoon cinnamon
6 ounces dark rum
6 cups brewed premium dark roast coffee

Mix butter, brown sugar and cinnamon together and divide mixture evenly among 6 warmed coffee cups. Add one ounce of rum to each cup and fill with hot coffee. Stir well to combine and serve.

Classic Caramel Cinnamon Walnut Coffee Cake

3/4 cup (1 1/2 sticks) unsalted butter, softened
1 cup granulated sugar
2 eggs
1 cup sour cream
2 cups all-purpose flour
2 teaspoons baking powder
1 teaspoon baking soda
1 teaspoon ground cinnamon, divided
1 teaspoon grated nutmeg, divided
1/2 teaspoon salt
3/4 cup firmly packed light brown sugar
1 cup coarsely chopped walnuts

Grease and flour a 9 x 13-inch pan. In a large bowl, beat the butter with an electric mixer at medium speed until fluffy; gradually add granulated sugar, beating well. Add eggs, one at a time, beating after each addition until blended. Add sour cream and mix well.

In a separate bowl, combine the flour, baking powder, baking soda, 1/2 teaspoon ground cinnamon, 1/2 teaspoon grated nutmeg and salt, and whisk to combine. Add gradually to butter mixture, beating well. Spread batter into prepared pan.

Combine the brown sugar, walnuts, 1/2 teaspoon cinnamon, and 1/2 teaspoon nutmeg in a small bowl. Sprinkle evenly over batter. Cover and refrigerate for at least 2 hours, or overnight.

Heat the oven to 350 degrees F and bake for 35 minutes, or until a wooden pick inserted in center comes out clean. 12 servings.

Croissant Ham Benedict with Citrus Hollandaise Sauce

4 large egg yolks, slightly beaten
1 tablespoon fresh lemon juice
1 tablespoon fresh orange juice
dash of salt
dash of white pepper
dash of cayenne pepper
1/2 pound (2 sticks) butter
6 croissants, split
12 slices thinly sliced Black Forest ham
6 poached eggs

To make the Citrus Hollandaise Sauce, place the egg yolks, lemon juice, orange juice, salt, white pepper and cayenne pepper in a food processor or blender, and blend thoroughly for one minute, until thick and creamy. Melt the butter in a small saucepan over medium heat. With the machine running, slowly pour in the hot butter. Blend until thickened, about 30 seconds. Transfer to an insulated container and keep warm. Makes about 2 cups.

Preheat the oven broiler and arrange the croissants, cut side up, on a baking sheet. Broil, watching carefully, just until the tops are lightly browned. For each serving, arrange both halves of a toasted croissant on a serving plate. Top with two slices of ham and one poached egg. Spoon some of the hollandaise sauce over the top.

Roasted New Potatoes with Sea Salt and Thyme

6 pounds baby red potatoes, each 1 ½-2 inches in diameter
1/3 cup olive oil
1 1/2 tablespoons coarsely ground sea salt
1/4 cup chopped fresh thyme

Preheat the oven to 350 degrees F. Quarter the potatoes and arrange in a single layer in a large roasting pan. Pour the oil over them and turn to coat well. Sprinkle with the salt and fresh thyme and gently turn again. Roast for 1 hour, turning occasionally while cooking, until tender.

Baked Tomatoes with Bacon Parsley Bread Crumbs

3 large ripe tomatoes, sliced in half
1/2 teaspoon salt
3 tablespoons grated Parmesan cheese
1/2 cup fresh bread crumbs
1 clove garlic, minced
1 tablespoon chopped fresh parsley
salt and pepper to taste
1/2 teaspoon dried oregano
1 tablespoon olive oil

Preheat oven to 400 degrees F. Cut the tomatoes in half, sprinkle with salt and drain cut side down in a colander, for about 10 minutes. Transfer to paper towels and drain.

Place tomato halves cut side up in a greased baking dish. Sprinkle with cheese, bread crumbs, garlic, parsley, salt, pepper, and oregano. Drizzle with olive oil. Bake for 20 minutes or until topping is lightly browned.

Memoirs of  Father's Day

If we remember our mothers for their loving, quiet influence, then our fathers must stand as unsung heroes. Too often relegated to practical, financial, logistical and sensible roles, we easily lose sight off their contributions, sacrifices and influences. It's our mothers who often bask in the recognition of a successfully brought up child, but somewhere, steadfast, proud, courageous, but out of the limelight, stand our fathers.

On Father's Day, we honor their sacrifices and commitment. Its first celebration in West Virginia, in 1908, was a one-time event to commemorate fathers who had been lost in a mine explosion, reports History.com. In 1909, Sonora Smart Dodd, raised by a widower, actively campaigned for a Father's Day in her hometown of Spokane, Washington. Her campaign produced results any father would admire: In 1910, Washington State held its first state Father's Day. But the holiday only spread slowly through the following decades—a delay often caused by fathers themselves.

Men scoffed at the sentimentality and attempts to commercialize fatherhood, leading to gifts ironically often paid for by the fathers, says History.com. Meantime, Mrs. Dodd had established a tradition of wearing a white rose to honor a deceased father and a red rose for a father still living.

In 1916, President Woodrow Wilson "honored the day by using telegraph signals to unfurl a flag in Spokane when he pressed a button in Washington, D.C.," History.com writes. Eight years later, President Calvin Coolidge encouraged states to observe Father's Day, purportedly calling it "the occasion to establish more intimate relations between fathers and their children and also press upon fathers the full measure of their obligations." June 19th slowly became a recognized and celebrated holiday, and in 1972, President Richard Nixon established the third Sunday in June as a national Father's Day—trailing Mother's Day by 58 years.

Party Timeline

One month before the brunch:

- Make or purchase the invitations.
- Finalize guest list and mail invitations.

3 weeks before the brunch:

- Finalize the menu, including drinks (carefully selecting the items you wish to make and those you wish to purchase).
- Create a look by selecting colors, mood, setting and, if necessary, entertainment.
- Order or gather the decorations and accessories.

2 weeks before the brunch:

- Make a shopping list for the food and liquor (see Shopping list).
- Order the food or any desert you do not wish to make.
- Order the Chocolate Mocha Pocket Watch Cakes or alternate dessert.
- Order flowers, and consider having them delivered the day before the brunch.

1 week before the brunch:

- Purchase all nonperishable food and liquor (see Shopping list).
- Create a music play list or purchase CDs.

3 days before the brunch:

- Decorate.
- Prepare the bar with glasses and liquor.
- Assemble all the serving dishes and set up the buffet table, if using one.

2 days before the brunch:

- Make the simple syrup for the cocktails and refrigerate.
- Chop walnuts for the coffee cake and cover tightly.

The day before brunch:

- Purchase perishable food (see Shopping list).
- Prepare the coffee cake batter and refrigerate.
- Set the table and lay out the serving dishes.
- Pick up the flowers or have them delivered.
- Make extra ice.
- Check that the bathroom is clean. Have fresh hand towels, soap and extra toilet paper on hand.

The morning of the brunch:

- Cut potatoes into small cube and immerse in water to prevent browning. Cover tightly and refrigerate until you are ready to bake.
- Chop parsley and garlic, grate parmesan, and cut tomatoes for the baked tomatoes.
- Chop thyme for potatoes.

Prior to guests' arrival:

- Prepare hollandaise sauce, covered and keep warm.
- Assemble croissant ham benedicts.
- Bake caramel cinnamon walnut coffee cake.
- Brew the coffee.
- Start the music.
- Prepare the coffee with buttered rum, including one for yourself!
- Light the candles.
- Enjoy!

How appropriate to keep your coffee gathering's takeaway gifts on the coffee table. A memorable gift combines individually wrapped coffee cups with a sample of unique coffee beans and measuring scoop.

No take-away gift will ever adequately express your appreciation to your father, which is why these small tokens go to the guests instead. The experience—the time and effort that created this day, customized for his hobby or event—is your gift to him.

Keeping to the theme of your father's well-remembered newspaper routine, why not give guests a subscription to a local or national newspaper? Or up the ante and give magazine subscriptions based on each guest's interests (available at www.magazines.com or amazon.com/magazines). For a more tangible take-away, purchase an issue of each magazine from a local bookstore. Order subscriptions from the cards inside, then roll the magazine or newspaper and tie with a beautiful ribbon. Add a gift card noting the upcoming subscription.

Vary it:
Wrap a bag of unique or unusual coffee beans in an oversized mug and saucer, with a coffee scoop. You can find these usually inexpensive items at a retailer of coffees or imported foods (see Resources).

Simplify it:
Who doesn't appreciate a gift certificate to a local or chain coffee house? Not a coffee drinker? No worries—try one of the many other types of drinks or food items available in these stores.

> "My father gave me the greatest gift anyone could give another person, he believed in me."
>
> —Jim Valvano

Seeing Stars

Life, liberty and the pursuit of happiness. These venerable words hold such profound public and personal meaning. We live them and we honor them. But on Independence Day, we turn to Founding Father John Adams, who wrote that the event be annually "solemnized with Pomp and Parade, with Shews, Games, Sports, Guns, Bells, Bonfires and Illuminations from one End of this Continent to the other from this Time forward forever more." And so, this Fourth of July, gather family and friends for fine, but informal food; a day of play; and a night of lights.

"We must be free
not because we claim freedom,
but because we practice it..."
—William Faulkner

At A Glance

Theme:
Chasing Stars

—m—

Setting:
A well-loved family home outside the city

—m—

Mood:
Casual, memorable, nostalgic, free; a celebration of summer's long days, cool nights and the American lifestyle

—m—

Colors:
Cadet blue, weathered white, cherry red

—m—

Flowers:
Small pots of white stephanotis and buckets of tall soft grass

—m—

Tastes:
The menu salutes the nontraditional. An effortless combination surf-n'-turf pasta and classic cheesecake fruit tart reinvents the Fourth of July feast.

—m—

Sounds:
Create a custom play list of your favorites. Remember that celebrations on the Fourth last longer than most. Patriotic music, while appropriate, can carry adverse effects if it grows overly long or political. Consider using classic American artists—Bruce Springsteen, Ray Charles, Neil Diamond, and Don McLean. A few others with American undertones in their tunes include Dave Matthews, The Fray, Third Eye Blind, Toby Keith, Willie Nelson, Jon Mayer and The Goo Goo Dolls. As a rule of thumb—generally, if you like it, your friends will, too.

—m—

Experience:
An all-day celebration of life, liberty and the pursuit of happiness. Treat guests to a innovative meal, convene a classic backyard croquet competition, and delight in a night of stargazing and s'mores.

Vary it: If the skies cloud over, draw up to a roaring fire pit, sip hot toddies and light sparklers.

Simplify it: Pile into the car and head out to see the local fireworks display. Pack a small picnic of drinks and snacks. Remember the blanket!

A Tale of Generation

Allow me to tell a tale of generations and memories, not so much mine, but those of the house. As esteemed and American as such things come, the house is an old charming country home—never forgotten, as its appearance might indicate, but just left to weather time out on its own.

We've loved this home for decades. It is our haven from city commotion, our old retreat, a place to recharge from the demands of the hectic modern world. It saw us through life stages, and gamely hosted our weekend visits as those evolved from the fishing reels, telescopes, and sleeping bags of young marries into family pursuits and pastimes of soccer balls, cell phones and birthday parties.

But this old refuge, covered now in overgrown vines and always encroaching signs of nature, still remembers all the little-kid camp-outs, freedom and fun, giggles of joy, chasing fireflies and wishing on shooting stars. That's where we'll spend this Fourth of July, walking through memories with the house, reconnecting, reinventing and rejuvenating our souls.

A cracked fountain, circa 1920, delights and soothes despite its age and over-grown foliage.

The Fourth of July—it conjures images of soft summer nights, distant fireworks, and festive gatherings of quietly jubilant loved ones. Unofficially the highlight of the season, it beckons us with effortless meals and informal fun.

The invitations set the tone, using any of three themes: stargazing, chasing fireflies or the awe-inspiring implications of the Fourth of July. No need to fuss with formality—a little imagination goes a long way.

The Invitation

Purchase small stargazer's maps, sold at most large bookstores. Print the party information on the back of the map, then roll and secure it with twine. Mail the map in small tubular containers sold at the post office or any craft store.

If you can find a small, inexpensive pair of children's binoculars (sometimes available at craft stores or dollar stores) throw those in for an unforgettable invitation.

Vary it

Purchase red, white and blue card stock paper, along with glittered letters and star-shaped stickers (found at most large stationery or party retailers). Add firefly buttons, strung and secured on a ribbon. Mail in thick envelopes.

Simplify it

Purchase a small horoscope roll, corresponding with each guest's birth month (found at any grocery or convenience store check out). Alternately, find online a copy of the Declaration of Independence, reduce it, print it, and roll it up. Attach the roll to a pre-made or handmade Fourth of July invitation. .

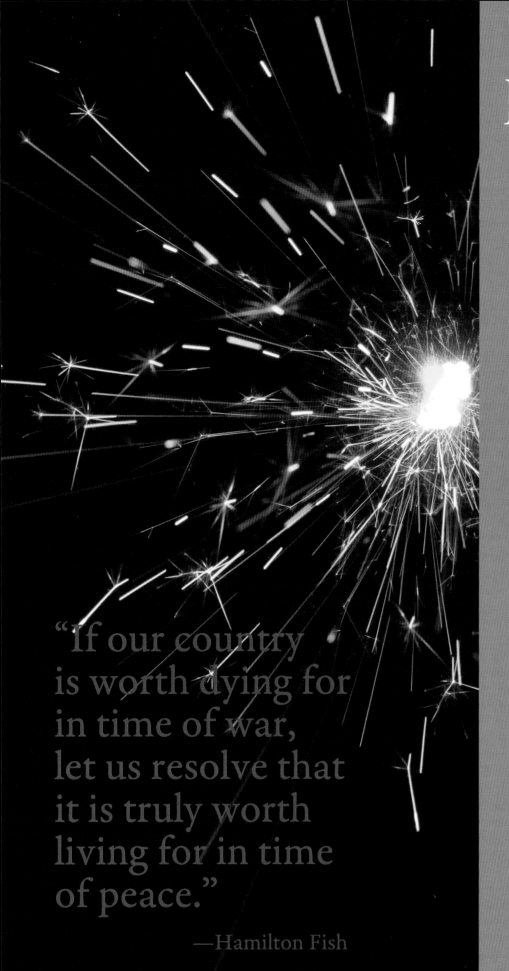

> "If our country
> is worth dying for
> in time of war,
> let us resolve that
> it is truly worth
> living for in time
> of peace."
>
> —Hamilton Fish

Essential Elements
of Entertaining
Religion, Politics and Friends

An old saying cautions us to "never discuss religion or politics in polite company." With good reason, too—although not an absolute, nothing kills a party faster than heated debates without winners. In a polarized world, few topics hold such power to hurt feelings and cause permanent rifts. Delivered properly, they educate and enlighten, but outside of a lecture hall, this rarely happens with a large group. Most of us speak with great passion regarding our views and beliefs, but once the dialogue starts, it's very hard to stop or redirect.

You needn't allow religious or political talk to take over. If it comes up, try these tips to help subdue the potential political tempest. The goal is to de-escalate the debate and highlight loved ones' bonds.

- Try to change the subject. At first, be subtle by initiating another topic or telling a humorous story related to the discussion, but with a punch line that moves away from the topic.

- Bring out the appetizers, announce dinner, ask for help clearing the table—do anything that breaks the mood and momentum.

- Remind your guests that this is a party, and you would not wish to see anyone get too emotionally involved in a conversation that hinders the evening's festivities.

- Enlist the aid of others, who can interrupt and separate the debaters for new, less-volatile chats.

- Start limiting the alcohol for the emotional. Nothing gets better with more of it.

- Reiterate that while this is a valuable debate, there are children around and that appropriateness and examples need to be upheld.

- Suggest the debaters find another time and place to continue the discussion.

If that doesn't work, remind yourself and others (if necessary) that, while you all may not share similar views, you do share other wonderful qualities—such as a friendship.

——— Restate that religion and politics are only two of virtually thousands of fascinating topics you can discuss.

If all else fails, and the conversation escalates, be blunt. Ask the debaters to stop and change the subject.

The Setting

Depart from the traditional barbeque and add a distinctive touch to this year's Fourth of July feast. Appetizers, mixed drinks and a fabric tablecloth lend a dash of panache to your fete. No one will see it coming! Drape your outdoor buffet with a white tablecloth, accented with a few smaller, blue- and linen-colored table coverings. Inexpensive rented bamboo chairs with white covers bring style, comfort and class. Because flowers may wilt in the summer heat, consider oversized galvanized (cleaning) buckets filled with potted long grass and miniature flags. (Later, replant the grass in your landscape). Fill small mason jars with battery-operated fireflies for subtle but elegant illumination as the daylight fades. Simple white plates, basket weave chargers, and plastic water and wine glasses give a genteel, refined feel, complemented by combined vintage-flag and solid-red napkins (see Resources).

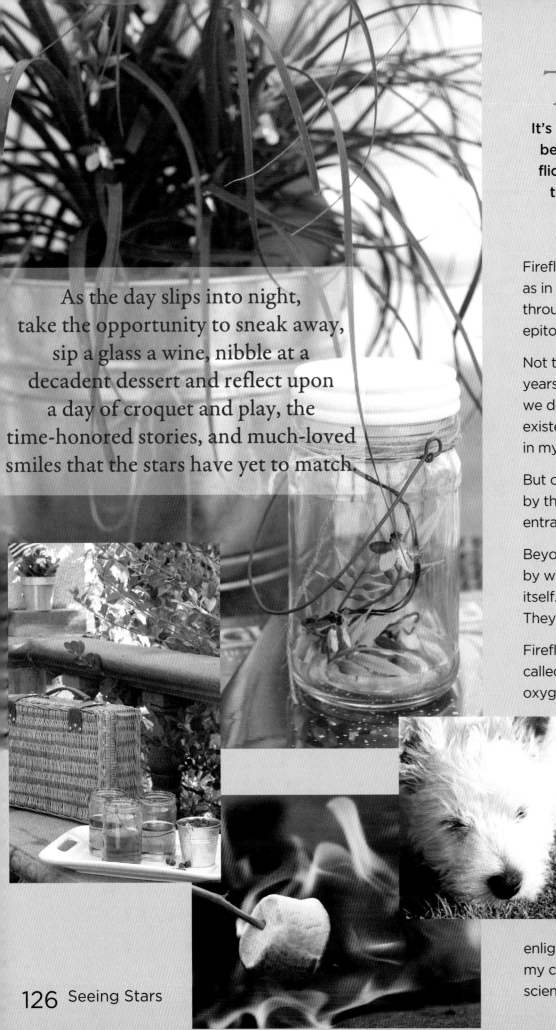

As the day slips into night,
take the opportunity to sneak away,
sip a glass a wine, nibble at a
decadent dessert and reflect upon
a day of croquet and play, the
time-honored stories, and much-loved
smiles that the stars have yet to match.

The Brilliant Firefly

It's a warm, sticky, summer evening. The sun has dropped behind the darkened hills. Your quest starts with a single flicker, then two, then suddenly, in a burgeoning brilliance, thousands of lightning bugs illuminate the evening sky. Their flashes synchronize in a hypnotic dance, a silent symphony that only nature could orchestrate.

Fireflies have captured the hearts of children for centuries, even as in turn, children capture them. Much like running barefoot through the grass, or licking a dripping ice cream cone, fireflies epitomize childhood and summer rites of passage.

Not that we all claim memories of fireflies. It was thirty-five years before I saw my first one. I grew up in the West, where we don't have these floating little candles. To me, they only existed in the occasional children's book and consequently, in my imagination.

But once I finally did spend a dark summer night surrounded by these magical little lanterns, their power to enchant and entrance grew clear.

Beyond enchantment, though, there lies a science. The process by which these little guys light up is as intriguing as the light itself. First the sad part: They don't do it to impress you. They do it to impress other fireflies and attract mates.

Fireflies convert one kind of energy into another in a process called bioluminescence, where the firefly's body combines oxygen with calcium, adenosine triphosphate (ATP), the chemical luciferin and an enzyme luciferase. This creates light, albeit a cold light, meaning the firefly doesn't use up energy by lighting up. Different species have different lights, and potential mates identify their own species by their lights.

Aside from mating, the bioluminescence process fascinates researchers who work to replicate it for use in projects ranging from medicine to painting.

Yet fireflies remain a symbol of things more intangible—a spark of wisdom, or prediction or enlightenment. To me, they are a symbol of warm nights, my children's laughter, and nature's unbounded ability to use science to create magic.

The Glory of the Game

Build energetic fun into the day with some time-honored outdoor games. (You may have to teach your kids!) Dust off the croquet set, reach down those badminton rackets and brush off the horseshoes. Want something more kid-friendly? Bring out the bean-bag toss, or teach them classic games like Capture the Flag, Red Rover, water balloon toss, scavenger hunts or hula-hoop contests.

(For more ideas, supplies and game rules, visit About.com or search in your browser for Classic Kids Outdoor Games).

"Those who won our independence believed liberty to be the secret of happiness and courage to be the secret of liberty."

—Louis D. Brandies

Shopping List

1 bottle blueberry vodka, such as Absolut Berri Açaí
1 bottle grapefruit club soda or flavored seltzer water
1 bottle fruity wine such as Gewürztraminers
1 large basket blueberries
2 limes
1 lemon
2 ripe cantaloupes
1 ripe honeydew
2 French bread baguettes
4 ounces chopped walnuts
1 pound beets (about 2 large)
6 ounces gorgonzola
1 small basket blackberries
1 small basket strawberries
1 small basket raspberries
3 large red bell peppers
1 large yellow bell pepper
1 large orange bell pepper
1 small jar of kalamata olives
1 medium zucchini
1 medium squash
1/2 cup fresh or frozen, thawed corn kernels
2 stalks celery
1 head garlic
1 bunch fresh mint
1 bunch fresh basil
1 small red onion
2 cups peeled, shelled edamame
1 pound green beans
1/4 cup sesame seeds
1 pound lump crab meat
1 cup prepared mango salsa
2 pounds flank steak
1 pound cooked, peeled, deveined medium shrimp
1 cup dry orzo pasta
2 cups chicken stock or broth
1/2 cup blue decorative sugar crystals
1 jar currant jelly
4 ounces feta cheese
8 prepared 4-inch cheesecakes or cream pies
1 loaf of fresh, crusty bread

The Essentials

8-10 water glasses
8-10 mason jar glasses (optional)
8-10 wine glasses
Small plates—crab cakes and crostini
8-10 soup bowls or small cups—soup
8-10 dinner plates
8-10 place settings or cutlery, including soup spoons,
   salad forks, dinner forks, knives and dessert forks
8-10 napkins (have a few extra on hand)
1-2 tablecloths—one necessary, the second
   for layering (optional)
3 serving trays—crab cakes, crostini,
   steak-shrimp-orzo
2 serving bowls—seasonal vegetables,
   steamed edamame-green beans
1 or 2 cake stands or serving trays for the tarts
1 large pitcher—blueberry sparklers

Staples (replenish if needed)

salt and pepper	brown sugar
granulated sugar	soy sauce
honey	distilled white vinegar
ground ginger	peanut oil
Balsamic vinegar	Dijon mustard
Worcestershire sauce	Old Bay spice mix
extra virgin olive oil	bread crumbs
butter	eggs
mayonnaise	

Menu
For 8 to 10

Signature Drink:
Blueberry Sparkler

—W—

Appetizer:
Crispy Crab Cakes Served with
a Peach-Mango Salsa
Classic Crostini Topped with Fresh Red Beets,
Gorgonzola Crumbles and Chopped Walnuts

—W—

Starter:
Chilled Seasonal Melon Soup
Garnished with Mint Leaves

—W—

Entrée:
Sliced Flank Steak and Shrimp
Served Over Lemon Orzo
Marinated, Sautéed Summer Vegetables
Sided by Steamed Edamame and Baby Green
Beans Sprinkled with Toasted Sesame Seeds

—W—

Dessert:
Mini Strawberry-and-Raspberry
Cheesecake Tarts
Mini Blackberry-and-Blueberry
Cheesecake Tarts

The Recipes

Blueberry Sparklers

1 lime
1 lime
1/2 cup blue sugar to rim the glasses
1/2 pint frozen blueberries
2 cups chilled blueberry vodka such as Absolut Blueberry
4 cups grapefruit flavored seltzer water or club soda
ice cubes

Cut the lime in half and pour the sugar into a small, shallow saucer. Run the cut lime around the edge of a cocktail glass and immediately put the glass in the saucer of sugar to rim the edge. Repeat with other glasses and set aside to dry. Drop a few frozen blueberry in the bottom of each glass and add 2 ounces vodka, 1/2 cup seltzer water and several ice cubes, being careful not to knock the sugar off the rims. Add a squeeze of lime and serve.

Mini Crab Cakes

1 pound lump crab meat, picked over for shells
3 eggs, lightly beaten
1/2 cup bread crumbs
1/2 cup chopped celery
1/2 cup fresh or frozen, thawed corn kernels
1 teaspoon Dijon mustard
1 teaspoon Worcestershire sauce
1/2 teaspoon Old Bay spice mix
2 tablespoons minced parsley
1/4 teaspoon salt
Additional bread crumbs for baking
1 cup prepared peach mango sauce

In a bowl, mix the crab, eggs and bread crumbs together, stirring gently. Add the bread crumbs, celery, corn, mustard, Worcestershire, Bay Spice and salt, and stir gently. Form into 18 small cakes and transfer to a baking sheet sprinkled with bread crumbs. Cover with plastic wrap and chill for one hour.

In a large heavy skillet, heat the oil over moderately high heat until it is hot but not smoking and sauté the crab cakes in batches, turning them once, for 2 to 3 minutes on each side or until they are golden. Transfer them to paper towels to drain. 18 pieces.

Classic Crostini Topped with Fresh Red Beets, Gorgonzola Crumbles and Chopped Walnuts

36 1/2-inch slices diagonally cut from two French bread baguettes
1/2 cup walnuts, chopped
1 pound beets (about 2 large), scrubbed and trimmed
1 cup water
1 tablespoon balsamic vinegar
1 teaspoon extra virgin olive oil
1/4 teaspoon freshly ground black pepper
1/4 teaspoon salt
6 ounces gorgonzola, crumbled
1 1/2 tablespoons mayonnaise

Preheat oven to 375 degrees F. Arrange the bread slices on a baking sheet and bake just until lightly toasted, 4 to 5 minutes. Cool on a wire rack and reserve. Pour the walnuts on the baking sheet and bake for 4 to 5 minutes, or until lightly toasted. Cool to room temperature and reserve.

Arrange the beets in a small baking dish and add water. Cover with lid or foil and bake for 45 to 50 minutes, or until tender when poked with a fork. Drain and cool. Use a paper towel to rub off the skins, cut the beets in quarters, and cut each quarter into thin slices. In a medium bowl combine the vinegar, olive oil, salt and pepper. Add the beet slices and toss gently to coat.

In a small dish, mash together the gorgonzola and mayonnaise with a fork. Spread each baguette slice with a heaping teaspoon of the Gorgonzola mixture; top with several beet slices and sprinkle with toasted walnuts. 36 pieces.

Honeydew Melon Soup

2 ripe cantaloupes, chilled
1 ripe honeydew melon, chilled
1 cup fruity wine such as Gewürztraminer
1 tablespoon fresh lime juice
fresh mint for garnish

Peel and dice the melons. Puree the melon in a blender or food processor until smooth and transfer to a bowl. Gently stir in the wine and lime juice. Serve in chilled bowls garnished with fresh mint.

Marinated Flank Steak

1 tablespoon olive oil
4 tablespoons honey
3 tablespoons distilled white vinegar
3/4 teaspoon ground ginger
3 garlic cloves, pressed through a garlic press
2/3 cup peanut oil plus extra for grilling
2 pounds flank steak

Combine soy sauce, honey, vinegar, ginger, garlic and oil in a small bowl and whisk until well combined. Pierce the steak all over the front and back with a sharp fork. Lay the steak in a shallow glass or ceramic dish, or in a heavy zip-lock bag. Pour the marinade over the steak, and then turn it over and coat the other side. Refrigerate all day, turning occasionally.

Preheat the grill for high heat. Put the grate on the highest level, and brush it lightly with vegetable oil. Grill for 15 to 20 minutes, turning once. When steak is cooked to your liking, remove it from the grill, allow it to rest for 5 minutes, and then slice it thinly against the grain. Serve immediately.

Shrimp and Lemon Orzo

1 tablespoon olive oil
1 cup uncooked orzo pasta
1 clove garlic, crushed
2 cups chicken stock or broth
zest from 1 lemon
1 pound peeled, deveined cooked medium shrimp

Heat the oil in a pot over medium heat. Stir in orzo, and cook 2 minutes, until golden. Add the broth and lemon zest and bring to a boil. Reduce heat to low and simmer 10 minutes, or until liquid has been absorbed and orzo is tender. Season to taste with salt and pepper and toss with shrimp.

Sesame Green Beans and Edamame

1/2 cup red wine or balsamic vinegar
1/3 cup olive oil
1 clove garlic, pressed through a garlic press
1 tablespoon sugar
1 teaspoon salt
1 pound fresh green beans, ends trimmed and
  lightly steamed
2 cups cooked, shelled edamame
1/4 cup finely diced red onion
1/2 cup chopped red bell pepper
1/4 cup sesame seeds, lightly toasted

Combine vinegar, oil, garlic, sugar and salt in a bowl and whisk until combined. Spoon the green beans, edamame, onion and red pepper into a serving dish and stir gently; drizzle the dressing over and stir. Allow to marinate for one hour, stirring occasionally. Sprinkle with toasted sesame seeds and serve.

Salad of Red Peppers, Yellow Peppers and Feta

2 tablespoons olive oil
2 red bell pepper, seeded and sliced
1 yellow bell pepper, seeded and sliced
1 orange bell pepper, seeded and sliced
salt and freshly ground black pepper, to taste
1/2 cup feta cheese, crumbled
4 tablespoons chopped fresh basil

Heat the oil in a skillet over medium heat. Add the peppers and sauté until tender and lightly browned. Remove from heat and season with salt and pepper. Cool to room temperature and transfer to a serving dish. Sprinkle with cheese and stir gently to combine. Garnish with chopped basil and serve.

Miniature Tarts with Fresh Berries

8 4-inch cream pies or cheesecakes purchased from
  the bakery
1/2 cup blueberries
1/2 cup blackberries
1/2 cup sliced strawberries
1/2 cup raspberries
1/2 cup currant jelly

Arrange the blueberries and blackberries on four of the pies. Arrange the strawberries and raspberries on the other four pies. In a small saucepan, heat the currant jelly until it melts. Cool briefly and brush the tops of the pies with the glaze.

Why July 4th?

Consider the implications of the Declaration of Independence. Fifty-six solemn delegates, on behalf of the people of thirteen small colonies and after much deliberation, chose "to dissolve the political bands which have connected them with another." Given the document's contents, the identity of "another" was clear.

The Founding Fathers would never mistake the portent of those words, which for them amounted to treason. They took this extraordinary step at a time when the British fleet had just sailed into New York Harbor with 30,000 soldiers and 10,000 sailors. Truly, as Benjamin Franklin so eloquently noted, "We must hang together, gentlemen . . . . else, we shall most assuredly hang separately."

And agree to this risk they did, mutually pledging "to each other our Lives, our Fortunes and our sacred Honor." In short, they endangered everything they owned or earned, their reputations and even their lives for this effort.

Today, we recognize that epic act on the Fourth of July. That was the day the delegates signed the document. Correct?

Incorrect. Actually, although we celebrate the Fourth, it doesn't mark the day of the signing. According to the National Archives, the Continental Congress voted for independence on July 2, but no one signed the document until August 2. Even then, the fifty-six delegates "eventually" signed over the next several months. In the end, the final signature was that of Thomas McKean of Delaware, affixed in or after January 1777.

The Library of Congress timeline says the Declaration was adopted July 4, after the July 2 vote for Independence. On July 6, the Pennsylvania Evening Post printed the document, and on July 8, in Philadelphia, it was first read to the public. On July 9, General Washington ordered it read to his troops, stationed in New York.

That July 2 decision prompted a (now much-quoted) July 3 letter from John Adams to his wife, Abigail, noting that "The Second Day of July 1776, will be the most memorable Epocha, in the History of America. I am apt to believe that it will be celebrated, by succeeding Generations, as the great anniversary Festival."

Today, we celebrate a great anniversary festival— on the Fourth. Question is, where did we get that date? According to the National Archives, that was the date on the written document.

A few other interesting facts about the events surrounding this venerable document:

The Declaration intended, in part, to "place before mankind the common sense of the subject, in terms so plain and firm as to command their assent, and to justify ourselves in the independent stand we are compelled to take," Thomas Jefferson wrote to Henry Lee in May 1825.

On September 11, 1776, British General Richard Howe met for a Staten Island Peace Conference with a delegation that included Franklin and Adams. It failed when Howe demanded the Declaration be revoked.

Jefferson, tasked with writing the Declaration, gave it to Adams and Franklin (and two other delegates) for editing before the "fair copy" was submitted to Congress on June 28, 1776. This scene, not the signing, is depicted in John Trumbull's painting, "Declaration of Independence," hanging in the rotunda of the U.S. Capitol. Trumbull only included delegates for whom he had likenesses, and included many who did not attend the presentation.

On July 4, 1826, fifty years after the date on the Declaration, Adams and Jefferson died within hours of each other.

"If you take advantage of everything America has to offer, there's nothing you can't accomplish".

—Geraldine Ferraro

A Story of Stars

A wispy, open-air tent adds fun to the stargazing event. I covered this 10- by 10-foot frame in mosquito netting, originally designed to cover a typical outdoor umbrella (find it at any outdoor furniture store). I added two Adirondack chairs; a sea-grass ottoman and rug; some fluffy, overstuffed pillows; a flag; some hanging glow-in-the-dark lanterns; and a spattering of astronomy and stargazing books for guidance. This canopy doubles as a great place to escape for a midday nap or private talk.

They guided sailors over vast and dangerous oceans; told the Greek gods the time and seasons; forecast troubles to discerning nomads; and outlined creatures, warriors and meaningful patterns for our storytelling ancestors. For millennia, we've turned to the stars for guidance, warnings, information and entertainment.

This Independence Day, revive this lost art. Grab a stack of blankets, a pair of binoculars (or a telescope if you can get one), good star map and insect repellent, and prepare for nature's finest mingling of science and art—and more.

A lesser-known gift of the stars is the sharing. My loved ones, now across a continent, can look up at roughly the same time I do and see the same stars, the same moon. We can wish together, but more often, we reminisce.

Each Fourth of July, my family went camping. Unlike most families who roughed it, we went no further than our own backyard. This was due mostly to my sister's astonishing array of allergies, my dad's dislike of sleeping on rocks and my mom's extraordinary fear of anything with more than two legs. Yet what defined this annual trek was my sister's unlimited ability to make us laugh, my dad's gifted knowledge of and

love for astronomy (the science) and astrology (the fun), and my mom's uncommon talent for delectable camp food.

On such nights, my parents would let us stay up a bit longer, no doubt hoping we would remember the eighty-eight constellations, the five-of-eight visible planets or the Roman mythology surrounding the globes and stars. Sad to say, we do not. I do remember the sharply damp, late nights, where you could almost feel the stillness. And in that stillness, I would wait . . . . wait . . . . wait . . . . until—there it went! A shooting star. I held a firm conviction that wishing upon that star meant all my dreams would come true. Over the years, that evolved from a pink Barbie bike for my birthday, to an invitation to an upcoming pool party, and then above all, to the chance that Jeremy Sharp would like me back. My hopes and expectations were generally short-lived, but even today, I am rewarded with the forever moment, the memory of laying in a sleeping bag and gazing at the stars as the embers glowed in our makeshift fire pit. I have strung together my collection of such memories, rather like a necklace, and I wear it lovingly each Fourth of July when I gaze at the stars. The heavens should shine so brilliantly as my necklace. I cherish it.

Party Timeline

One month before the party:

-w- Make or purchase the invitations.

-w- Finalize guest list and mail invitations.

3 weeks before the party:

-w- Finalize the menu, including drinks (carefully selecting the items you wish to make and those you wish to purchase).

-w- Create a look by selecting colors, mood, setting and, entertainment, if necessary.

-w- Order or gather the decorations and accessories.

2 weeks before the party:

-w- Make a shopping list for the food and liquor (see Shopping list).

-w- Order the food or any desert you do not wish to make.

-w- Order flowers, and consider having them delivered the day of the party.

1 week before the party:

-w- Assemble or purchase take-away gifts and wrap them.

-w- Purchase all nonperishable food and liquor and charcoal, if necessary.

-w- Purchase sparklers.

-w- Create a music play list or purchase CDs.

-w- Purchase grasses for the table.

3 days before the party:

-w- Decorate.

-w- Prepare the bar with glasses and liquor.

-w- Assemble all the serving dishes and set up the buffet table, if using one.

2 days before the party:

-w- Prepare the honeydew melon soup. Cover tightly and refrigerate.

The day before party:

-w- Purchase perishable food (see Shopping list).

-w- Set out the table in the yard.

-w- Set out the yard games.

-w- Pick up flowers or have them delivered.

-w- Make extra ice.

-w- Check that the bathroom is clean. Have fresh hand towels, soap and extra toilet paper on hand.

The morning of the party:

-w- Set the table (if the party is outdoors).

-w- Assemble the mini crab cakes. Cover tightly and refrigerate.

-w- Marinate the flank steak.

-w- Cut the peppers, trim the green beans, and chop onions for pepper salad and sesame green beans and edamame. Cut beets.

-w- Cover and refrigerate.

Prior to guests' arrival:

-w- Assemble pepper salad and green beans and edamame.

-w- Assemble red beet crumbles.

-w- Heat the current jelly and brush on the tarts.

-w- Assemble shrimp and lemon orzo.

-w- Start the grill.

-w- Turn on the music

-w- Prepare the Blueberry Sparkler, including one for yourself!

-w- Light the candles.

-w- Enjoy!

Take Away Gifts

The take-away gift caps the evening's festivities. It combines the light-hearted fun of a day of play and a night of wishing upon the stars. Charm your departing guests with a gift to stimulate their minds, their tastes and, well, their gardens.

Gift them with numbered galvanized-metal flowerpots, bursting with a potted geranium (perfect for planting in the garden later); a classic 1920s-era handmade lollipop; a miniature book on astrology; or each guest's personal horoscope guide (see Resources).

Vary it:
Blend a jar of homemade chocolate-chip cookie mix, complete with a wooden spoon secured to the top and directions to use it. Tie with a beautiful ribbon.

Simplify it:
Fill a clear container with glow-in-the-dark stars to hang on children's ceilings or on the underside of dog houses. Both will appreciate the ambience (see Resources).

"The greatest lesson we can learn from the past . . . . s that freedom is at the core of every successful nation n the world."

—Frederick Chiluba

Lights, Camera, Action!

As the sky transcends to the perfect shade of lavender, share a laugh, a tear, perhaps a bowl of popcorn.

Nature has staged its final act for the day, the ultimate example of classic theater. And that's your cue. You have set your scene: a small concession stand deals a steady stream of popcorn and candy, friends gather on carefully arranged blankets and a hush settles over the crowd as all eyes turn to the big screen. The film begins.

Tonight's gift to your guests, your friends, promises enchantment but also perspective. You offer an enduring classic movie to remind them of days gone by, or of a world where complexities grow simple and endings are always happy.

"Louis, I think this is the beginning of a beautiful friendship."
—Rick, played by Humphrey Bogart, in "Casablanca"

Theme:
Stars in the Dark

Setting:
A well-used, well-loved, romantic backyard.

Mood:
Fun, inspired, graceful, classic, and relaxed

Colors:
Midnight black, sultry white, sunset yellow

Flowers:
An abundance of sunflowers, alstros, daffodils and potted yellow daisies or mums.

Tastes:
The menu features an elegant evening summer picnic, replete with the freshest of ingredients plucked straight from the local farmer's market.

Sounds:
A custom playlist features multiple eras of much-loved theatrical tunes. Charm guests of any generation with such collections as *The Hollywood Sound, Hollywood's Greatest Hits, Hollywood's Best* (from the thirties, forties or fifties), or the original sound track from "Casablanca." These melodies span decades, yet remain favorites for any generation of movie-goers.

Experience:
A rented video screen, or an oversize sheet attached to a garage or fence. A projector and popcorn. Enjoy a night under the stars with individual blankets, savory picnic boxes, and a evening of classic stars—under the stars.

Vary it: Outdoor cinema not possible? Consider holding the outdoor picnic and then moving the movie indoors for comfort and ease.

Simplify it: When warm summer nights blend with guests and a good time, movies may end up too quiet of a pastime. If so, keep the concession stand running, but bring out one of the many movie-related board games available at any toy store. Or search online bookstores or toy stores, and ensure ahead of time that you stay in the game.

"I have a dream too, but it's about singing and dancing and making people happy. It's the kind of dream that gets better the more people you share it with. And I found a whole group of friends who have the same dream, and that makes us sort of like a family."

— Kermit the Frog, in "The Muppet Movie"

Life gives us family, but gifts us with friends. We surround ourselves with them, understanding that people—family and friends—are our truest path to happiness.

Among this handful of precious people, we grow through a life of laughter, tears, humility, frustration, successes, failures, and life's joys and sorrows.

Amid these special people, we give and take support, love and the comfort that comes from long familiarity. We cherish and are cherished, and this knowledge softens our perplexing worlds with a deep meaning. We don't take this lightly.

These are the ones with whom we walk our life's journey. For this reason, we celebrate occasions that allow us to draw closer. We call these friends a gift, and we call this gift happiness.

I love creating intimate spots for friends or loved ones to sneak away to. These are where some of the best conversations can be had and meaningful catching up can be done. This old garden bench on the side of the house is donned with an extra blanket and pillows invite guests to sit and make themselves comfortable.

"It's Showtime"

Can anything capture the imagination, the emotions, the attention like classic cinema? Movies tell our story, alter our perspectives, make us think. They allow us to reminisce, marking our life milestones: "I went to see Godfather with my friends in my senior year!" Or, "My parents took us to see Dumbo on my sixth birthday." Your backyard night at the movies will delight, inspire and entertain your guests. Should your invitations do any less?

The Invitation

Much in the way movie houses tailor real cinema tickets to the currently showing movie, these clever replicas will easily customize for the film you choose for your event. Hand-letter the occasion, date, time, place and RSVP information. Enclose in small colored envelopes and mail (see Resources).

Vary it

Why not craft your own ticket? Purchase colored cardstock paper and cut into ticket-size pieces. Or, using your computer, print any of the many clip-art ticket designs out there onto your card stock, and cut to ticket size. Hand-letter the party information where pertinent, and insert into an oversize box of candy (heat-resistant types—Dots, Ju Ju Candy, Skittles, or Hot Tamales—work best). Add a little extra candy from a reserve box to eliminate rattling. Reseal the box with tape and affix the addresses. Place stamps directly onto the box, and mail.

Simplify it

Check your local party-supply store for Hollywood theme party supplies (or search their sites online). Purchase invitations, fill out pertinent information, and enclose in a padded envelope with a handful of unpopped popcorn kernels. Address and send. Alternately, see if you can find invitations featuring the movie or star you will show. Then complete as noted above.

"The summer night is like a perfection of thought."
— Wallace Stevens

Showy Setting

Your guests are assured the best seat in the house; each couple or family has their own blanket, pillows and picnic box. The spots are designated with wooden address numbers tied to small lawn stakes (see Resources).

The picnic boxes keep everything you need close and convenient. The wooden, caulk board boxes (children's storage boxes – see Resources) feature the written menu and are filled with extra plates, serving utensils, soft drinks, flowers and a couple boxes of candy. (If you are substituting with different boxes or pails consider writing the menu on paper and attaching it with a pretty ribbon.

Take refugee from the heat with a custom blended margarita and the soothing sound of a nearby fountain. *If you do have a water feature, be sure to have a couple bottles of bug spray and citronella candles on hand to avoid lots of unexpected guests.

These small details will not go unnoticed and are sure to make the evening unforgettable.

How does a classic become a classic?

It's A Wonderful World for films that reach classic status. Our hallowed classics challenge us, move us, thrill us and comfort us in their steadfastness. They represent our national identity, reflect our culture and tap into our thoughts at a given moment.

But what earns a film the "classic" moniker? Research helps not at all. While a handful of aficionados split hairs on an exact definition, most sources toss the term around loosely. Some say classic covers films from the Hollywood studio-system era, which ended in 1960. But then how does one explain the iconic "The Godfather" (1972) or "Star Wars" (1977). Can anyone say "Dr. Zhivago (1965)?

According to Reel Classics LLC, true classics model established standards, but tantalize the imagination—without graphic sex, violence, or other technical or special effects. They achieve this through a perfect balance of story line, characters and timing.

Story Line

In "Fenimore Cooper's Literary Offenses," the inimitable Mark Twain took to task Cooper's Deerslayer tale and

offered nineteen rules governing literary art in fiction. One rule states that "the episodes of a tale shall be necessary parts of the tale, and shall help to develop it." Cooper's episodes, he said, "have no rightful place in the work, since there was nothing for them to develop." As author of several classics (with a nod to Cooper's, as well), Twain knew what drives a story line.

ReelClassics goes further. "Classic movies use compelling stories and characters, or snappy dialogue, or high production values (cinematography, editing, shot composition, scoring, sets and costuming), or good acting, or some combination." Hollywood's Production Code, it writes, which controlled depictions of "sex, violence and immoral behavior on the screen," forced Tinseltown to blend these components into subtle but unparalleled creativity.

In the end, classics simply render a story, rather than tell it. A plot or narrative unfolds in layers, allowing viewers to savor it and look forward to what will happen next. This is the essence of great storytelling.

Character

The bulk of Twain's literary rules focus on the story's characters, requiring first that "the personages in a tale shall be alive, except in the case of corpses," with readers (or viewers) able to tell them apart.

Truly, no matter how good one's story line, without authentic and believable characters, the story will fail. Imagine how pallid The Godfather would be without Michael Corleone, whose character ranged from war hero to the brutal leader of a crime syndicate—and did so believably. Each episode pushes him away from his former self and toward the new, fulfilling another Twain requirement that "the characters in a tale shall be so clearly defined that the reader can tell beforehand what each will do in a given emergency."

The characters make or break great films. They become the storyteller, the means by which the audience will identify with, and ultimately love or hate the movie.

Timing

Dare we say it? Timing is everything. This holds true with movie debuts, whether through the time of year or the events of the time. Various films over the years, for example, recount the life, or death, of George Armstrong Custer, with two classics: 1942's "They Died With Their Boots On" and 1970's "Little Big Man." Many critiqued Errol Flynn's 1942 version for its glorified portrayal of Custer—but the United States had just gone to war. By contrast, Dustin Hoffman's Little Big Man depicts Custer as something of a buffoon—but America was tired of war.

Likewise, "Titanic" owes part of its success to its Christmas 1997 release, a time of economic security, and vacationing viewers who sought refuge from holiday stress or boredom.

Finally, "Inherit the Wind," fictionalizing the 1925 Monkey Scopes Trials, debuted as a play in 1955 to discuss McCarthyism, its authors said. In 1960 it found its way to film, starring the comfortable but colorful Spencer Tracy as the maverick Henry Drummond, and released to an America questioning authority. It became a classic. A second rendering, to 1988's corporately comfortable culture, did not fare as well.

Classics speak to the times, but through their other elements transcend the times, too. Timing isn't everything, but without it, a film may find itself Gone With the Wind.

Essential Elements of Entertaining
It's About Time

You look chic, stylish and welcoming. An exquisite buffet fills your side table and your party décor invites elegant good times. The scene calls for only one more thing. The guests. Ten minutes past the appointed hour, they begin to arrive. With warm hellos and hugs, they greet you, then head into your home for an evening of your legendary hospitality. They were merely fashionably late.

Etiquette lore says the term fashionably late grew popular early in the nineteenth century to imply the distinguished art of being tardy. Today, it means the same thing, although etiquette mavens give it mixed reviews.

Some say being fashionably late implies your own importance, that something occurred and unavoidably detained the irreplaceable you. A fashionably late person knows how to allow enough guests to arrive before making his own entrance.

Others consider fashionably late something of a courtesy, depending upon local customs, the event and the host. It allows the party to get underway with a steady stream of guests, rather than a rush at the appointed hour. But it can also delay a carefully planned dinner.

As a rule of thumb, consider anything beyond five to ten minutes—at the most—unacceptable and disrespectful. Your host invested time, effort and a budget into an evening's food, décor and entertainment. Tardiness alters the time-frame for everyone else. Lateness implies a disregard for others' time compared with your own, a disinterest in the event, and a disrespect for its importance.
Despite these implications, many people simply want to know: How late is fashionable?

Estimates vary depending upon the source, but after thirty minutes, you've surpassed "acceptable" for a large party. And an arrival this late unquestionably requires a call to the host.

With dinner parties and large group meetings, you may arrive ten to fifteen minutes late before you exceed acceptable. And you still owe a phone call. For meetings with another person or for most other parties, you're testing acceptability at five minutes past due. You needn't call for a five-minute delay.

Open houses, cocktail parties and other "drop-by" parties generally have a flow of guests. Unless otherwise specified, you can arrive—and leave—at any time during designated hours.

Now for two universal rules:

1. No exceptions, no excuses for being late to weddings, funerals or most performances.

2. Conversely, don't arrive early to dinner parties or engagements held at a private residence. If you do find yourself running ahead of time, sit in the car and wait until the designated time.

Getting guests to go home

Can anything steal the magic of your evening like a guest who won't go home? Generally, you can gauge which guests might overstay and prepare ahead. After all, these are the crème de la crème of your friends, else why would you invite them? Simply add an end time to the invitation.

But if your friends enjoyed your event so much that they forget the time, or you find yourself with some who just won't get on the exit train (the flow of guests who quickly follow the first departure), try these time-honored tips on pointing them due home.

First, remember your manners. Remain gracious and polite. Anything less reflects poorly on you, not them. Besides, if you like them enough to invite them, you like them enough to keep.

Stick to a pre-planned excuse or strategy devised with your spouse or another loved one, and keep your stories straight. Imagine the awkwardness when you describe a relaxing weekend ahead only to hear your spouse mention your early morning flight.

Pre-determine a departure time, and starting winding things down about forty-five minutes ahead of that. Offer guests coffee or tea, or pass out bottles of water. This polite segue usually leads people to start wrapping up their conversations.

Approach groups of guests with a little arm stretch and a sincere thank you for their coming. Mention what a great evening it has been.

Cap your list of subtle hints by handing out your take-away gifts. Add such conversation-enders as, "Be careful getting home. We always enjoy your company—let's do this again soon."

If these polite tricks fail, bring out bolder measure. Start cleaning up. Gather the dishes, take out the trash and blow out the candles. Most people won't want to stick around and wash dishes, and will head for the door. Just remember not to get beat at your own game. Politely refuse offers of help, or you'll just prolong the evening.

If, unbelievably, that doesn't work, ask your guests to leave. Diffuse tension with your wit and humor: "I am so sorry to wrap this up, but I have a debriefing with Scotland Yard first thing in the morning."

And if even then, they won't leave, turn off the lights, say goodnight and tell them to lock up when they leave.

The Top Movie Quotes of All Time

We all do it. We pepper our daily conversations with quips and quotes from the big screen, with no real regard of the saying's true source.

In 2005, the American Film Institute released its *100 Years...100 Movie Quotes*, which it calls the top movie quotes of all time. You'll find the entire list on AFI's website, but below, we offer the Top 10.

When your movie guests gather, let them argue for others that missed the list.

1. "Frankly, my dear, I don't give a damn."
   – Gone With the Wind, 1932

2. "I'm going to make him an offer he can't refuse."
   – The Godfather, 1972

3. "You don't understand! I coulda had class. I coulda been a contender. I could've been somebody, instead of a bum, which is what I am." – On the Waterfront, 1954

4. "Toto, I've got a feeling we're not in Kansas anymore."
   – The Wizard of Oz, 1939

5. "Here's looking at you, kid." – Casablanca, 1942

6. "Go ahead, make my day." – Sudden Impact, 1983

7. "Bond. James Bond." – Dr. No, 1962

8. "May the Force be with you." – Star Wars, 1977

9. "Fasten your seatbelts. It's going to be a bumpy night."
   – All About Even, 1950

10. "You talking to me?" – Taxi Driver, 1976

The Top 25 Movies of All Time
(from the American Film Institute's *100 Years...100 Movies*)

1. Citizen Kane (1941)
2. Casablanca (1942)
3. The Godfather (1972)
4. Gone With the Wind (1939)
5. Lawrence of Arabia (1962)
6. The Wizard of Oz (1939)
7. The Graduate (1967)
8. On the Waterfront (1954)
9. Schindler's List (1993)
10. Singin' In the Rain (1952)
11. It's a Wonderful Life (1946)
12. Sunset Blvd. (1950)
13. The Bridge on the River Kwai (1957)
14. Some Like It Hot (1959)
15. Star Wars (1977)
16. All About Eve (1950)
17. The African Queen (1951)
18. Psycho (1960)
19. Chinatown (1974)
20. One Flew Over the Cuckoo's Nest (1975)
21. The Grapes of Wrath (1940)
22. 2001: A Space Odyssey (1968)
23. The Maltese Falcon (1941)
24. Raging Bull (1980)
25. E.T. The Extra-Terrestrial (1982)

What starts out as a patch of green grass is transformed into an al fresco theater under the stars.

Outdoor picnic blankets and pillows, individual dinner boxes, a movie screen, petite concession stand and vintage popcorn popper complete the scene.

The flowers are cleverly displayed in oversized popcorn boxes that conceal the vase.

"Deep summer is when laziness finds respectability."

— Sam Keen

"A perfect summer day is when the sun is shining, the breeze is blowing, the birds are singing, and the lawn mower is broken."

— James Dent

Shopping List

2 750-ml bottles blanco or silver 100 percent
  agave tequila
½ pound baby carrots
2 large tomatoes
1 English cucumber
1 bunch parsley
1 bunch fresh chives
1 bunch celery
1 head garlic
1 head butter lettuce
20 limes
10 oranges
1 pound button mushrooms
2 large red bell peppers
1 large yellow bell pepper
1 large orange bell pepper
2 pounds baby tomatoes
1 pound baby onions
2 pounds red new potatoes
2 pounds assorted lettuces
2 small avocados
1 small red onion
1 11-ounce can mandarin oranges
1 3-ounce can sliced black olives
1 bottle Italian dressing
1 small jar mayonnaise
6 cups (48 ounces) beef broth
1 small bottle agave nectar
1/2 pound cooked lobster meat
20 extra-large fresh shrimp
2 pounds tenderloin steak
10-12 small French rolls
20-24 large cookies
1/2 gallon ice cream, your favorite flavor
1 ½ teaspoons dried saffron
1 pound sweetened flaked coconut
4 ounces sliced almonds
1 pound long-grain white rice
1 box sea salt or Kosher salt
4 ounces grated Parmesan cheese
Soda
Popcorn
Candy

The Essentials

10 – 12 margarita glasses
10 – 12 bottles of water
10 – 12 small soup bowls for the gazpacho
10 – 12 small salad plates for mixed green salad
10 – 12 dinner plates
10 – 12 place settings of cutlery, including salad forks,
  dinner forks, and knives
1 small serving bowl for saffron rice
1 small serving bowl for mixed green salad
1 medium serving bowl for gazpacho soup
1 small plate/bowl for the grilled parmesan and
  garlic bread
1 large serving tray for New England lobster rolls
1 large serving tray for the steak and shrimp kabobs
1 cake stand for ice cream sandwiches
10 – 12 popcorn boxes
10 – 12 napkins (have a few extra on hand)
1 tablecloth
5 – 6 large baskets or boxes to hold
  the individual picnics

Staples (replenish if needed)

salt
freshly ground black pepper
all-purpose flour
milk
butter
eggs
extra virgin olive oil
granulated sugar

Menu
For 10 to 12

Signature Drink:
Perfect Lime and Orange Margaritas

Appetizer:
Petite New England Lobster Rolls

Starter:
Summer Chopped Gazpacho

Salad:
Mixed Green Salad with Avocado, Red Onion,
Oranges and Candied Almonds

Entrée:
Grilled Steak and Shrimp Kabobs with Assorted
Peppers, New Potatoes, Mushrooms
and Cherry Tomatoes

Accompaniments:
Saffron Rice with Fresh Herbs
Grilled Parmesan Garlic Bread

Dessert:
Homemade Ice Cream Sandwiches

The Recipes

Perfect Lime and Orange Margaritas

Ground sea salt or Kosher salt
1 lime
¼ cup (2 ounces) blanco or silver 100 percent agave tequila (or more or less to suit your taste)
3 tablespoons fresh lime juice
2 tablespoons fresh orange juice
1 teaspoon agave nectar

Pour a 1/4-inch layer of salt onto a small plate. Cut the lime and run the cut side around the rim of a margarita glass. Dip the top of the glass in the salt to coat, and set aside to dry.

Fill a small cocktail shaker with ice. Add the tequila, lime juice, orange juice and agave nectar, and shake for 30 seconds. Add ice to the glass and strain the margarita over the ice. Garnish with a wedge of the lime. 1 serving.

Petite New England Lobster Rolls

For the *choux* puffs:
1 cup all-purpose flour
1/8 teaspoon salt
½ cup milk
½ cup water
1/3 cup butter
4 eggs

For the lobster salad:
½ pound cooked lobster meat, chopped
½ cup mayonnaise
2 stalks celery, finely chopped
1 ½ teaspoons chopped parsley
3 tablespoons finely chopped red bell pepper
salt and pepper to taste
fresh butter lettuce leaves

In a medium bowl, combine the flour and salt with a whisk. In a heavy saucepan over medium-high heat, combine the milk, water and butter and bring to a boil. Add the flour mixture and stir quickly with a wooden spoon. When the mixture becomes dry and no longer clings to the side of the pan, remove from the heat and cool for two minutes. Add the eggs one at a time, stirring well after each addition.

Preheat the oven to 400 degrees F. Spoon the choux mixture in generous teaspoon-sized balls on a parchment paper-lined baking sheet and bake for about 12 minutes, until firm and lightly browned. Cool on a wire rack. Makes about 5 dozen puffs.

To make the lobster salad, combine the ingredients in a medium bowl and refrigerate until needed.

To make the lobster rolls, split the choux puffs in half with a sharp knife. Fill with a generous teaspoonful of lobster salad, top with lettuce and reassemble the puffs. Makes about 5 dozen appetizers.

Summer Chopped Gazpacho

6 cups chilled beef broth
1 English cucumber, peeled and chopped
1 cup chopped fresh tomatoes
1 cup finely chopped celery
1 cup finely chopped baby carrots
1 small can sliced black olives, drained
salt and pepper to taste
2 tablespoons finely chopped fresh parsley

Combine the broth and vegetables, add salt and pepper if needed, and stir in the chopped parsley. Serve in chilled bowls.

Green Salad with Avocado, Red Onion, Oranges and Candied Almonds

1/2 cup sliced almonds
1/4 cup sugar
2 pounds assorted lettuces
2 small avocados, peeled and cut in 1-inch pieces
1 small red onion, peeled and sliced in ¼ inch slices
1 11-ounce can mandarin oranges, drained
Italian dressing

To make the candied almonds, line a baking sheet with parchment paper and set aside. Sprinkle the sugar in a cast iron skillet and heat over a medium-high flame, swirling occasionally, until the mixture melts. Quickly add the almonds and stir with a silicone spatula to coat the almonds with the sugar. Continue to cook and stir just until the sugar mixture turns caramel-colored. Remove from the heat and quickly spoon the almonds onto the parchment, spreading as thinly as possible. Allow to cool completely; break the almonds into small pieces and store in a glass jar for up to 5 days until ready to use.

To make the salad, combine the salad greens, avocado, red onion rings and oranges and dress lightly with the salad dressing. Sprinkle with the candied almonds just before serving.

Grilled Steak and Shrimp Kabobs with Assorted Peppers, New Potatoes, Mushrooms and Cherry Tomatoes

20 extra-large fresh shrimp
2 pounds tenderloin steak, cut into 1-inch cubes
1 pound button mushrooms, cleaned
1 large red bell pepper, seeds and stem removed and
  cut in 1-inch pieces
1 large yellow bell pepper, seeds and stem removed
  and cut in 1-inch pieces
1 large orange bell pepper, seeds and stem removed
  and cut in 1-inch pieces
2 pounds baby tomatoes
2 pounds red new potatoes, halved and parboiled
1 pound baby onions, peeled and parboiled
extra virgin olive oil
salt and pepper

Preheat the grill to medium-high heat. Thread each skewer with one ingredient, brush lightly with olive oil and sprinkle with salt and pepper. Cook to desired doneness, remove from skewers and serve on a large platter.

Saffron Rice with Fresh Herbs

6 cups water
1 tablespoon butter
1 teaspoon salt
1 1/2 teaspoons dried saffron
3 cups long-grain white rice
1 1/2 teaspoons finely chopped fresh chives
1 1/2 teaspoons finely chopped parsley

In a large saucepan over medium heat, add the water, salt and butter and heat over high heat until the butter melts. Add the saffron and turmeric and stir until combined. Add the rice and stir well. Heat to boiling and reduce the heat to low. Cover and cook for 20 minutes, or until most of the liquid has been absorbed by the rice. Remove from heat and leave covered for up to 30 minutes. To serve, fluff the rice and spoon into a serving bowl; sprinkle with chives and parsley.

Garlic-Parmesan Bread

½ cup butter, softened
½ cup grated Parmesan cheese
2 cloves garlic, peeled and minced
10 small French rolls, sliced crosswise and lengthwise

Preheat the grill. Combine the butter, Parmesan cheese and garlic; spread the mixture on the inner sides of the baguette slices. Spray two large pieces of aluminum foil with baking spray and arrange 10 bread halves on each piece of foil, cut side down. Wrap tightly and cook on the top rack (not on direct heat) for about 5 minutes, or until lightly browned. Unwrap and serve. 10 servings.

Homemade Ice Cream Sandwiches

2 1/2 cups sweetened flaked coconut
1/2 gallon ice cream, your favorite flavor
20 large cookies

To toast the coconut, heat the oven to 350 degrees F and spread the coconut on a foil-lined cookie sheet that has been lightly sprayed with baking spray. Bake the coconut for 10 to 15 minutes, stirring once, until lightly browned. Remove from the oven and cool the baking sheet on a wire rack.

To assemble the sandwiches, line two cookie sheets with parchment paper or waxed paper. Spoon 1/4 to 1/3 cup ice cream on one cookie and spread to the edges. Top with another cookie, smooth the sides if necessary, and roll the edges in toasted coconut. Arrange the cookies on the prepared baking sheet and freeze for at least two hours.

Party Timeline

One month before the dinner:

- Make or purchase the invitations.

3 weeks before the dinner:

- Finalize the menu, including drinks (carefully selecting the items you wish to make and those you wish to purchase).
- Create a look by selecting colors, mood, setting, and if necessary, entertainment.
- Purchase or reserve to rent projector and movie screen.
- Select the movie or movies you wish to show.
- Order or gather decorations and accessories.

2 weeks before the dinner:

- Make a shopping list for the food and liquor (see Shopping list).
- Order the food or any desert you do not wish to make.
- Order flowers, and consider having them delivered the day of the dinner.

1 week before the dinner:

- Assemble or purchase take-away gifts and wrap them.
- Purchase all nonperishable food and liquor (see Shopping list).
- Assemble candy and popcorn for the concession stand.
- Create a music play list or purchase CDs.

3 days before the dinner:

- Decorate.

2 days before the dinner:

- Prepare the bar with glasses and liquor.
- Assemble all the serving dishes and set up the buffet table
- Make the candied almonds for the salad and store in a covered container at room temperature.

The day before the dinner:

- Buy remaining perishable food (see Shopping list).
- Squeeze limes and oranges for margaritas.
- Bake choux puffs for lobster rolls.
- Make the ice cream sandwiches and freeze.
- Set the table.
- Pick up the flowers or have them delivered.
- Make extra ice.
- Check that the bathroom is clean. Have fresh hand towels, soap and extra toilet paper on hand.

The morning of the dinner:

- Set up the movie screen or attach a sheet to wall.
- Set up the projector and test to be sure it is working and volume is set to the proper level.
- Set up concession stand and set out any candy that won't melt.
- Make the lobster salad and refrigerate.
- Make the gazpacho and refrigerate.
- Make the garlic-Parmesan butter and refrigerate.
- Finish preparing the food.
- Pop some popcorn.

Two hours before the dinner:

- Thread the shish kebab ingredients on the skewers and refrigerate. Bring tenderloin to room temperature for one hour before grilling.

Prior to guests' arrival:

- Start the music or movie, depending on desired start time.
- Mix a batch of margaritas, including one for yourself!
- Set out remaining candy.
- Light the candles.
- Enjoy!

"When you smiled you had my undivided attention. When you laughed you had my urge to laugh with you. When you cried you had my urge to hold you. When you said you loved me, you had my heart forever."

— Unknown

Take Away Gifts

Like films, your take-away gifts can range from high to low budget. Unlike most films, funds won't affect quality.

Nothing says movies like a collection of memorabilia. Try loading a children's chalk board storage box (see Resources) with two screen-printed T-shirts, a bowl of gourmet popcorn (sealed), a candy-filled, reproduction movie-reel tin, a couple of classic movies (purchased used for a couple of dollars—see Resources), a dozen "Admit One" tickets, and a black-and-white movie photo. Mix to match to your budget.

Vary It:
You've already asked guests about their favorite movies, right? How else would you know what to show? Use those answers now. Search out something unique to the movie— or find a copy of the movie itself. Remember, used costs less.

Simplify It:
Invite each guest to a movie without you via a movie-house gift card. Personally, I love gift cards. These one-stop gifts, contrary to current etiquette comments, are very personal. They favor your loved one with choice. Find gift cards at your guests' favorite theaters or at the grocery store.

TASTING IN TUSCANY

As late summer meanders into autumn and the sun sets just slightly earlier each evening, you can catch the occasional whiff of the coming cooler weather. Fall is in the air, the cusp of the seasons, when nature starts to relinquish her aging greenery for that sudden burst of abundant color. Before the harvest heralds the deeper cold, not to mention the coming holidays, we rush to savor one last slice of summer. We gather our friends for one final moment of play, a celebration of the autumnal equinox, with fine food and wines and above all, memories in the making.

"Wine makes every meal an occasion, every table more elegant, every day more civilized."

—André Simon

AT A GLANCE

Theme:
The Intrigue of Italy

Setting:
A shaded flagstone veranda and backyard garden.

Mood:
Contemplative, enlightening, comfortable, refined and memorable. Rich colors set off the natural fabrics and fibers to create an atmosphere drenched in Italian inspiration. Relaxed seating, antique garden statues, hanging lanterns, and a timely sunset provide the perfect backdrop for an enchanted evening.

Colors:
Cypress green, saffron gold and accents of garnet red.

Flowers:
Rust colored hydrangeas, red amaranth and wild berries

Tastes:
Time-honored Tuscan cuisine, with an emphasis on regional ingredients and techniques, for a rustic, plentiful Italian feast.

Sounds:
A custom play list featuring a wide variety of provincial music like *The Best of Andrea Bocelli: Vivere*, the well-recognized and loved Italian tenor releases his greatest hits in this album. *Italia* is another complimentary choice, featuring Chris Botti, a trumpet player whose music crosses between jazz and classical. For a lighter fare, tap into Putumay Present's *Italian Café* Or if you seek the fun or traditional, let your guests stomp to the beats of Italian favorites collected in *Bella Tuscany*, *Dinner in Italy* from Angelo Petisi or *That's Amore* from the Italian Tenors.

Experience: Stomp and Taste
Begin building anticipation for the unique experience of grape-stomping with a creative invitation that asks your guests whether they prefer red or white wine. At the event, guests will wash their feet, then step into individual buckets of red or white grapes, depending upon their preferences. Later, the grapes will be refined and made into personal bottles of wine (more details on the following page).

Vary it: If sloshing around in grape juice is a little too physical or messy, hire a local sommelier to conduct one of the many types of wine-tastings (listed on the following page).

Simplify it: Gather ye amateurs and have some fun leading your own wine-tasting. Find books or websites with suggestions for buying, trying, tasting and rating different varieties of wine—and see what happens

It is often said that the sun shines differently in Tuscany than in any other place in the world. With its seemingly insatiable supply of olives, spectacular architecture, renowned cuisine, delicate lavender fields, captivating hillside towns, romantic vineyards and celebrated wines, it's no wonder thousands are lured there each and every year.

Traveling to Tuscany is to visit a world untouched by time, where its wines are synonymous with poetry, its country-side with jewels, and its food with an intimate journey. Here reside people who are genuine and engaging, who appreciate a history few will ever know, and who value traditions and family above all. Few places in the world embody such an authentic lifestyle or leave such enduring impressions on those who experience it.

Matthew and Meg Spencer
Cordially invite you to spend the
Afternoon stomping, sampling
and savoring a variety of wines
and accompaniments.
Saturday, September 18th
4:00 p.m.

"Wine brings to light the hidden secrets of the soul,
gives being to our hopes, bids the coward flight,
drives dull care away, and teaches new meanings
for the accomplishment of our wishes."
—Horace

AUTUMN'S HARVEST BECKONS

Setting the tone, the feel and the mood of such a unique event starts with the invitation. As I've said before, your guests will take their cue from your presentation. In this case, the invitation determines whether guests say, "You want me to what?" or "Oh, what fun!" For this event, creative and fun trumps elaborate and expensive invitations.

The Invitation
Purchase iron-on transfer paper from your local craft store. Design your invitation on your computer—you can even hand-letter, then scan it in. **Remember to use editing software to mirror the image before you print!** Then print the invitation onto the transfer paper and in turn, iron the design onto inexpensive cotton cocktail napkins. Stain each with a red-wine ring in one corner. Enclose each napkin in a square envelope with proper postage.

Vary it
Purchase several small individual bottles of inexpensive wine at your local market or wine merchant. Empty the contents—maybe even enjoy! Wash the bottles, let dry and then replace the label with a personalized one (available at craft stores) giving party details (see Resources). Or create your own label, using extra large stickers or name tags. Wrap each bottle in bubble wrap, and ship in a small box.

Simplify it
Send a very simple, brown bottle bag (found at any liquor store) with the party details written on the front. This is a great option if you are encouraging your guests to bring a bottle of their favorite wine.

Essential Elements of Entertaining
Toasting Through the Ages

Oh, the fine art of the proper toast. These carefully chosen and highly public words reflect the dignity, the solemnity, the significance and even the joie de vivre of an occasion. To make a toast is an honor. To receive a toast is a gift. And to witness a toast is an often moving memory in the making.

Some trace the tradition of toasting to ancient Greece, and then through history as a means to test for poison. The purported idea, according to Snopes.com, which debunked the poison angle, was to tap glasses and slosh liquid between celebrants' drinks. Poison thus would be discovered. More likely, Snopes' researchers say, many would see using one's own glass as a sign of hostility, since passing a communal cup was often the norm. In Britain, researchers noted, when the host received the nearly empty cup, a piece of spiced toast absorbed the last drops and was consumed by the host.

Clinking glasses may have originated as a means of adding sound to the multisensory act of toasting, once individual glasses became the norm. More to the point, though, touching glasses with those nearest you brings each person into a community of those who participate in the toast. It also brings the wine full circle—"On a deeper level, the wine is also being re-communed with itself," Snopes says. From being one in the bottle, the wine is separated into glasses and brought symbolically back together again through toasting.

Tips on Toasting

Those short, eloquent, pithy toasts you see in the movies are actually the result of good writers, practice and showmanship. You can do likewise. A toast is an honor—it should be genuine, heartfelt, informed and focused on the recipient and the occasion. The following tips for toasts apply whether the occasion is for four or 400 people.

Be Ready for Your Turn

Wedding toasts come in a hierarchy, generally best man, groom, bride, fathers, mothers, and finally, friends and other family members. For all other occasions, typically, the host toasts first, followed by other guests. To get everyone's attention, stand and gently tap your wine goblet or water glass.

Be Brief and to the Point

Guests at weddings and showers may expect a brief personal story preceding the toast, but for smaller gatherings, consider saving stories for another time. Listeners can go glassy eyed at even a light play-by-play of your college experience—just give a little background, make the group laugh and finish it up. Most toasts are successful with a quote or sincere statement.

Be Appropriate

This is the most important, the make-or-break, of all toast guidelines. Without it, your toast will haunt you each time you see the recipients again, if you ever do see them again. But with an appropriate toast, the group will laugh at your gentle humor, applaud and cheer your sincere wish, and emulate you when they next toast another. A key to appropriateness is to know your audience. With large or unknown crowds, always, always lean toward the side of caution. Inevitably, a gathering of someone's friends and family will blend ages, ethnicities, cultures, beliefs and preferences. Jokes at someone else's expense are never appropriate—remember, you can never remake a first impression or undo offending someone. In fact, if you don't naturally use humor in your rapport, avoid it in your toast. Use a quote or a sincere wish instead. If it is a small gathering and you know your audience fairly well, you have a lot more leeway. But again, remain sensitive to age, gender, religions and ethnic backgrounds.

Be Prepared

For good or bad, toasts are memorable, and since they pay tribute to a person or an occasion, plan ahead. Whether your toast is for newlyweds or a company party, jot down what it is you want to say, practice it, think about it and try to memorize it. (Avoid note cards if possible.) If your toast is for a more intimate group, identify why or what you're toasting, and look up some relevant quotes or words of wisdom (see References for some online sources).

Be Clever
No one wants to hear an overused joke, so make your toast authentic and personal—even funny, if you can do so without offense. Recount a humorous short story or an anecdote that captures the honoree's personality.

Be Positive
This is a celebration, not a therapy session. A festive occasion is not the time nor place for your resentments and unresolved conflicts, even jokingly. Never has this maxim held more true: "If you don't have something nice to say, don't say it at all." Think of your toast as a greeting card—would you buy it if it weren't uplifting or funny?

Be Sober
Above all, stay sober—or stay away from the microphone. One drink may help you relax, but no refills until after you've impressed with your eloquence. Very few positive things come from inebriation, especially when public speaking is involved. A special occasion requires restraint and decorum.

Toasting is an essential and anticipated part of many celebrations, so have fun and use your best judgment. Remember: be brief, be witty, be positive—and use a toast to honor the occasion.

A SPECTACULAR SETTING

On one of the last warm days of summer, signal the season's close by gathering friends for an evening of wine-tasting—and the long-forgotten art of grape-stomping. Several large tubs contain a bounty of red and white grapes, a small bench for resting and a basket of wines ready for savoring.

Nothing says an intimate evening with friends like a perfectly aged side door and weathered garden statue.

Highlight your buffet tables with regional cheeses and hors d'oeuvres, accented with flowers atop a statue pedestal. Tantalize those wine-tasting buds with a bowl of fresh artichokes and figs, and a basket filled with extra wine (historically, straw often insulated wine). Include extra glasses, cutlery and bottles of water.

A "clean up" station, consisting of a comfortable chair and water bucket, stands ready for pre- and post-stomp foot-washing. Place lemon citrus soaps, a scrub brush and wrapped personal towels nearby.

How elegant the clean dinner table, adorned only with simple strips of linen cloth, a low-profile floral arrangement, and authentic Italian dishware.

Ambience and light flicker from a dozen inexpensive lanterns swaying gently in the late afternoon breeze.

Both attractive and functional, open frames encase the wine rating cards and act as a clipboard.

Carry your wine-based theme to the dessert table, with this oversized almond cake and chocolate butter cream disguised as a wine barrel. Surrounded by Champagne grapes, this clever cake doubles as a unique conversation piece.

"THE WINES THAT ONE BEST REMEMBERS ARE NOT NECESSARILY THE FINEST THAT ONE HAS EVER TASTED, AND THE HIGHEST QUALITY MAY FAIL TO DELIGHT SO MUCH AS SOME FAR MORE HUMBLE BEVERAGE DRUNK IN MORE FAVORABLE SURROUNDINGS."

—H. Warner Allen

Shopping List

1 head garlic
1 bunch fresh sage
1 lemon
1 medium carrot, peeled and finely chopped
1 medium celery stalk, finely chopped
1 yellow onion
1/2 pound cauliflower
1/2 pound thin asparagus
1/2 pound grape or cherry tomatoes
1 English cucumber
1/4 pound White Beech mushrooms or other small mushrooms, cleaned and stems trimmed
1 yellow bell pepper
1 orange bell pepper
1 loaf French bread
1 pound ground lean pork
1 1/2 pounds sweet Italian sausage links
1/2 cup good quality red wine
2 cups canned, whole peeled tomatoes, with the juice
1 15-ounce cans cannellini or white kidney beans, drained
1 3.8-ounce can sliced black olives, drained
1/3 cup Italian salad dressing
1 pound gemelli pasta grated Parmesan cheese
1/2 teaspoon freshly ground black pepper
2 green onions, trimmed and sliced

Staples (Replenish if needed)

Sea salt
Freshly ground black pepper
Extra virgin olive oil
Canola oil
Butter

The Essentials

6 water glass
6 wine glasses
6 coffee cups (if desired)
6 small side plates for white bean spread and cheeses
6 salad plates
6 dinner plates
6 place settings of cutlery, including salad forks, dinner forks, knives and dessert forks
1 small serving bowl for white bean spread
1 small serving bowl for roasted red peppers
1 small serving bowl for marinated artichokes
1 small plate/bowl for assorted olives
1 large serving tray for cheeses
1 basket for cut bread/crackers
1 cylindrical server or vase for bread sticks
1 large salad bowl for salad
1 medium serving tray for sausage
1 large serving bowl for pasta
1 cake stand for dessert
1 small serving tray for cookies
6 napkins (have a few extra on hand)
1 tablecloth

MENU
For 6

Appetizers:
White Bean Spread Drizzled with a Fresh Sage Oil Served with Golden Fresh-baked Crostini, Assorted Italian Olives, Roasted Red Peppers and Marinated Artichokes

Starter:
An Assortment of Cheeses, including Hard, Soft, Mild and Savory Varieties
Toasted Breads and Skinny Breadsticks

Salad:
Big Autumn Salad Comprised of Marinated Vegetables

Entrée:
Gemeli Pasta with a Porcini Ragu

Accompaniments:
Grilled Sausages Browned and Served with Ragu Sauce, Fresh Parmesan and Parsley

Dessert:
Prepared Wine-barrel Cake and Ginger Snap Cork Cookies, Dessert Wine and Coffee

The Recipes

Tuscan White Bean Spread with Sage-Infused Olive Oil and Fresh Crostini

1 15-ounce cans cannellini or white kidney beans, drained
1 clove garlic, peeled and roughly chopped
1 1/2 teaspoons lemon juice
1 tablespoon olive oil
1/2 teaspoon salt
1/4 teaspoon freshly ground black pepper
Sage-Infused Olive Oil (recipe follows)
fresh sage leaves for garnish

Crostini (recipe follows)

Combine the beans, garlic and lemon juice in a food processor. With the motor running, slowly add the olive oil and process until smooth. Scrape down the sides, add the salt and pepper and process again. Taste and adjust seasonings if necessary. Spoon into a bowl and serve at once or refrigerate for up to three days. Just prior to serving, garnish with fresh sage leaves and serve with crostini.

Sage-Infused Olive Oil

1/2 cup extra virgin olive oil
1/4 cup chopped fresh sage

Warm the olive oil over low heat in a small saucepan and add the sage. Cook for 20 minutes, stirring occasionally. Remove from the heat and rest for four hours. Pour through a fine wire-mesh strainer, pressing on the sage to extract the flavor. Discard the sage and use the oil at once or refrigerate, covered, for up to two weeks. Makes 1/2 cup.

Crostini

1 loaf French bread, ends trimmed and cut crosswise into
   1/4-inch-thick slices
extra virgin olive oil

Preheat the oven to 400 degrees F. Arrange the bread slices on a baking sheet and generously brush with olive oil. Turn the slices over and repeat brushing with olive oil. Bake for about 6 to 8 minutes until the crostini are lightly browned, turning once. Cool on a wire rack before serving.

Gemeli Pasta with Autumn Harvest *Ragu* Sauce

3 tablespoons extra virgin olive oil
4 tablespoons butter
1/2 yellow onion, finely chopped
1 medium carrot, peeled and finely chopped
1 medium celery stalk, finely chopped
1 pound ground lean pork
1/2 teaspoon salt
1/2 teaspoon freshly ground black pepper
1/2 cup good-quality red wine
2 cups canned, whole peeled tomatoes, with the juice,
   coarsely chopped
2 cloves garlic, peeled and minced
1 pound gemelli pasta
grated Parmesan cheese

Heat the olive oil and butter in a heavy-bottomed sauce pot over medium heat, add the onion and cook until the onion is lightly browned. Add the carrot and celery and continue cooking until just tender. Add the pork, breaking it up as you stir. Add the salt and pepper and cook, stirring occasionally, until the pork is thoroughly cooked and begins to brown. Add the wine and cook until it is nearly evaporated. Add the tomatoes

and garlic and stir until combined. Once the mixture starts to bubble, turn the heat down to low. Simmer, partially covered, for 2 hours, stirring occasionally. Check the seasonings and adjust if needed.

Heat a large pot of water to boiling over medium high heat. Add the pasta and cook, stirring occasionally, until just tender. Drain and spoon into heated pasta bowls or plates. Top the pasta with some of the sauce and garnish with grated Parmesan cheese.

Grilled Sweet Italian Sausages

Canola oil
1 1/2 pounds sweet Italian sausage links

Prepare the grill for cooking over medium-hot charcoal or moderate heat for gas, and lightly brush the grill rack with the canola oil. Grill the sausages for 10 to 12 minutes (covered only if using a gas grill) turning several times until cooked through and evenly browned. Transfer to a warmed platter and serve. 6 servings.

Italian Marinated Vegetable Salad

1/2 pound cauliflower, cut in florets
1/2 pound thin asparagus, trimmed and cut diagonally in
   1-inch pieces
1/2 pound grape or cherry tomatoes, halved
1 English cucumber, cut in thin slices
1 3.8-ounce can sliced black olives, drained
1/4 pound White Beech mushrooms or other small
   mushrooms, cleaned and stems trimmed
1/2 yellow bell pepper, peeled, seeded and cut in
   1/2-inch pieces
1/2 orange bell pepper, peeled, seeded and cut in
   1/2-inch pieces
1/3 cup Italian salad dressing
1/2 teaspoon salt
1/2 teaspoon freshly ground black pepper
2 green onions, trimmed and sliced

Heat a large pot of water to boiling over medium high heat. Add the asparagus and cook just until it becomes bright green and is barely tender, about two minutes. Remove with a slotted spoon to bowl of ice water. Repeat the process with the cauliflower florets, cooking for about 3 minutes or until just tender. Remove with a slotted spoon to the ice water. Drain the asparagus and cauliflower, pat dry on paper towels and reserve.

In a large salad bowl, combine the asparagus and cauliflower with the remaining vegetables, the salad dressing and salt and pepper; stir gently to combine. Cover and refrigerate for two hours. Just before serving, gently stir the salad and sprinkle the green onions on top.

How to Host a Wine Tasting

The only thing more purely enjoyable than a gathering of your dear friends is that gathering with a wine-tasting party to toast, taste and test a variety of reds and white wines. Whether you invite the curious novice or the experienced connoisseur, or both, you're bound to walk away with greater appreciation and expertise in wine's types, tastes and price points.

Types of tastings

- The Vertical Wine-Tasting
- The Horizontal Wine-Tasting
- Old World versus New World Wine-Tasting
- The Price Point or Priceless Wine-Tasting
- The "Big Eight" Wine-Tasting

Create or buy tasting cards (see Resources) that specify the type of wine, the vineyard, the year and a brief description of the wine (usually found on the wine's label). Each guest should have his own card. In a basic tasting, merely use a simple grid to mark or rate each wine. More complex tastings should leave room to record the wine's appearance, aroma and flavor—as well as ratings of favored bottles.

Regardless of their wine-tasting experience and knowledge, your guests may recognize some selections and have biases based on prior use and price. I always recommend a blind testing format, which keeps the focus on taste. Soak the lower half of the bottle and remove the label, or simply buy inexpensive wine bags to mask the bottles (these make great host or take-away gifts). Just remember which bottle is which. Try folding and attaching the removed label to the bottom of each bottle.

It is customary to start with drier wines and move to the sweeter wines. Likewise, tradition begins with white wines, then progresses to light reds and ends with full-bodied red wines. Always start with younger wines and move to the more mature ones.

Pour approximately 2 ounces of wine per person, per glass, ensuring guests get through all the bottles without growing inebriated.

Provide plenty of plain bread and water, allowing guests to cleanse their palates between wines. And don't forget buckets for spitting or dumping the ones your friends don't like.

What You Need:

Four to six bottles of wine

Wine glasses—one per guest

A loaf of plain bread for cleansing palates between wines

A pitcher of water for rinsing glasses and palates between wines

Cards for describing and recording each tasted wine

Brown paper bags or wine bags to disguise the different wines

Pens

Appetizers to sample before or after the tasting. (Eating between wines skews the flavor and aroma of the wine.)

The Vertical Wine-Tasting

A vertical wine tasting compares a series of wines from one winery, but from successive years. This teaches just how unique wine can be from year to year.

You may feature Clos Du Val's Napa Valley Cabernet Sauvignon from 2003, 2004 and 2005. Each year has distinctions in flavor, color and aroma, resulting in characteristic differences. With age as the only testing variable, guests will grow very aware of the producer's style and techniques. This focuses on what the aging process can do for a particular type of wine.

The Horizontal Wine Tasting

The horizontal tasting focuses on a single year's wine from multiple producers. Try the 2005 Cabernet Sauvignon from four to six Napa Valley wineries, and sample them side-by-side.

You could serve the 2005 Clos Du Val Napa Valley Cabernet Sauvignon, the 2005 75 Wine Company Cabernet Sauvignon, the 2005 Carpe Diem Cabernet Sauvignon, and so on. Consider using wines from one region or create more variety by featuring a Cabernet each from Washington, Chile, California and Australia from 2005—the choices are wide open.

Old World vs. New World Wines

Have some fun with history—compare the "Old World" wines (from Europe—France, Italy, Germany, Austria, Spain) with the same variety of "New World" wines (from North America, South America, South Africa, New Zealand and Australia). With vineyards and techniques dating back hundreds of years, Old World wines pride themselves on the delicate subtlety and refined restraint (elegance) in flavor that comes from mature soil and perfected methods. But "New World" vintners, with fewer years' experience, bring a bolder, more valiant wine by assertively blending different varieties for a bigger, fruiter outcome. Try to feature similar grapes and styles when comparing Old World and New World wines—for example, an Italian Bordeaux with a California Cabernet Sauvignon.

The Price Point or Priceless Wine-Tasting

This is a taste of the bottom line. The Price Point tasting helps guests differentiate between wines within the same price range. Set a budget you're comfortable with and purchase a variety of wines within it. This tasting builds an admiration for the distinct differences between wines in a particular price range.

The more complex Priceless tasting, on the other hand, compares various wines of differing prices—for example, a $9 Chardonnay compared with a $60 Chardonnay, and so on. Uncommonly fun, this teaches us how we so commonly equate price to quality, when quality can be subjective. Definitely conduct this one blind, letting guests focus on the wines without false associations with price.

The Big Eight Wine-Tasting

The "Big Eight" refers to the eight (four red and four white) most common and recognized wine varieties in the world. This tasting is by far the most comprehensive of all, allowing your friends to methodically discover the differences between grapes, varieties and blends. Tasted side by side, guests will find their true preferences.

The four primary red wines are Cabernet Sauvignon, Pinot Noir, Merlot, and Syrah/Shiraz, while the four primary white wines are Chardonnay, Riesling, Sauvignon Blanc and Pinot Gris/Pinot Grigio. For this tasting, you may want to consider comparing all "New World" or all "Old World" varieties for more consistency.

Party Timeline

One month before the party:

- Make or purchase invitations.
- Finalize the guest list and mail invitations.

3 weeks before the party:

- Finalize the menu, including wine selections. (Carefully select the items you wish to make and those you wish to purchase).
- Create a look by selecting colors, mood, setting and entertainment, if necessary.
- Order or gather the decorations and accessories including custom wine labels.

2 weeks before the party:

- Make a shopping list for the food and liquor (see Shopping list).
- Order the food or any desert you do not wish to make.
- Order the cake and cookies.
- Order flowers, and consider having them delivered the day of the party.

1 week before the party:

- Assemble or purchase take-away gifts and wrap them.
- Purchase all nonperishable food and liquor (see Shopping list).
- Create a music playlist or purchase CDs.
- Prepare the sage-infused olive oil.

3 days ahead:

- Decorate.
- Assemble all the serving dishes and set up the buffet table if using one.

2 days before the party:

- Make the white bean spread.
- Make the olive mixture.

The day before the party:

- Purchase perishable food (see Shopping list).
- Set the table and lay out the dishes.
- Prepare the wine bar with glasses, wine bottle covers, and rating sheets
- Wash grapes and dry. Place grapes in large galvanized buckets.
- Set up foot cleaning station
- Hang Lanterns
- Pick up flowers or have them delivered.
- Make extra ice.
- Check that the bathroom is clean. Have fresh hand towels, soap and extra toilet paper on hand.

Prior to guests' arrival:

- Start the music.
- Open bottles of wine to allow them to breathe.
- Pour a glass for yourself!
- Light the candles.
- Enjoy!

"In wine there is wisdom,
   in beer there is strength,
in water there is bacteria."

— David Auerbach

Handcrafted Chianti
from the cellar of
Matthew Spencer
2009

TAKE AWAY GIFTS

A take-away gift is by no means necessary, but is a simple, creative gesture of affection and appreciation for your guests. Inexpensive and true to your theme, these small tokens set a final tone to your evening.

A great memento from an evening of drinks, food and laughter is a set of photo drink coasters. Consider adding a list of the wines tasted or recipes used for the evening in place of the pictures. This will personalize the gift, and later allow your guests to reminisce about the evening; they can also later replace the inserts with their own photos.

Vary it

A simple and very unexpected gift, tie an issue of *Food & Wine, Wine Spectator* or similar magazine with a ribbon and a gift card for a year's subscription. With every issue, guests are reminded of the fine food and fun at your wine-tasting soirée.

Simplify it

Everyone can enjoy an extra bottle of wine, particularly one adorned with custom, personalized wine labels. Created and purchased online (see Resources) these labels are inexpensive, can be purchased in quantities of ten, and are ready for shipping in one to two days. They turn a simple bottle of wine into a keepsake.

Formally *Frightful*

An elegant masquerade for adults combines spectral decor, bewitching cheer and a cultivated menu. Guests will revel in a ghoulishly good time, and celebrate this colorful holiday with style.

"Shadows of a thousand years
Rise again unseen,
Voices whisper in the trees
Tonight is Halloween."

—Dexter Kozen

At A Glance

Theme:
Things That Go Bump in the Night

Setting:
An old church converted into a beautiful home or alternately,
any living room.

Mood:
Seasonal, festive and fun. White pumpkins, creepy owls, luminous
lanterns, a jubilant witch, scattered bones, and eerie fog scare up
an unsettling evening of celebratory entertaining.

Colors:
Midnight black, ghostly white and fiery orange

Flowers:
In lieu of fresh flowers, head to your local craft store for faux black and
purple leaves and berries, bagged moss and dried grass. Collect dried
leaves in a variety of autumn colors from your yard.

Tastes:
The menu features the heartier flavors and offerings of autumn,
from crispy cranberry-Brie appetizers to a creamy pumpkin soup
and a savory pork roast topped with a ruby red plum sauce.

Sounds:
A custom play list features a mélange of macabre music, like
*Halloween Howls, Halloween Hits, The 13th Hour, Classics from the
Crypt,* and *Out of the Darkness.* These will chill you with a lively—
or not!—range of tunes, from the fun traditional songs
to the dark, instrumental classics.

Experience:
Create a spooky experience by recruiting the services of a ghost
hunter. Invite him to bring the tools of his trade and investigate
if your house is also a home to otherworldly beings.

Vary It: Hire a local historian to lead a haunted walk through a local
cemetery or history-rich neighborhood.

Simplify It: Give your guests a prescient peek at their futures by
retaining a fortune teller, palm reader or tarot card reader.

"Where there is no imagination, there is no horror"
—Arthur Conan Doyle, Sr.

Halloween is so much more than an occasion; it's an event. Once considered a ghostly holiday for tiny witches and goblins, Halloween has emerged as a full-blooded, grown up nod to the macabre. Today, it stands as one of few socially acceptable times to stray from the norm, take that risk, and perhaps show a delightfully fun-loving side of yourself that no one else ever gets to see.

Halloween stirs the imagination, ignites fears from within, and unearths one's own forebodings. Whether we admit it or not, most of us love a good fright every so often—scaring us to death makes us feel alive!

And so, as the light of day fades into the dark of night, and shadows begin to form from the light of the moon, invite your guests to join you for an evening of masquerade, mystery and revelry. Allow for an abundance of candles to illuminate the room and chase away the shadows. Trees wrapped in lights, spooky spiders, ravenous rats, bewitching bats, frightful frogs and creepy cats will kindle an eerie ambience. Just be sure not to get too carried away!

A Spirited Start

Set the ghostly tone and enchant your guests with Halloween magic, beginning with the party invitation. It teases the imagination and builds anticipation for a hauntingly fun affair and a frightfully delicious feast!

The Invitation

Purchase card stock paper, and decorate with cut-out chandeliers and selectively placed bats (stickers). Print the invitation from a computer, then re-copy on a copy machine to achieve the final look.

Vary it

Roll up a card stock paper invitation and place it inside a small tube-shaped vial (available at any craft or container store) with a few plastic spiders and a little moss. Attach a clear address label and mail the plastic tubes as they are—with the proper postage.

Simplify it

Use pre-made Halloween invitations, but lend a personal touch by stretching white spider webbing across the front.

A small side table supports a unique wire tree adorned with a few tea-light candles and a family of crows. Scattered across the table are plastic vials filled with fake spiders and moss.

The Tradition of Pumpkin Carving

An Irish folk tale is said to have inspired the modern-day jack-o'-lantern. According to legend, a man named Jack—who was something of a cheapskate, a drunkard and a practical joker—convinced the devil to climb a tree. Once the devil was in the tree, Jack surrounded it with crosses, trapping the demon there. In exchange for removing the crosses so he could get down, Jack made the devil promise not to take his soul when Jack died.

When Jack passed away, however, he was denied entrance to heaven because of his stinginess, pranks and drinking. When he tried to get into hell, the devil reminded him of their deal and told Jack he was doomed to forever wander through the cold darkness. When Jack complained that he couldn't see, the devil tossed him a burning ember from hell to light his way, which was then placed in a hollowed-out turnip to last longer. Thus, Jack's lanterns were born. Because pumpkins grew more bountifully than turnips in America, the tradition eventually evolved into pumpkin lanterns—often carved with spooky or silly faces.

Essential Elements of Entertaining
Over or Under Decorating?

Balancing the right mix of party decorations to convey a theme—without overdoing it—is a time-honored art. But with only a few well-planned accents and accessories you can transform your lovely home into a haunted haven for the spectral set.

First, make a list of each area you will use for the party, much like you would do when decorating your house or accessorizing an outfit. Consider the walkway and entrance to your home, the foyer, the dinner or buffet table, those console and coffee tables, the bar and the bathroom. View each of these areas as separate sections, just as you would an outfit with a dress, hair and makeup, jewelry, shoes, a coat and purse. Each area can display unique features, but must carry a common link, whether color, texture or theme. When decorating for a party, pick one major theme and build on it. Create the Halloween party around witches, for example, and use decorations throughout that relate to those fiendish folks. Keeping this kind of focus helps limit excess.

Second, list and describe the main focus for each area you plan to decorate. (Next to each photo, I have listed the items used).

Third, carefully look over each section, once you've decorated. If one item stands out too much, remove it. It's over the top.

Fourth, the best rule of thumb—think practical. Did your embellishments leave enough room to set down plates and glasses? Did you space items so that guests can see easily across the table? Can a guest set down a drink on that side table without knocking things over? If décor adversely affects function, take away a few items.

Fifth, scout your home for anything you can use to enhance the theme—lamps, jars, candlesticks, books, clothing and other accessories. Be daring! Experiment! Have fun! You'll surprise yourself.

Finally, and most important, *caveat emptor*. Remember your budget and avoid buyer's remorse. Only use what you can reuse or live with for years to come. Seek out items that will refurbish for future themes. Spend your money on those few items, and accent with cheaper novelties from craft or toy stores, and large department stores.

Spooky Settings
Accents Add an Otherworldly Aura

Flickering candle lanterns line the steps, illuminating the outside entryway. Pumpkins and black wooden candelabras adorn the dinner table, with accents of owls, lanterns and dried leaves.

Faux leaves and berries simplify the buffet design, and a selectively placed rubber cat and plastic spiders add an ominous ambience.

A console table, unneeded for functional duties, holds an old dictionary (turned to a picture of skeletal human), a rubber frog, moss-filled jars (one with a plastic skeletal head), dried leaves and candy bones.

The coffee table continues our theme, with a toy fortune ball, some distinctive black books, tied grasses, and an inexpensive bone necklace.

Spirits of another kind fill the bar, including bottles of gin, vodka, whiskey and club soda. Let the liquors' natural colors shine through, or concoct an eerie and ominous brew with a touch of food coloring. Give new life to liquors with personalized labels bearing creepy alternate names. The bathroom sanctuary stashes a coat rack draped with white and black witch robes, and a hat and extra brooms.

I highlighted the fireplace as a natural focal point by installing an old happy witch.

"When witches go riding,
    And black cats are seen,
The moon laughs and whispers,
    'tis near Halloween."

—Author unknown

"Clothes make a statement. Costumes tell a story." —Mason Cooley

A selection of spirits, spiked with a touch of food coloring, populate the bar; spooky new labels decorate the liquor bottles.

A toy fortune ball, distinctive black books, tied grasses and an inexpensive bone necklace rest peacefully on a coffee table.

The fireplace warms a jubilant witch, while tying together the décor theme.

Dress up any bottle of liquor with a mini pet costume.

Real science-lab beakers become intriguing drink glasses (see Resources).

Roll napkins, and tie with twine, moss and candy bones.

Haunting
Halloween History

Back beyond the Monster Mash, the tricks and treats, the one night each year of unrestrained ghoulishness and glee lies a holiday deeply rooted in history and religion. Halloween first appeared more than 2,000 years ago as Samhain, a Celtic new year celebration marking the November 1st beginning of the calendar year. Samhain demonstrated gratitude to Celtic gods for a bountiful and successful year. Rituals included large bonfires, into which the Celts sacrificed animals and crops. Dancing and adoring oneself in an animal head and skins tricked and confused lingering souls presumed to be walking the earth—and began the tradition of donning a costume.

Tricks for Treats

By the seventh century, Pope Boniface IV had designated November 1st as All Saints Day, a general celebration of Christian saints. Over time, All Saints Day replaced Samhain and became known as All Hollows Day. The Catholic Church later designated November 2nd All Souls Day to honor the lives of loved ones who had passed on, which was celebrated with lively parties and parades. Wealthy individuals would deliver food and treats to those less fortunate, and in turn, the recipients prayed and wished well for the deceased family members of the gift givers. Celebrants believed that the more prayers said for their deceased relatives, the less likely their spirits were to remain on earth haunting the living. The "souls' cakes" delivered to the less fortunate eventually became the modern day ritual of trick-or-treating.

Witches: Good, Bad, Reviled, Revered—and Endlessly Fascinating

One of Halloween's most enduring characters and costumes is that of the witch. Ugly and evil, a witch generally has bad teeth, warts and pallid skin; wears a black gown with a pointed hat; keeps a frog or a black cat; and cackles with maniacal laughter.

But witches weren't always considered ugly or evil. In ancient times, witches often became healers or wise women of the community. The word "witch" derives from the Old English word "wicca," a term applied to male and female members of an ancient pagan tradition. Wicca reveres masculine, feminine and earthly aspects of God, and its traditions involved both heaven and earth, and the next world and this world. But those beliefs often conflicted with church teachings, leading to the condemnation of witches.

Throughout history women accused of witchcraft faced trumped-up charges and trials, and execution, often in unsavory ways. Healers frequently faced suspicions of witchcraft, particularly if they failed to save a well-connected patient from a fatal disease.

Prejudice and persecution against witches reached a particularly fevered pitch in the seventeenth century, when ignorance and confusion lead to chaos and the deaths of thousands of suspected witches in Europe and America. Perhaps one of the most well-documented accounts of the mass hysteria against witches is found in the Salem (Massachusetts) witchcraft trials of 1692 and 1693. At that

Menu

For 8

The Signature Drink:
Mad Scientist's Punch

Appetizers:
Crispy Puff Pastry Tarts Filled with
Melted Brie Cheese and Cranberry Sauce,
Crispy Pecans Roasted in a Salty-Sweet
Ginger-Cinnamon Mixture

Starter:
Creamy Homemade Pumpkin Soup

Salad:
Baby Spinach Salad Drizzled with Homemade
French Dressing and Topped with Crispy Bacon
and Bleu Cheese Crumbles

Entree:
Roasted Pork Tenderloin with
Ruby Red Plum Sauce

Accompaniments:
Wild Rice Pilaf, Assorted Muffins
and Breadsticks

Dessert:
Cupcakes, Coffee and Assorted Liqueurs

Shopping List
1 medium and 2 large onions
1 pound fresh spinach
Several sprigs fresh thyme
1 bunch fresh parsley
1 head garlic
6 slices bacon
2 1-pound pork tenderloins
1 package frozen puff pastry
8 ounces canned whole berry
  cranberry sauce
32 ounces canned pumpkin puree
76 ounces chicken broth or stock

4 ounces apple cider or juice
4 ounces plum preserves
2 ounces apricot preserves
1 4-ounce wedge Brie cheese
2 ounces bleu cheese
4 ounces heavy
  whipping cream
1 package wild rice
1 package long grain rice
1 pound large pecan halves
Bakery muffins and breadsticks
Prepared cupcakes

The Essentials
8 water glass
8 wine glasses
8 science beakers (optional)
8 coffee cups (if desired)
8 small side plates for brie tarts
  and crispy pecan mixture
8 soup bowls
8 salad plates
8 dinner plates
8 place settings of cutlery,
  including salad forks, dinner
  forks, knives and dessert forks
1 large serving trays for roasted
  pork tenderloin

2 medium serving trays for the
  wild rice and assorted muffins
1 large salad bowl for
  spinach salad
1 large serving bowl for
  pumpkin soup
1 small serving bowl for crispy
  pecan mixture
1 cylindrical server or vase for
  bread sticks
1 large salad bowl for salad
1 cake stand or large serving
  tray for cupcakes
8 napkins (have a few extra
  on hand)
1 tablecloth

Staples (replenish if needed)
salt
freshly ground black pepper
granulated sugar
brown sugar
ground ginger
cinnamon
ground mustard
dried thyme

dried rosemary
vegetable oil
Worcestershire sauce
soy sauce
ketchup
vinegar
butter
eggs

The Recipes

Mad Scientist's Punch
For an authentic touch, serve this drink in genuine glass science-laboratory beakers (see Resources for ordering information).

2 cups top-quality silver tequila
2 cups fresh-squeezed orange juice
1 cup orange liqueur such as Grand Marnier or Cointreau
1 cup Limoncello
1 cup sour mix
4 cups ice cubes

Combine the ingredients in a punch bowl or other serving container. Ladle into glasses. Makes 8 servings; recipe can easily be multiplied.

Puff Pastry Tarts with Brie and Cranberry Sauce

1 cup canned whole berry cranberry sauce
1 puff pastry street
1 4-ounce wedge Brie cheese, chilled and cut in

Preheat oven to 375 degrees F. Thaw puff pastry sheet flat and roll gently with a rolling pin to make a 10-inch square. Cut the puff pastry sheet into 25 2-inch squares and press each square into a greased mini muffin tins. Place 1" slice of brie in the center of each puff pastry and then top with a spoonful of the cranberry sauce. Bake 10-12 minutes, or until puff pastry corners are toasted light brown. Let cool 5 minutes before serving. Makes 2 dozen.

Spiced Pecans

1 teaspoon water
1 egg white
1 pound large pecan halves
1 cup granulated sugar
1 teaspoon ground cinnamon
1 teaspoon salt
1/2 teaspoon ginger

Preheat the oven to 225 degrees F. In a large bowl, beat the water and egg white together until frothy. Add the pecans to the bowl and stir until the nuts are coated with the mixture. In a small bowl, combine the sugar, cinnamon, salt and ginger. Sprinkle the sugar mixture over the pecans, stirring until the nuts are coated. Spread the nuts on a lightly greased cookie sheet and bake for one hour, stirring occasionally. Remove from the oven, cool in the pan on a wire rack. When completely cool, store in an airtight container.

Baby Spinach Salad with Bacon and Bleu Cheese
For the dressing:
1 cup vegetable oil
1/4 cup sugar
1/3 cup ketchup
1/4 cup vinegar
1/2 teaspoon salt
2 teaspoons Worcestershire sauce
1 medium onion, peeled and grated

For the salad:
1 pound fresh spinach, torn in pieces
6 slices bacon, cooked and crumbled
2 ounces bleu cheese, crumbled

Whisk the dressing ingredients together in a small bowl and refrigerate. Just before serving, drizzle some of the dressing over the bacon and toss gently. Add the bacon and bleu cheese and serve immediately.

Creamy Pumpkin Soup

6 cups chicken stock
1 1/2 teaspoons salt
1/2 teaspoon freshly ground black pepper
4 cups pumpkin puree
1 cup chopped onion
1/2 teaspoon chopped fresh thyme
1 clove garlic, minced
1/2 cup heavy whipping cream
1 teaspoon chopped fresh parsley

In a large, heavy saucepan heat the stock, salt, pepper, pumpkin, onion, thyme and garlic. Bring to a boil and reduce heat to low; simmer for 1 hour uncovered. Puree the soup in a food processor or blender and return to pan; heat to simmering. Stir in the heavy cream. Pour into soup bowls and garnish with fresh parsley.

Pork Tenderloin with Plum Sauce

For the pork:
1/2 cup soy sauce
2 garlic cloves, minced
1 tablespoon ground mustard
1 teaspoon dried thyme
1 teaspoon ground ginger
1/2 cup apple cider or juice
2 pork tenderloins (about 1 pound each)

For the sauce:
1/2 cup plum preserves
1/4 cup finely chopped onion
1/4 cup apricot preserves
2 tablespoons brown sugar
2 tablespoons apple cider or juice
2 tablespoons soy sauce
2 tablespoons ketchup
1 garlic clove, minced

In a small bowl, combine the soy sauce, garlic, mustard, thyme, ginger, apple cider or juice, and garlic. Pour 3/4 cup of the mixture into a large resealable plastic bag and reserve the rest in a small bowl. Add the pork to the bag, seal it and turn to coat; refrigerate for at least 2 hours. Cover and refrigerate remaining marinade for basting.

Preheat the oven to 425 degrees F. Drain and discard marinade from pork. Place tenderloins on a rack in a shallow roasting pan. Bake for 40-45 minutes or until a meat thermometer reads 160 degrees F, basting several times with the reserved marinade.

In a small saucepan, combine the sauce ingredients and bring to a boil over medium-high heat. Reduce heat and simmer, uncovered, for 10 minutes or until flavors blend. Let pork stand for 5 minutes before slicing. Serve with plum sauce.

Wild Rice Pilaf

3 1/2 cups chicken stock or broth
3/4 cup uncooked wild rice
1 cup uncooked long grain rice
1 large onion, chopped
1 garlic clove, minced
1/2 teaspoon dried rosemary, crushed
1/2 cup butter
1/4 teaspoon pepper

In a large saucepan over medium-high heat, bring the broth to a boil. Add the wild rice; reduce heat. Cover and cook for 30 minutes. Add long grain rice; cook 20-25 minutes longer or until liquid is absorbed and rice is tender.

Meanwhile, in a large skillet over medium heat, sauté the onion, garlic and rosemary in butter until the onion is tender. Stir in the rice and pepper. Transfer to a greased, shallow 2 quart baking dish. Cover and bake at 350 degrees F for 25-30 minutes. Fluff with a fork before serving.

Party Timeline

1 month before the party:

🦇 Make or purchase the invitations.

🦇 Finalize guest list and mail invitations.

3 weeks before the party:

🦇 Finalize the menu, including drinks (carefully selecting the items you wish to make and those you wish to purchase).

🦇 Create a look by selecting colors, mood, setting and entertainment, if necessary.

🦇 Order or gather the decorations and accessories.

2 weeks before the party:

🦇 Make a shopping list for the food and liquor (see shopping list).

🦇 Order the food and any desert you do not wish to make.

🦇 Order custom cupcakes.

🦇 Order flowers, and consider having them delivered the day of the party.

1 week before the party:

🦇 Decorate.

🦇 Assemble or purchase take-away gifts and wrap them.

🦇 Purchase all nonperishable food and liquor (see Shopping list).

🦇 Create a music play list or purchase CDs.

🦇 Prepare the spiced pecans and store in an airtight container.

3 days before the party:

🦇 Prepare the bar with glasses and liquor.

🦇 Assemble all the serving dishes and set up the buffet table, if using one.

2 days before the party:

🦇 Prepare the salad dressing, pumpkin soup and plum sauce, and refrigerate.

1 day before the party:

🦇 Purchase remaining perishable food (see Shopping list).

🦇 Set the table and lay out the dishes.

🦇 Prepare the bar with glasses and liquor.

🦇 Pick up flowers or have them delivered.

🦇 Make extra ice.

🦇 Check that the bathroom is clean. Have fresh hand towels, soap and extra toilet paper on hand.

The morning of the party:

🦇 Prepare puff pastry tarts, cover and refrigerate.

🦇 Chop onions for the salad and pumpkin soup. Cover in a separate bowl and refrigerate.

🦇 Chop thyme, garlic, and parsley for soup and tenderloin. Keep separate, cover and refrigerate.

🦇 Cook bacon and crumble. Refrigerate.

Prior to guests' arrival:

🦇 Start the music.

🦇 Prepare the Mad Scientist's Punch, including one for yourself!

🦇 Put on your costume, relax and have fun!

🦇 Light the candles.

🦇 Enjoy!

Can any gift surpass the one carefully chosen for its elegance and practicality? I like to give favors my guests find delightful and useful. For Halloween, fill black woven baskets with seasonal fruit candles. Wrap them in black paper with torn black netting and accent with dried leaves, moss, plastic spiders, bones and basic twine.

Vary it
Scare up a book of local haunted houses, neighborhoods, or cemeteries and wrap it with a detailed map of the area (found at your local book store or online). It's a fascinating look at little-known history and legends.

Simplify it
Instead of history, give the future. Tarot cards let guests 'read' their own personal outlooks, year after year (available online).

Birds of a Feather

Thanksgiving. The very word conjures thoughts of autumn scents and colors, longstanding traditions, warm feelings, memories of past gatherings, abundant food and simply belonging. It embodies harvest, home, joy in small things, and our shared experiences. But even more, it elicits a humble and deeply felt gratitude for what's good in our worlds. This, of all holidays, calls for reflection. Thanksgiving evokes a solemn, but joyful expression of our appreciation for what we have.

It is a holiday to celebrate home, not so much of the structural kind, but of the intrinsic kind. Homes, however humble, are the cornerstone of lives, our havens, and within its walls live our victories and defeats, love and heartbreak, joys and fears, and most of all, the people we cherish.

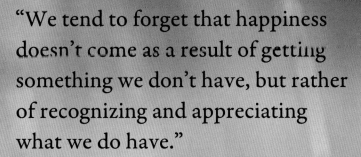

"We tend to forget that happiness doesn't come as a result of getting something we don't have, but rather of recognizing and appreciating what we do have."

—Frederick Keonig

At A Glance

Theme:
A season of gratitude

Setting:
Anyplace with a roof overhead and a floor beneath. It is simple. It is home.

Mood:
Inspired, hearty, polished, joyful, relaxed, reflective, thankful. To the scents of brewing coffee and baking apple muffins, gather your loved ones for a mouthwatering meal and joyous celebration of each other.

Colors:
Chestnut brown, vintage cranberry and soft pewter

Flowers:
A fusion of red and orange dahlias, purple thistle and Solenostemon plants.

Tastes:
Rustic, hardy and slightly unconventional. This Thanksgiving, propose a brunch instead of dinner.

Sounds:
A custom playlist that can encompass the personal interests of any generation of guests. For a traditional tone of jazz, try It's *De-Lovely – The Authentic Cole Porter Collection* with other legendary performers. Or if you seek more modern songs, try the classic vocals in Bette Midler's *The Rose*, or *The Devine* album. For a more upbeat background blend, tap into Sting's *Live in Berlin*, performed with the Royal Philharmonic Orchestra. Finally, for lively, and sometimes soulful, mood music, offer the artsy vibes of The Piano Guys.

Experience:
Eloquence at its best is short and undiluted with unneeded words. Jot down on small gift cards what you each appreciate most. Read them or hang them from a small tree you'll call your symbolic tree.

Vary it: Inelegant as it may sound, few things will bond a family like an annual Turkey Trot. Many towns hold an official one Thanksgiving morning, but if not, propose your own. Not athletic? A multiplayer board game – Trivial Pursuit anyone?

Simplify it: For guests who are children—or who enjoy a childlike sense of play—craft Christmas wish lists to be sent to Santa. This also can go into your mental cache of possible presents.

Thoughtful Gestures

Nothing fires up the family phone lines like the anticipation of a holiday gathering, which is why family and friends rarely expect a written invitation. Imagine the fun when you go to the trouble to not just hand-write a request for the pleasure of their presence, but you do so creatively. Certainly, such a prelude will help build the spirit of the gathering.

The Invitation

An invitation needn't be slick for an event that celebrates our humble thanks. Find simple card stock paper and glue a medium-size feather to the top. Your theme? Birds of a Feather will be thankful together. Handwrite the basic information:

Birds of a Feather
Please gather with us for Thanksgiving Brunch
Thursday, November 28th 10:00 a.m.
Sveum Residence
5690 W. Pine Ave.

Vary it

Remember five-finger turkeys? Using simple cardstock, paint or stamp the palm of a child's hand, with fingers spread out. Attach little feathers to the top of the outline created from the pointer, index, ring and pinky fingers. Make an eye and little gobble on the thumb. Handwrite the same inscription.

Simplify it

Purchase a small amount of straw from a craft store. Pull out several strands, tie together with a velvet ribbon and attach it to a small note card.

"As we express our gratitude, we must never forget that the highest appreciation is not to utter words, but to live by them." —John F. Kennedy

Sociable Setting

I love Thanksgiving for its purity and simplicity. It is a celebration not rooted in a gift exchange, nor is it a holiday in which guests expect a creative menu. On this day, friends and family gather to simply be grateful for the moments spent savoring not just an abundant and delicious meal, but the company of those we love most. And don't forget—some of you may savor your moments tuning in to the game.

Like a breath of the waning autumn weather, capture the look with outdoor statues, freshly cut vines, and faux pheasant feathers. This motif suggests a less formal and more organic feel, a naturalness you'll find reflected in the mood of the day.

The mantle décor is understated, with sparse leaved vines and an assortment of candles.

A Tree of Gratitude

The act of gratitude—giving thanks, showing appreciation, and recognizing our own good fortune—is indeed an art. Far from innate, we must practice it to perfect it. Early on, someone must teach us to see what we have, however small or large, and be grateful for it. Sadly, some do it better than others.

With three young children, I continually strive for opportunities to teach this art, while remaining always mindful of my own chance to feel and show it.

While gratitude is good for its own sake, it comes with added benefits. Appreciation goes hand-in-hand with happiness—it elevates human emotion, or emotional intelligence, to a level that considers others. It cultivates feelings of love, satisfaction, empathy, joy and compassion. People with appreciation for what they have lead healthier and happier lives, with stronger ties to friends and family.

My family's quest to visualize this feeling, to make it tangible, led to our Gratitude Tree tradition. On the first day of November, I set up an old metal tree that, once upon a time, I sprayed with gold glitter. (In retrospect, I don't recommend doing that.) Next to the tree, I place a basket that I've filled with simple brown gift tags (see Resources). Each day, each family member writes on a card something for which they are grateful. I strive to never impose my thoughts or suggestions, and instead allow them to write what's most important to them. We attach the cards to the tree.

On Thanksgiving Day, after a hearty meal and lively conversation, we take the leaves (gift cards) off the tree and read each one aloud. Some are funny, some self-serving and some are breathtaking.

After the evening has wound down, I quickly label the cards with a name and date, bundle them and place them in a small box where I save them. Some day, we'll look through those and marvel at the simple changes that reflect a life-time of growth, maturity and hopefully, gratitude.

> "Not what we say about our blessings, but how we use them, is the true measure of our thanksgiving."
> —W.T. Purkiser

I am thankful for: Our Puppy —Morgan 2011

Essential Elements of Entertaining

How to fix common food disasters when everything goes wrong

Cooking disasters happen to everyone at one time or another, regardless of your skill level or preparation. Julia Childs, a world-renown chief, often made common mistakes. Her charm and wit made them humorous and endearing. With that said, the best way to avoid the most common food catastrophes is to avoid cooking a new dish for your celebration. This is Cooking 101—cooking a new dish right before a gathering is like cramming for an exam the night before. Countless things can arise when you don't know what to expect. The item may take longer to cook, taste bad, be extremely time-consuming, curdle, or at the very least, look very different than the photo-shopped picture in the book.

Instead, if you must use a new recipe, try making the item a few days ahead to be sure it turns out the way you wish. Second, read recipes and ingredient lists all the way through. Nothing puts the kibosh on an impending meal like "marinate overnight."

Finally, have a back-up plan or alternate item you can quickly prepare. (Even resorting to frozen pizzas, albeit awkward, can save a meal—I can personally attest to this.) And just in case, have take-out menus handy.

Remember, most cooking disasters are fixable. So when things start to go wrong, keep calm and don't breathe a word of it—most people will never know if you don't call attention to it.

And now, in the spirit of Thanksgiving sharing, we offer these tips to help ensure cooking success:

1. **Do as much prep work ahead of time** I always try to plan a menu that lets me make most of the items the day before. Also, keep extra ingredients on hand in case you need to add to the recommended serving size.

2. **Don't try to alter recipes, equipment or techniques** Odds are there is a very good reason why ingredients are added in a particular order or cooked at a certain temperature.

3. **Be vigilant of food and contamination** Put perishables quickly into the fridge, and never reuse knives and cutting boards after preparing poultry or meat. Never undercook meat, poultry or seafood. Hedge on the side of caution here—slightly overcooked food has never sent friends to the ER.

4. **Recovering overcooked foods**

Poultry—meat—seafood. The solutions to this one vary based upon the degree of overcooking or burning that occurred. For poultry and meat, slice them and add small amounts of chicken or beef broth, respectively, over the pieces. This reintroduces some moisture into the meat. If that doesn't work, try serving the meat over noodles or rice, which can redirect the focus away from it. For poultry or seafood, add some Cajun spices and call it "blackened."

Pasta—rice. For clumped rice or pasta, try submerging the mass into hot water that contains a couple of tablespoons of olive oil. If needed, separate with your fingers (cooking utensils will break the pasta up). Be careful not to burn yourself.

Vegetables. Overcooked vegetables are hard to salvage, particularly root vegetables. Watch these carefully. If vegetables cook beyond the point of serving, all you can really do is to puree them into a soup. Add broth or milk, and some seasonings. Have some frozen peas or corn on hand as a substitute.

5. **Speeding up cooking times** Depending on the product, you can usually cook smaller items faster than larger ones. For poultry and meats, remove them from their wrappers and cut them in half, quarters or into the portions you will serve. For most meat, you can raise the temperature to 500 degrees F and add one to one-and-a-half cups of beef broth. Cover tightly with foil. For pork or chicken, set the temperature between 425 degrees F and 450 degrees F. Top with a little butter and add about a half of a cup of chicken broth or white wine to the pan. Cover tightly with foil to help steam the meat and prevent drying. Check before serving to ensure the chicken is not pink. If all else fails, slice the chicken into smaller pieces, add a little butter and microwave on High for 5 minutes.

6. **Salvaging burned items** For soups and sauces you must react quickly. Once you realize the ingredients are scorching at the bottom of the pan, immediately transfer the soup or sauce into another pan—without touching or scraping the bottom of the pot. Taste the soup or sauce to see if it has a scorched flavor or a lot of burned residue. If it does, you're sunk. This isn't a fixable mistake. Have a Plan B.

For burned meat or poultry (remove the skin if it has any), cut away any burned areas and slice. For poultry, try adding a touch of chicken stock or white wine. For meat, add a little olive oil and steak sauce. Let it absorb for a minute or two. If you can't slice it, then it's too far gone to salvage.

7. **When food is too salty** This is the most common food mishap, and luckily it's the easiest to fix. First, try peeling and cutting a potato into large pieces, and add them to your soup or sauce for 15 minutes. If it is still too salty, try adding 1 teaspoon of sugar at a time until the flavor is neutralized. If it's meat or a vegetable that are too salty, try straining them, then quickly rinsing with water or chicken stock.

8. **Too sweet.** One teaspoon at a time, add lemon juice. It will cut the sweet flavor.

9. **Too sour.** Counter sour with sweet by adding white or brown sugar, honey or syrup, one tablespoon at a time.

10. **Too spicy.** There are many fixes for meals that end up too spicy. The simplest is to add broth or tomato sauce (or diced pineapple) to soups or salsas, and adjust the rest of the seasoning. If those aren't an option, try adding a natural coolant—dairy—in the form of sour cream, plain yogurt or milk.

11. **Too acidic.** Counter with fat found in oil or butter, and add it in small amounts.

12. **Too mild.** Quite simple. If it's meat, poultry or seafood try, steak sauce, soy sauce or Italian salad dressing. Soups can get a little kick from Tabasco or other hot sauce (be very careful not to overdo it). Cajun seasoning and basic salt also work well

13. **Too runny.** Mix together a small amount of cornstarch and water in a little bowl. This will form a paste. Add the paste, one teaspoon at a time to the soup or sauce until it thickens.

14. **Too thick.** Add water, broth or tomato sauce a little at a time.

15. **Too lumpy.** If your sauce is lumpy because of the eggs you've added, then it's curdled and nearly impossible to save. Toss it. If it is lumpy from other ingredients, try whisking briskly. If that doesn't work, try straining the sauce. Finally, as a last resort, put it into a blender. (Remember, never blend hot items in a closed blender or food processer. The heat will cause eruption and burns.)

16. **Too soggy.** When you over-dress the salad, transfer it to a different bowl. A lot of dressing will stay at the bottom, so carefully lift the salad out instead of pouring it. If it is still too dressed, transfer to a salad spinner and gently give it a couple spins. If it still needs more removed, add some cubed bread, which soaks up much of the dressing.

17. **Fallen or broken cake.** Make enough cakes, and you're bound to have a few that fall apart. If your cake cracks or breaks apart when removing it from the pans, try "gluing" it back together first. Push the pieces back together, then freeze. Often, they will reattach themselves. Simple cracks or breaks can also be pushed together, and covered by frosting or fruit. Just be sure not to transfer the cake once this has been done.

If your cake, however, has a sinkhole with craters taken out, then you'll need to be more creative. Try filling the hole with fruit or whipped cream. If that won't work, cut the cake into small, even squares. Serve with fruit, whipped cream or ice cream. You will salvage your cake and draw compliments for your cleverness.

The best fix for a food mishap is a sense of humor. Remember, you will care far more than your guests will, and they will take their cues from you. The best dinner party I have ever attended was the result of a food-kitchen fire (minor) disaster. In the end, we enjoyed pizza on blankets in the living room, formal attire and all.

"Gratitude is when memory is stored in the heart and not in the mind."

—Lionel Hampton

On this autumn day, we stop for a moment to take a genuinely close look at our good fortune, however large or small, and to express our deep appreciation for it. 'Tis the season to be grateful.

Even the chairs dress well, with simple pinecone garlands and burlap sacks stamped with each guest's first initial. This can also serve as a seating arrangement if you have a larger gathering. The sacks become herbal-potpourri takeaway gifts for your guests.

Cut ivy and candle groupings create a seasonal mantle.

Above: Take away gifts are wrapped in a square piece of burlap. Fabric is folded like an envelope and secured with fifteen safety pins, ribbon, feathers and small charms from a craft store.

"Not all of us can do great things. But we can do small things with great love."

—Mother Teresa

Left; A old French-pastry rack lets your friends help themselves—and frees up counter space.

Above: Prepare drinks ahead of time to keep yourself among your guests and out of the kitchen.

Shopping List

1 quart blood orange juice
1 quart apple juice
1 cup apple cider
1 tablespoon lemon juice
1 liter sparkling water
1 bottle vodka
1 bottle triple sec
2 oranges
8 canned, frozen or fresh cherries
2 cups cranberries
1 pound baby spinach leaves
1 small onion
1 medium leek
1 red bell pepper
1 green bell pepper
4 tart baking apples,
  like Granny Smith
8 large grapefruits
2 20-ounce packages fresh
  diced potatoes with onion
1/4 pound pancetta
1 pound link sausages
1 1/2 pounds thick-sliced bacon
1/3 cup grated Parmesan cheese
1/2 cup shredded
  Provolone cheese
1 cup chopped pecans
3 cups steel-cut oats (regular,
  not quick cooking)
1 1/2 dozen eggs
1 8-ounce container
  whipping cream
1 small carton milk
1/2 pound butter
1 can pumpkin puree
1 pound powdered sugar
2 loaves French bread
1 pint maple syrup

The Essentials

6 water glasses
6 wine glasses (optional)
6 juice glasses
6 coffee cups (optional)
1 pitcher—Blood Orange Splash
6 small plates—Grapefruit Wedge
Brulée (optional)
6 bowls—Cinnamon Pecan
  Oatmeal
6 individual pedestals—Apple
Crisp Muffins (optional)
6 dinner plates
6 chargers (optional)
6 place settings of cutlery,
  including soup spoons, dinner
  forks, knives and dessert forks
6 napkins (have a few extra
  on hand)
1 tablecloth in white or cream
1 large scarf (for optional layering)
1 small serving tray—
  Grapefruit Wedges
1 large serving tray—Pumpkin
French Toast
1 large serving bowl—
  Cinnamon Pecan Oatmeal
1 gravy boat—Apple Cider Syrup

Staples (replenish if needed)

all-purpose flour
granulated sugar
brown sugar
baking powder
baking soda
cornstarch
cinnamon
nutmeg
allspice
salt
freshly ground black pepper
vegetable oil
extra virgin olive oil
vanilla extract

Menu

For 6

Signature Drink:
Blood Orange Splash

Appetizer:
Grapefruit Wedges Brulée

Starter:
Cinnamon Pecan Oatmeal with
Cranberry Reduction

Entrée:
Pumpkin French Toast with Apple Cider Syrup
Pancetta, Spinach and Provolone Baked Omelet

Accompaniments:
Maple Glazed Sausage and Bacon
Crunchy Golden Hash Browns with
Leeks and Peppers

Dessert:
Apple Crisp Streusel Muffins

The Recipes

Blood Orange Splash

1/3 cup blood orange juice
1/4 cup sparkling water
2 ounces vodka
1 tablespoon triple sec
1 tablespoon simple syrup*
Orange slice and cherry for garnish

Combine the juice, sparkling water, vodka, triple sec and simple syrup in a tall glass and stir gently. Spear a pick with the cherry and orange slice to garnish. 1 serving.

(*Note: To make simple syrup, combine equal parts sugar and filtered water in a saucepan and heat over medium flame until sugar is dissolved. Cool to room temperature and store in the refrigerator.)

Cinnamon Pecan Oatmeal with Cranberry Reduction

For the oatmeal:
1 cup chopped pecans
3 cups steel-cut oats (regular, not quick-cooking)
9 cups water
3 cups apple juice
1 tablespoon cinnamon

For the cranberry reduction:
2 cups water
2 cups cranberries
1 1/2 cups sugar
1/2 cup brown sugar
2 teaspoons ground cinnamon

To toast the pecans, preheat the oven to 350 degrees F. Spread the nuts on a baking sheet, and toast them in the oven until they begin to smell toasted and fragrant, about 5 minutes. Reserve. (Can be done one day ahead. Store pecans in a tightly covered container at room temperature.)

Bring the water and apple juice to a boil in a large saucepan over medium-high heat. Stir in the oats and reduce heat to medium low. Simmer uncovered for 25 to 30 minutes, stirring occasionally, until liquid is absorbed and oats are tender.

While the oatmeal is cooking, combine the water, cranberries, sugar, brown sugar and cinnamon in a heavy medium saucepan over medium-high heat and bring to a boil. Reduce heat and simmer, stirring frequently, for about 20 minutes or until volume is reduced by about a third. Remove from heat. When cool, puree sauce in processor. Cover and keep warm. (Sauce can be made one day ahead and stored in the refrigerator, tightly covered.)

To serve, pour the oatmeal in a tureen or individual serving bowls. Sprinkle with chopped pecans and spoon some of the cranberry reduction on top.

Pumpkin French Toast with Apple Cider Syrup

For the apple cider syrup:
1/2 cup sugar
1 tablespoon cornstarch
1 teaspoon ground cinnamon
1 cup apple cider
1 tablespoon lemon juice
2 tablespoons butter

For the French toast:
4 eggs
1/2 cup canned pure pumpkin puree
1/2 cup whipping cream
1/2 cup milk
2 teaspoons ground cinnamon
1 teaspoon ground nutmeg
2 tablespoons sugar
1 tablespoon butter
1 teaspoon vegetable oil
16 1-inch thick slices French bread
sparkling sugar

To make the syrup, whisk together the sugar, cornstarch, and cinnamon in a saucepan. Stir in the apple cider and lemon juice. Cook over medium heat until mixture begins to boil, and continue cooking until the syrup thickens. Remove from heat and stir in the butter until melted. Keep warm. In a shallow bowl, whisk together eggs, pumpkin puree, cream, milk, cinnamon, nutmeg and sugar. (Mixture can be prepared the night before and stored, tightly covered, in the refrigerator.)

Heat the butter and oil in a skillet over medium heat. Dip the bread quickly on both sides into the egg mixture, place in the hot skillet and cook for 1 to 2 minutes on each side, until lightly browned. Keep warm in the oven and repeat with remaining bread. Sprinkle with sparkling sugar and serve immediately with apple cider syrup.

Pancetta, Spinach and Provolone Baked Omelet

10 eggs
1/3 cup grated Parmesan cheese
1/4 cup milk
1/2 teaspoon salt
1/4 teaspoon freshly ground black pepper
1 tablespoon extra virgin olive oil
1/4 cup finely chopped onion
1/4 pound pancetta, chopped
3 cups baby spinach leaves, stems removed
1/2 cup shredded Provolone cheese

Preheat oven to 350 degrees F. In a medium bowl, whisk together the eggs, Parmesan cheese, milk, salt and pepper. Reserve.

Brush a 12-inch ovenproof skillet with olive oil and heat over medium flame. Add the onion and pancetta and cook, stirring occasionally, for 5 to 6 minutes or until lightly browned. Pour off the grease and add the spinach, cooking and stirring until all the leaves are wilted. Remove from heat.

Pour the egg mixture over the spinach. Sprinkle shredded cheese on top. Bake for about 20 minutes or until puffy and lightly browned on top. Cut into wedges and serve.
8 servings.

Maple Glazed Sausage and Bacon

1 pound sausage links
1 1/2 pounds thick-sliced bacon
1 1/2 cups maple syrup
2/3 cup packed dark brown sugar
1 teaspoon ground allspice
1 teaspoon ground cinnamon

In a large skillet, cook sausage links until browned. Drain, clean skillet and cook the bacon until browned and crispy; drain and clean skillet. Combine syrup, brown sugar, cinnamon and allspice in the skillet and stir until combined. Bring to a boil over medium-high heat. Add the sausages and cook and stir for about 3 minutes, or until glazed. Use a slotted spoon to remove the sausages to a platter. Add the bacon to the skillet and cook and stir for about 3 minutes, or until glazed. Transfer the bacon to the platter and serve.

Crunchy Golden Hash Browns with Leeks and Peppers

2 20-ounce packages fresh diced potatoes with onion
1 1/2 teaspoons vegetable oil
1 medium leek, white and pale green part only, chopped
1/2 red bell pepper, finely diced
1/2 green bell pepper, finely diced
salt and freshly ground black pepper to taste

In two batches, spread the potatoes on a large cutting board and dice. Brush a large skillet with vegetable oil and heat over a medium flame until hot. Add half of potatoes, leek and peppers and cook, turning every few minutes, until potatoes are lightly browned. Season to taste with salt and pepper. Transfer to a serving dish, keep warm, and repeat with remaining potatoes, leeks and peppers.

Apple Crisp Streusel Muffins

For the muffins:
2 cups all-purpose flour
1 cup sugar
1 teaspoon baking powder
1/2 teaspoon baking soda
1/2 teaspoon salt
2 eggs
1/2 cup butter, melted
1 teaspoon vanilla
1 1/2 cups chopped, peeled tart apples like Granny Smith

For the streusel topping:
1/3 cup packed brown sugar
1 tablespoon all-purpose flour
1/8 teaspoon ground cinnamon
1 tablespoon cold butter

For the icing:
3/4 cup confectioners' sugar
1 tablespoons milk
1 teaspoon butter, melted
1/8 teaspoon vanilla
pinch of salt

Preheat oven to 375 degrees F. Line 12 muffin cups with paper baking cups. In a large bowl, combine the flour, sugar, baking powder, baking soda and salt. In a separate bowl, combine eggs, butter and vanilla. Stir the butter mixture into dry ingredients just until moistened. Stir in apples and fill each muffin cup three-quarters full.

In a small bowl, combine brown sugar, flour and cinnamon in a small bowl. Cut in butter until crumbly. Sprinkle over batter. Bake for 15 to 20 minutes, or until a toothpick inserted in center comes out clean. Cool for 5 minutes before removing from pan to a wire rack to cool completely. Combine glaze ingredients in a small bowl and drizzle over muffins. Makes 1 dozen.

Grapefruit Wedges Brulée

8 large grapefruits
2/3 cup dark brown sugar
1/2 teaspoon cinnamon
1/4 teaspoon salt

Preheat the broiler and position the oven rack near the top of the oven. Cut grapefruit in half crosswise, and cut again lengthwise to make four wedges. Repeat with remaining grapefruit. Arrange grapefruit wedges with one cut side up on a baking sheet. Combine the brown sugar, cinnamon and salt and press the mixture on the cut side of the grapefruit. Broil just until sugar mixture starts to melt, about 1 or 2 minutes, watching carefully to avoid burning. Arrange grapefruit on a platter and serve at once.

Party Timeline

One month before the brunch:

- Make or purchase the invitations.
- Finalize guest list and mail invitations.

3 weeks before the brunch:

- Finalize the menu, including drinks (carefully selecting the items you wish to make and those you wish to purchase).
- Create a look by selecting colors, mood, setting and entertainment, if necessary.
- Order or gather the decorations and accessories.

2 weeks before the brunch:

- Make a shopping list for the food and liquor (see Shopping list).
- Order food or any desert you do not wish to make.
- Order flowers, and consider having them delivered the day before the brunch.

1 week before the brunch:

- Assemble or purchase take-away gifts and wrap them.
- Purchase all nonperishable food and liquor (see Shopping list).
- Create a music play list or purchase CDs.

2 days before the brunch:

- Decorate.
- Prepare the bar with glasses and liquor.
- Assemble all the serving dishes and set up the buffet table, if using one.
- Make the simple syrup for the cocktails and refrigerate.

The day before brunch:

- Purchase remaining perishable food (see Shopping List).
- Set the table and lay out serving dishes.
- Pick up the flowers or have them delivered.
- Toast the pecans for the oatmeal and store, tightly covered, at room temperature.
- Make the cranberry reduction sauce for the oatmeal and store, tightly covered, in the refrigerator.
- Dice onions, leeks, and red and green peppers for the hash browns, and store separately, tightly covered, in the refrigerator.
- Chop onions and pancetta, tear spinach, shred Provolone cheese for omelet, and store separately, tightly covered, in the refrigerator.
- Make extra ice.
- Check that the bathroom is clean. Have fresh hand towels, soap and extra toilet paper on hand.

The night before the brunch:

- Prepare the batter for the pumpkin French toast and store, tightly covered, in the refrigerator.

The morning of the brunch:

- Finish dicing the potatoes, and store, tightly covered, in the refrigerator.
- Cut the grapefruit, seal, tightly covered, in the refrigerator.
- Slice oranges for garnish on the Splash cocktails. Seal and refrigerate.

Prior to guests' arrival:

- Start the music.
- Prepare the Blood Orange Splash cocktails, including one for yourself!
- Light the candles.
- Enjoy!

Take Away Gifts

1: How Many People Does It Take to Make a Difference,
by Dan Zadra and Kobi Yamada
This is, hands down, one of my favorite books. It's said to "inspire you to discover and celebrate your special gifts and, above all, share them with a world that truly needs it." A small coffee table book filled with quotes, thoughts and goal setting questions, it can gift your guests with renewed perspective and purpose.

Vary it:

Luggage Tags. At a time of year when so many of us travel, a few personalized luggage tags can come in handy. Found at any craft store, you can add old pictures, beautiful fabrics, quotes or anything else of meaning to the recipient.

Simplify it:

Rum or cider with a side of mulling seasoning warms your guests from the inside on these cold November nights. Fill a small pouch with mulling spices and attach it to a small bottle of spiced rum or 1/2 gallon of locally made cider.

"Gratitude makes sense of our past, brings peace for today, and creates a vision for tomorrow."   —Melody Beattie

Resources

Grocery List

Fruit
Apples
Bananas
Berries
Grapes
Lemons
Melons
Oranges

Vegetables
Broccoli
Carrots
Celery
Cucumbers
Garlic
Lettuce
Mushrooms
Onions
Peppers
Potatoes
Spinach
Tomatoes
Zucchini
Zucchini

Paper Goods
Aluminum Foil
Plastic Wrap
Paper Towels
Toilet Paper
Tissues
Garbage Bags
Household Cleaner
Dish Soap
Laundry Soap
Tooth Paste
Soap
Personal
Personal

Snacks
Chips
Cookies
Crackers
Nuts
Popcorn
Pretzels
Candy

Dairy
Cream
Half and Half
Milk
Butter
Eggs
Cream Cheese
Cheese
Yogurt

Frozen
Appetizers
Dough
Pizza
Meat
Fruit
Vegetables
Ice Cream
Pastries

Meat & Fish
Bacon
Beef
Chicken

Sauces & Oils
Sauces & Oils
BBQ Sauce
Oil
Vinegar
Cooking Wine
Soy Sauce
Salad Dressing
Salsa
Dip
Pasta Sauce
Peanut Butter
Jelly
Honey
Ketchup
Mustard
Mayonnaise
Pickles

Extras

Grains
Cereal
Granola
Pasta
Rice

Baked Goods
Muffins
Bagels
Bread
Tortillas

Baking & Spices
Flour
Sugar
Baking Soda
Vanilla
Chocolate
Cinnamon
Cayenne Pepper
Chili Pepper
Garlic Powder
Thyme
Oregano
Parsley
Rosemary
Salt
Pepper

Canned
Soup
Tomatoes
Beans
Vegetables
Fruit
Broth

Beverages
Water
Coffee / Tea
Juice
Soda
Tonic / Soda Water
Mixer
Beer
Wine

Bar List

Bar
Celery
Cocktail Onions
Fruit Slices
Green Olives
Maraschino Cherries
Lemon Slices
Lime Slices
Salt

Ice

Extras

Beer
Pilsner
Pale Lager
Dark Lager
Porter
Stout
Dark Lager
Cabernet Sauvignon
Stout

Soda
7-up / Sprite
Pepsi / Coke
Diet
Root Beer
Dr. Pepper
Mt. Dew
Other

Liquor
Beer
Red Wine
White Wine
Champagne
Brandy
Bourbon
Vermouth
Flavored Liquor
Gin
Rum
Scotch
Tequila
Triple Sec
Vodka
Whiskey

Champagne

Wine
Red Wine
Chardonnay
Merlot
Pinot Noir
Syrah
Sangiovese
Zinfandel
Blend

White Wine
Chardonnay
Gewurztraminer
Pinot Grigio
Sauvignon Blanc
Riesling
Blend

Mixers
Club Soda
Diet Soda
Seltzer
Tonic Water
Diet Tonic Water
Mixer
Soda
Diet Soda
Water
Cranberry Juice
Grapefruit Juice
Orange Juice
Tomato Juice
Lime Juice
Worcestershire Sauce
Tabasco Sauce

Seating

Round Tables

30" Seats 2 – 4
36" Seats 4
48" Seats 6 – 8
60" Seats 8 – 10
72" Seats 10 - 12

Tablecloth Size

90"
96"
108"
120"
132"

Square Tables

36" x 36" Seats 4 – 6
48" x 48" Seats 6 - 8
60" x 60" Seats 8 – 10
72" x 72" Seats 10 – 12

Tablecloth Size

96" x 96"
108" x 108"
120" x 120"
132" x 132"

Rectangular Tables

30" x 48" Seats 6 - 8
30" x 72" Seats 8 - 10
30" x 96" Seats 10 – 12

Tablecloth Size

90" x 108"
90" x 132"
90" x 156"

Budgeting for Every Occasion

Location
Venue Cost / Rental _____

Invitation
Save the Date _____
Invitations _____
Printing Costs _____
Inserts for Invites _____
Unusual boxing or Tubes _____
Stamps / Postage _____
Misc. _____

Décor
Candles _____
Spot Lighting _____
Lamps / Sting Lights _____
Outdoor Tent _____
Rented Tables / Chairs _____
Rented Furniture _____
Purchased / Rented Dishware _____
Purchased / Rented Service Pieces _____
Tablecloths _____
Napkins / Napkin Rings _____
Fabric / Pillows _____
Misc. _____

Table Décor
Buffet Table Décor _____
Misc. _____

Flowers
Flowers _____
Vases _____
Florist / Delivery _____
Tips _____
Misc. _____

Music
Band _____
Musician(s) _____
CD's _____
Tips _____
Misc. _____

Drinks
Beer _____
Wine / Champagne _____
Hard Alcohol _____
Mixers / Soda _____
Bottled Water _____
Ice _____
Bartender _____
Tips for Bartender / Servers _____
Misc. _____

Food
Hors d' Oeuvres _____
First Course _____
Main Course _____
Dessert _____
Condiments _____
Delivery _____
Cater / Chef _____
Servers _____
Tips for Cater / Chef / Servers _____
Misc. _____

Gifts
Welcome Gifts _____
Takeaway Gifts _____
Valet _____
Bathroom Supplies _____
Clean Up _____
Tips _____
Misc. _____

Vendors

Company_____

Contact Name_____

Address_____

Phone_____E-mail_____

Referred By_____

Notes

Company_____

Contact Name_____

Address_____

Phone_____E-mail_____

Referred By_____

Notes

Guests

Mr. and Mrs._____

Address_____

Phone_____E-mail_____

Invitation Sent_____

Will Attend_____Will Not Attend_____

Notes

Mr. and Mrs._____

Address_____

Phone_____E-mail_____

Invitation Sent_____

Will Attend_____Will Not Attend_____

Portion Control

Number of Guests	4 -6	8 – 10	12	24
Drinks				
Soda, Juice, Soda/tonic	1 oz bottle	2 bottles	2 bottles	3 bottles
Water	4-8 small bottles	8 – 16 bottles	12-20 bottles	24 - 40 bottles
Beer*	12 bottles	18 bottles	24 bottles	36 bottles
Wine**	3-4 bottles	5-6 bottles	7-8 bottles	12–16 bottles
Ice	4 pounds	6 pounds	10 pounds	20 pounds
Lemons/limes	3 each	3 each	4 each	5 each
Cheese***	2 pounds	3 pounds	4-5 pounds	8-10 pounds
Crackers	1-2 boxes	2-4 boxes	4 boxes	8 boxes
Appetizers'	12-24 pieces	24-40 pieces	36-48 pieces	72-96 pieces
Dessert				
Pie	(1) 9-inch	(1) 9-inch	(2) 9-inch	(3) 9-inch
Layer cake	(1) 8 inch	(1) 8-inch	(1) 8-inch	(2) 8-inch

Consider a variety of light and dark - domestic and foreign beer

** *Consider a variety of white and red – depending on the type of food
served and time of the year – purchase more of one variety over another.*

*** *Consider a variety of hard, aged, blue and soft cheese*

Conversion Charts

Liquid Conversions

U.S.	METRIC
1 tsp	5 ml
2 tbs	15 ml
2 tbs	30 ml
3 tbs	45 ml
1/4 cup	60 ml
1/3 cup	75 ml
1/3 cup + 1 tbs	90 ml
1/3 cup + 1 tbs	100 ml
1/2 cup	120 ml
2/3 cup	150 ml
3/4 cup	180 ml
3/4 cup + 2 tbs	200 ml
1 cup	240 ml
1 cup + 2 tbs	275 ml
1 1/4 cups	300 ml
1 1/3 cups	325 ml
1 1/2 cups	350 ml
1 2/3 cups	375 ml
1 3/4 cups	400 ml
1 3/4 cups + 2 tbs	450 ml
2 cups (1 pint)	475 ml
2 1/2 cups	600 ml
3 cups	720 ml
4 cups (1 quart)	945 ml (1,000 ml = 1 liter)

Weight Conversions

U.S.	METRIC
1/2 oz	12 g
1 oz	28 g
1 1/2 oz	43 g
2 oz	57 g
2 1/2 oz	71 g
3 oz	85 g
3 1/2 oz	100 g
4 oz	113 g
5 oz	142 g
6 oz	170 g
7 oz	200 g
8 oz	227 g
9 oz	255 g
10 oz	284 g
11 oz	312 g
12 oz	340 g
13 oz	368 g
14 oz	400 g
15 oz	425 g
1 lb	454 g

Oven Temperatures

FAHRENHEIT	CELSIUS
250	120
275	140
300	150
325	165
350	180
375	190
400	200
425	220
450	230
475	240
500	260
550 (broil)	290 (broil)

Reflections of Christmas

Invitations

Large white or kraft colored gift tag – Hobby Lobby – hobbylobby.com
Mistletoe - local florist or grocery store
Faux mistletoe – Hobby Lobby – hobbylobby.com
Mailbox or padded envelope – Container Store – containerstore.com

Vary It

Page from an antique book – local antique store or eBay – ebay.com
Crystallized branch – Hobby Lobby – hobbylobby.com
Raffia ribbon – Hobby Lobby – hobbylobby.com
Padded envelope – Container Store – containerstore.com

Simplify it

Any card or party retailer

Table

Tablecloth
Lavender satin duvet cover – Z Gallerie – zgallerie.com
Placemats
Antique book pages taped together – a local antique store or eBay – ebay. com

Napkins

Lavender polyester – Z Gallerie – zgallerie.com
Napkin Rings – glass beads Z Gallerie – zgallerie.com

Dishware

Dinner plates – Lavender rimmed – Z Gallerie – zgallerie.com
Salad plates – Lavender rimmed – Z Gallerie – zgallerie.com
Small, beaded rectangular silver tray, round, beaded silver cake stand
  and round, clear glass beaded cake stand – Target – target.com.
Small and large rectangular silver trays - Pottery Barn – potterybarn.com
Large Round, sterling silver tray – a local antique store or eBay – ebay.com
Large silver ice bowl – Pottery Barn – potterybarn.com

Glassware

Wine glasses – Crystal (homeowners)
Water glasses – Crystal (homeowners)
Crystal decanters (homeowners)
Small silver cups and saucers – Crate and Barrel – crateandbarrel.com
Tapered Glass shot glasses – Crate and Barrel – crateandbarrel.com
Silverware – Waterford "Powerscourt" – Macy's – macys.com
Crystal Candlesticks- Crystal (gas) Orvis – orvis.com
Sterling silver candelabras – a local antique store or eBay – ebay.com
Candles – Bed Bath and Beyond – bedbathandbeyond.com
Mercury glass candleholders and pedestals – Pottery Barn – potterybarn.com
Silver ball tree - Z Gallerie – zgallerie.com
Newspaper shades – West Elm –westelm.com
Beaded crystal votives in various sizes – Z Gallerie – zgallerie.com
Votive candles – various sizes – Hobby Lobby – hobbylobby.com

Glass rope garland – Smith and Hawken – Target.com
Beaded crystal ball ornaments (hung from the mantel)
  Z Gallerie – zgallerie.com

Flowers

Crystal garland and pics – Hobby Lobby – hobbylobby.com
Evergreen and pinecone garland and pics – Hobby Lobby –hobbylobby.com
Over- sized pinecones – a local greenhouse or florist
Christmas trees – Hobby Lobby – hobbylobby.com
Glass and crystal tree ornaments Pottery Barn – potterybarn.com –
  Hobby Lobby – hobbylobby.com – Target – target.com
Light spheres in various sizes – Save on Crafts – saveoncrafts.com
Newspaper tree rope – West Elm – westelm.com
Petite child's chandelier (on tree) – Target – target.com
Various birds nests – Artisan Center – artisancenterdenver.com or
  eBay –ebay.com
Various bird cages – a local antique store or eBay – ebay.com
Small and large feathered birds – Hobby Lobby – hobbylobby.com
Cotton snowballs - Pottery Barn – Potterybarn.com
Twig and wire basket (hung from the door and wall) – Hobby Lobby –
  hobbylobby.com
Glass domes – Target – target.com
Battery- operated strand of lights – Hobby Lobby – hobbylobby.com

Music

itunes - apple.com/itunes - Barns and Nobel – barnsandnobel.com -
Amazon - amazon.com

Gift Wrap

White, Silver, and brown wrapping paper – Container Store –
  containerstore.com
Antique book pages taped together - a local antique store or eBay –
  ebay.com
Silver, purple and brown ribbon – Container Store –
  containerstore.com
Evergreen pics and wreaths, silver and crystal pics, nests, birds and
  petite picture frames – Hobby Lobby – hobbylobby.com

Takeaway Gifts

Recordable CD's – Target – target.com

Vary it

Mitten and hat sets – Target – target.com

Items not listed belong to the homeowner who graciously allowed us
to use their home.

Arctic Freeze

Invitations
> Pale Blue Stock paper, stamps, ribbon, faux snow, stickers and empty icicle
> ornament – Hobby Lobby – hobbylobby.com
> Clear plastic box – Container Store – containerstore.com

Vary It
> Clear plastic ornament and gift card – Hobby Lobby – hobbylobby.com
> CD size mailing box – Container Store – containerstor.com

Simplify it
> Any card and party retailer

Table
> Tablecloth
> Blue snagged silk - cut to fit – JoAnn Fabric – joann.com
> Faux fur throw - Target – target.com

Napkins
> Blue Cotton – Crate and Barrel – crateandbarrel.com
> Napkin Rings – Crystal beaded – Bed Bath and Beyond –
> bedbathandbeyond.com

Dishware
> Chipped looking glass dishes – Z Gallerie – zgallerie.com
> Serving Pieces – Chipped looking glass – Z Gallerie – zgallerie.com
> Serving Tray – Silver – Target – target.com
> Cake Stand – clear – Target – target.com

Glassware
> Champaign glasses - Z Gallerie – zgallerie.com
> Martini glasses – Z Gallerie – zgallerie.com
> Silver glass tea cups and saucers – Create and Barrel – crateandbarrel.com
> Silverware – curved – World Market – worldmarket.com
> Candlesticks – stacked looking ice cubes – Z Gallerie – zgallerie.com
> Candles- Bed Bath and Beyond

Accessories
> Tall, hollow glass trees – West Elm – westelm.com
> Hollow glass snowmen – West Elm – westelm.com
> Little polar bears and penguins – Z Gallerie – zgallerie.com
> Glass Blocks _ Hobby Lobby – hobbylobby.com
> Ornaments – Hobby Lobby – hobbylobby.com
> Faux snow and snowballs _ Pottery Barn – potterybarn.com
> Spice rack for malt toppings – Target – target.com
> Led wire branches – Save-On Crafts – save-on-crafts.com
> Large plastic igloo – Pets Mart – petsmart.com
> Large Stiffed Husky – Kazoo and Co. – kazzotoys.com
> Slippers – Faux suede – Target –target.com

Flowers
> Vases – Clear glass – Crate and Barrel – crateandbarrel.com
> Filler – Faux snow – Pottery Barn – potterybarn.com

Music
> itunes - apple.com/itunes - Barns and Nobel – barnsandnobel.com
> Amazon - amazon.com

Gift
> Gift Wrap
> Blue paper, white and blue ribbon – Container Store – containerstore.com
> Beaded pics and plastic icicle rope – Hobby Lobby – hobbylobby.com

Takeaway Gifts
> Knit gloves – Target – target.com
> Serendipity Frozen Hot Chocolate – Serendipity – serendipity3.com

Items not listed belong to the homeowner who graciously allowed us
to use their home.

The Love Letter

Invitations

    Vintage designed post cards – Cavallini Papers – paper-source.com

Vary It

    For inspiration try one of these websites -Brainyquote.com, thinkexist.com
    or quotations.about.com

Simplify it

    Any card or party retailer

Table

    Napkins
    World Market – worldmarket.com
    Stamp and wax – Hobby Lobby – hobbylobby.com
    Napkin Rings – twine sealed with a wax stamp

Dishware

    White porcelain – World Market – worldmarket.com
    Dishes with gold angel wings – Ballard Designs
    Gold Plastic Chargers – Hobby Lobby – hobbylobby.com

Glassware

    Wine glasses – Crate and Barrel – wax seal melted to the front
    Water glasses – repurposed candleholders tied with twine and a wax seal
    Gold tea cups – Bed Bath and Beyond – bedbathandbeyond.com
    Silverware - Waterford "Powerscourt" – Macy's – macys.com
    Candlesticks – antique candelabra – Wisteria
    Votives – Hobby Lobby – hobbylobby.com
    Candles – Bed Bath and Beyond – bedbathandbeyond.com

Flowers

    Beaded garland – Hobby Lobby – hobbylobby.com
    Cone shaped baskets (hung from the back of chairs) – Hobby Lobby –
    hobbylobby.com

Music

    itunes - apple.com/itunes. - Barns and Nobel – barnsandnobel.com -
    Amazon - amazon.com

Accessories

    Wooded gold wings – Ballard Designs – ballarddesigns.com
    Queen of Hearts paper crown – Vintage Diana – vintagediana on Etsy
    Wax and wax stamps – Hobby Lobby – hobbylobby.com

Takeaway Gifts

    Bed Sheet – Bed Bath and Beyond- bedbathandbeyond.com
    Large square basket – World Market – worldmarket.com
    Soaps, lotions, and bath oils – Santa Maria Novella –
    santamarianovellausa.com
    Flower Petals – Hobby Lobby – hobbylobby.com
    Chocolate – Ghirardelli – ghirdelli.com
    Movie – Barns and Nobel – barnsandnobel.com

Vary it

    Leather notebook - Leelanau Trading Co – leelanautradingco.com

Items not listed belong to the homeowner who graciously allowed us
to use their home.

Enchanted Easter Eve

Invitations

    Large, hollow plastic eggs -Target –target.com

    Jelly beans –Any retailer that carries candy

    Mailing box – Container Store – containerstore.com

Vary It

    White card stock paper, plastic grass and faux flowers – Hobby Lobby –
      hobbylobby.com

    Mailing box – Container Store – containerstore.com

Simplify it

    Any card or party retailer

Table

    Tablecloth

    White tablecloth – Pottery Barn –potterybarn.com

    2nd tablecloth – fuchsia duvet cover and matching pillows– Bed Bath and
      Beyond – bedbathandbeyond.com

    Placemats - straw pot liners cut open – Home Depot – homedepot.com

Napkins

    Green cotton – Crate and Barrel – crateandbarrel.com

    Napkin Rings - twine

Dishware

    Dinner plates – World Market –worldmarket.com

    Salad plates – Two-toned melamine – Crate and Barrel –crateandbarrel.com

    Checkered platters, tea set and three-tiered serving dish – MacKenzie
      Childs – neimanmarcus.com

    White square platter and cake platter – Crate and Barrel –
      crateandbarrel.com

    Small silver tray – Two's Company – twoscompany.com

Glassware

    Wine glasses – green, hand-blown glass – Anthropologie –
      anthropolgie.com

    Water glasses – etched, clear glass – The Lark – thelarkdenver.com

    Miniature garden tools – Hobby Lobby –hoobylobby.com

    Silverware – Waterford "Powerscourt" – Macy's – macys.com

    Candlesticks- Sculptured glass – Pottery Barn – potterybarn.com

    Candles – Bed Bath and Beyond – bedbathandbeyond.com

    Lamp Shades – Lamp shades – Hobby Lobby – hobbylobby.com

    Moss sheeting and floral wire – Hobby Lobby – hobbylobby.com

Flowers

    Garland – beaded, pink and green garland – Hobby Lobby –
      hobbylooby.com

    Vases - small, clear glass – Target – target.com

    Cone shaped wire and twig baskets (hung from the back of chairs) Hobby
      Lobby – hobbylobby.com

    Ribbon – Pink and Orange – Container Store – containerstore.com

Music

    itunes - apple.com/itune - Barns and Nobel – barnsandnoble.com

    Amazon – amazon.com

Accessories

    Moss covered bunnies – The Lark – thelarkdenver.com

    Black Urns –Smith and Hawkins – Target – target.com

    Empty silver frame – Hobby Lobby – hobbylobby.com

    Hanging flower vases – City Floral – cityfloralgreenhouse.com

    Large striped gazebo – Z Gallerie – zgallerie.com

Gift Wrap

    Hot pink wrapping paper and pink / orange ribbon – Container Store –
      containerstore.com

    Plastic grass and flowers – Hobby Lobby – hobbylobby.com

    Zinc plant markers – City Floral –cityfloralgreenhouse.com

Takeaway Gifts

    Baskets and breakfast treats – World Market – worldmarket.com

Vary it

    Unique variety of cocktail Jelly Beans – Beau Coup – beau-coup.com

Simplify it

    Silver –plated picture frame –Pottery Barn –potterybarn.com

    Plastic grass and flowers – Hobby Lobby – hobbylobby.com

    Zinc plant markers – City Floral –cityfloralgreenhouse.com

Items not listed belong to the homeowner who graciously allowed us
to use their home.

Nesting

Invitations

Blue and striped card stock paper – Hobby Lobby – hobbylobby.com
Birds nest, bird and raffia ribbon – Hobby Lobby – hobbylobby.com
Square mailing box – Container Store – containerstore.com

Vary It

Blue Yarn – The Lambshoppe- thelambshoppe.com
Mailing box – Container Store – containerstore.com

Simplify it

Any card or party retailer
Feathers – Hobby Lobby – hobbylobby.com

Table

Tablecloth
White tablecloth – Bed Bath and Beyond – bedbathandbeyon.com
Bird and floral fabric – cut to fit - Ralph Lauren – Calico Corners – calicocorners.com

Napkins

Vintage – local antique store or eBay.com

Dishware

Blue and white, birds and nest plates and bowls – Perrier – Perrier.com
Blue and white, birds and nest tea set and cups – Perrier – Perrier.com
Cake Stand – small iron bird bath – local antique store or eBay.com
Beverage decanter – Classic Hostess – classichostess.com

Glassware

Wine glasses – Crate and Barrel – crateandbarrel.com
Water glasses – Crate and Barrel – crateandbarrel.com

Silverware

Assorted antiques – local antique store or eBay.com
Small twig nests – Hobby Lobby –hobbylobby.com

Flowers

Cone shaped twig baskets (hung from the back of chairs) Hobby Lobby – hobbylobby.com
Initial tags – antique hotels keys – eBay – ebay.com
Feathers – Hobby Lobby – hobbylobby.com
Silver vases – Two's Company – twoscompany.com

Music

itunes - apple.com/itunes - Barns and Nobel – barnsandnobel.com
Amazon – amazon.com

Accessories

Infant bumble bee onesie and burp cloth – Little e
Assorted Blue and white knitted ware – Nordstroms – Nordstrom.com
Wicker baskets – World Market – worldmarket.com
Wicker rocking chairs – Home Depot – homedepot.com
Vintage inspired large birdcage – Ballard Designs – ballarddesigns.com
Blue Yarn – Debbie Bliss – The Lamb Shoppe – thelambshoppe.com

Gift Wrap

Vintage sewing patterns – eBay – ebay.com
Striped wrapping paper and ribbon – Container Store – containerstor.com
Bumble Bee wrapping paper – Peaceful Valley Gifts – PeacefulValleyGifts.com
Twig nests, birds, and little eggs – Hobby Lobby – hobbylobby.com

Takeaway Gifts

Months of seeds – Red Envelope – redenvelope.com
Treat bags – Target – target.com

Vary it

Milk bath, soaps, scented candles – L'Occitane – usa.loccitane.com
Lavender tea bags – Lavender Dreams White Tea – Teavana – teavana.com

Simplify it

Cone shaped twig baskets (hung from the back of chairs) Hobby Lobby – hobbylobby.com
Initial tags – antique hotels keys – eBay – ebay.com
Feathers – Hobby Lobby – hobbylobby.com

Items not listed belong to the homeowner who graciously allowed us to use their home.

Pearls of Wisdom

Invitations
> Pink card stock paper, half-round pearl adhesives, and cameo sticker –
> Hobby Lobby – hobbylobby.com
> Mailing box or envelope – Container Store – containerstore.com

Vary It
> Pink card stock paper and lace trim – Hobby Lobby – hobbylobby.com
> Costume brooch or cameo – eBay – ebay.com
> Mailing box – Container Store – containerstore.com

Simplify it
> Any card or party retailer
> Loose pearl beads – Hobby Lobby – hobbylobby.com
> Mailing box or envelope – Container Store – containerstore.com

Table
> Tablecloth
> Pale pink cloth - cut-to-fit – Joann Fabric – joannfabric.com
> Pink floral cloth – cut-to-fit – Calico Corners – calicocorners.com

Napkins
> Pink cotton – Bed Bath and Beyond – bedbathandbeyond.com
> Napkin Rings – faux strand of pearls wrapped around napkin –
> AmeriMark – amerimark.com

Dishware
> Dinner plates – Monogrammed, gold-rimmed China – local antique store or
> eBay – ebay.com
> Ivory porcelain chargers – Pottery Barn – potterybarn.com
> Antique floral bowls – local antique store or eBay – ebay.com
> Ivory serving bowls, platters and large tray – Crate and Barrel –
> crateandbarrel.com
> Wooded cake stand - eBay – ebay.com
> Sterling silver tea set – local antique store or eBay – ebay.com

Glassware
> Glass domes – local antique store or eBay – ebay.com
> Wine glasses – etched, gold –rimmed crystal wine and champagne glasses
> –local antique store or eBay – ebay.com
> Water glasses – hand-blown clear glass cups – Anthropologie –
> anthropologie.com
> Silverware – Assorted antiques – local antique store or eBay.com
> Petite Iron urns – Watson and Co – watsonandco.com
> Miniature boxwood trees and table wreath – local green house
> Porcelain table bust – Ballard Designs – ballarddesigns.com
> Multiple strands of faux pearls and cameos – AmeriMark –
> amerimark.com
> Dried boxwood wreaths (hung from the back of chairs)– Tended Thicket –
> thetendedthicket.com

Music
> itunes - apple.com/itunes - Barns and Nobel – barnsandnoble.com
> Amazon – amazon.com

Accessories
> Large ceramic busts – Ballard Designs – ballarddesigns.com
> Hanging curtains from gazebo – World Market – worldmarket.com
> Hanging candle chandelier – local antique store or eBay – ebay.com
> Moss sheets (covering old chair) - Hobby Lobby – hobbylobby.com
> Leather notebook – Leelanau Trading Co – leelanautradingco.com

Gift Wrap
> Pink wrapping paper, floral wrapping paper and pink ribbons –
> Container store – containerstore.com
> Lace and linen napkins and handkerchiefs – local antique store or
> eBay – ebay.com
> Cameo stickers and pearl rope – Hobby Lobby – hobbylobby.com
> Embellished slippers - Goody Goody Slippers – goodygoodyshoes.com

Takeaway Gifts
> Bath salts, candle, lavender eye pillow and foot lotion – L'Occitane –
> usa.loccitane.com
> Napkins and handkerchiefs – local antique store or eBay – ebay.com

Vary it
> Spa CD's, notepads and pencil sets and plated silver trays – Barns and
> Nobel –barnsandnobel.com or Target – target.com

Simplify it
> Embellished slippers – Goody Goody Slippers – goodygoodyshoes.com
> Decorative box – Container Store – containerstore.com
> Faux pearls and brooch - AmeriMark – amerimark.com

Items not listed belong to the homeowner who graciously allowed us
to use their home.

A Proper Gentleman

Invitations
    Ivory handkerchiefs – Macy's – macys.com
    Iron on decals – Hobby Lobby – hobbylobby.com or Target – target.com
    Brown kraft paper envelopes and leather buttons – Hobby Lobby –
        hobbylobby.com

Vary It
    Masculine patterned card stock paper – Hobby Lobby – hobbylobby.com

Simplify it
    Any card or party retailer

Table
    Tablecloth
    Wool plaid - cut-to-fit – Ralph Lauren - Calico Corners – calicocorners.com

Napkins
    Wool houndstooth - cut-to-fit – (exposed seam) with small leather buttons
        sewn onto the side – Calico Corners – calicocorners.com
    Leather buttons – Hobby Lobby – hobbylobby.com
    Silver Platter and tea set – local antique store or eBay – ebay.com

Dishware
    Dinner plates – Lenox - Bed Bath and Beyond – bedbathandbeyond.com
    Salad plates – Lenox - Bed Bath and Beyond – bedbathandbeyond.com

Glassware
    Wine glasses – Crate and Barrel – crateandbarrel.com
    Water glasses – Crate and Barrel – crateandbarrel.com
    Coffee cups and saucers – Lenox - Bed Bath and Beyond –
        bedbathandbeyond.com
    Small silver cups and saucers – Crate and Barrel – crateandbarrel.com
    Silverware – Waterford "Powerscourt" – Macy's – macys.com

Flowers
    Vases – Silver-plated children's tea set – Amazon – amazon.com
    Old coffee sack (surrounding center piece flowers) – eBay – ebay.com
    Various ties (hung from the back of chairs) – borrow some from your dads,
        husbands or brothers closet.

Music
    itunes - apple.com/itunes - Barns and Nobel. - barnsandnobel.com.
    Amazon - amazon.com

Accessories
    Espresso maker – Elektra Semi Automatic – Elekta – elektrasmi.com
    Empty silver picture frames – Hobby Lobby – hobbylobby.com
    Black poster board and chalk (black poster board acts like a chalk board
        when written on with chalk) – Hobby Lobby – hobbylobby.com
    Vintage shoehorn – A local antique store or eBay – ebay.com

Gift Wrap
    A collection of old shirts, ties, suspenders, and belts are repurposed from
        things your father no longer wants or visit your local charity.

Takeaway Gifts
    Subscription to a local newspaper or magazine – Barns and Noble –
        barnsandnoble.com - magazines.com or amazon.com/magazines
    Ribbon and gift cards – Container Store – containerstore.com

Vary it
    Oversized coffee cups, saucers and coffee scoops – Crate and Barrel –
        crateandbarrel.com
    Ribbon – Container Store –containerstore.com

Items not listed belong to the homeowner who graciously allowed us
to use their home.

Chasing Stars

Invitations

    Stargazers map – Barns and Nobel – barnsandnobel.com – skymaps.com

    Childs binoculars – Land of Nod – landofnod.com or Amazon – amazon.com

    Mailing tube – Container Store –containerstore.com

Vary It

    Red, white or blue card stock paper, glittered letters and star stickers –
      Hobby Lobby – hobbylobby.com

    Firefly buttons and ribbon – JoAnn Fabric –joannfabric.com

    Mailing box – Container Store – containerstore.com

Simplify it

    Any card or party retailer

    Horoscope roll sold at most grocery stores and 7-11

Table

    Tablecloth

    White tablecloth – Bed Bath and Beyond – bedbathandbeyond.com

    Linen and blue cloth – cut-to-fit - (draped across the middle of the table)

    Joann Fabric – joannfabric.com

Napkins

    Vintage flag inspired napkins – Wisteria – wisteria.com

Dishware

    Dinner plates – Target – target.com

    Soup bowl buckets – Target – target.com

    Wicker chargers –Pottery Barn – potterybarn.com

    Small and medium white serving trays – Target – target.com

    Wicker serving tray - Pottery Barn – potterybarn.com

Glassware

    Wine glasses – clear etched plastic – The Lark – thelark.com

    Water glasses – clear etched plastic – The Lark – thelark.com

    Silverware – Waterford "Powerscourt" – Macy's – macys.com

    Battery- operated fireflies in a mason jar

    Galvanized silver cleaning bucket – Home Depot- homedepot.com

    Potted grass – local green house

    Miniature flags – Michael's – michaels.com

Music

    itunes - apple.com/itunes - Barns and Nobel –barnsandnobel.com.

    Amazon - amazon.com

Accessories

    Large 10X10 mosquito net tent –Sports Authority – sportsauthority.com

    Hanging glow and the dark star lanterns – Amazon – amazon.com

    Overstuffed, outdoor pillows – Bed Bath and Beyond –
      bedbathandbeyond.com

    Sea Grass rug – Pottery Barn –potterybarn.com

    Sea Grass ottoman – Z Gallerie – zgallerie.com.

    American Flag – Target – target.com

    Large telescope – Best Buy – bestbuy.com or Toys R us – toysrus.com

    Wicker picnic basket – Amazon – amazon.com

    Croquet set, badminton net, horseshoes or beanbag toss – Target –
      target.com – Sports Authority – sportsauthority.com

Takeaway Gifts

    Galvanized metal flowerpot – Anthropologie – anthropologie.com

    All-day-lollipop – Dylan's Candy Bar – dylanscandybar.com

    Miniature astrology book – Barns and Nobel – barnsandnobel.com

Vary it

    Large seal-tight jar and ribbon– Container Store – containerstore.com

    Wooded spoon – any local grocery store

Simplify it

    Jar of glow-in-the-dark-stars – Amazon – amazon.com

Items not listed belong to the homeowner who graciously allowed us
to use their home.

A Night Under the Stars

Invitations

    Movie ticket invitations –ticketprinting.com (type in concert ticket)

Vary It

    Yellow card stock paper – Hobby Lobby – hobbylobby.com

    Oversized candy boxes – Bed Bath and Beyond – bedbathandbeyond.com

Simplify it

    White and red card stock paper – Hobby Lobby – hobbylooby.com

    Unpopped popcorn kernels – Any grocery store

    Mailing envelope – Container Store – containerstore.com

Table

    Tablecloth

    Arden Black –cut-to-fit fabric – Ballard Designs – ballarddesigns.com

Napkins

    Black cotton – World Market – worldmarket.com

    Napkin Rings – raffia – Hobby Lobby – hobbylobby.com

Dishware

    Dinner plates – Black rim – Target – target.com

    Salad plates – Black rim – Target – target.com

    Soup bowl buckets – Target – target.com

    Large Beverage decanter– Classic Hostess – classichostess.com

    Wicker silverware basket - eBay – ebay.com

    Serving tray, serving bowls and cake stand – Crate and Barrel – crateandbarrel.com

    Glass pitcher – Crate and Barrel – crateandbarrel.com

    Wicker serving tray – Pottery Barn – potterybarn.com

Glassware

    Martini glasses – Clear Polycarbonate – William- Sonoma – William-sonoma.com or Crate and Barrel – crateandbarrel.com

    Water glasses – Clear Polycarbonate – William- Sonoma – William-sonoma.com or Crate and Barrel – crateandbarrel.com

    Silverware – Waterford "Powerscourt" – Macy's – macys.com

    Yard Stands (comes with hanging solar lights) Home Depot – homedepot.com

    Wooded numbers (painted black) – Hobby Lobby – hobbylobby.com

    Wooden chalkboard tubs –Smith and Hawken – target.com

Flowers

    Tall galvanized flower cans – Save-On-Crafts – save-on-crafts.com

    Raffia Ribbon – Hobby Lobby – hobbylobby.com

    Black Urns – Target – target.com

Music

    itunes - apple.com/itunes - Barns and Nobel – barnsandnobel.com. Amazon - amazon.com

Accessories

    Outdoor Throws – Arden Black – Ballard Designs – ballarddesigns.com

    Outdoor throw pillows – Home Depot – homedepot.com

    Concession Stand (converted from a child's grocery stand – top fabric made) – Target – target.com

    Outdoor Theater System – Frontgate – frontgate.com

    Black fabric – cut-to-fit – JoAnne Fabric – joannefabric.com

    Popcorn boxes and butter pitcher – World Market – worldmarket.com

Takeaway Gifts

    Wooden chalkboard tubs –Smith and Hawken – target.com

    Screen T –shirts – Hollywood Mega Store – hollywoodmegastore.com

    Popcorn bowl – World Market – worldmarket.com

    Tin movie reel – Hollywood Mega Store – hollywoodmegastore.com

    Classic movie – Barns and Nobel – barnsandnobel.com – Amazon – amazon.com – eBay –ebay.com

    Admission tickets – Hollywood Mega Store – hollywoodmegastore.com

    Black and White movie photos - Hollywood Mega Store – hollywoodmegastore.com

Vary it

    Classic movies - Barns and Nobel – barnsandnobel.com – Amazon – amazon.com – eBay –ebay.com

Simplify it

    movie gift card – a local movie theater of most grocery stores.

Items not listed belong to the homeowner who graciously allowed us to use their home.

Tasting In Tuscany

Invitations
White cotton cocktail napkin – World Market – worldmarket.com
Iron on decals – Hobby Lobby – hobbylobby.com or Target – target.com
Mailing box or envelope – Container Store – containerstore.com

Vary It
Small, individual wine bottles – A local liquor store
Personalized wine labels – Bottle Your Brand – bottleyourbrand.com
Large, printable stickers – Hobby Lobby – hobbylobby.com
Mailing box – Container Store – containerstore.com

Simplify it
Brown bottle bag – A local liquor store

Table
Tablecloth
3 cut-to-fit burlap stripes spaced across the table – JoAnn Fabric –
joannfabric.com

Napkins
Saffron yellow cotton – Crate and Barrel – crateandbarrel.com

Dishware
Dinner plates – Souleo Provence – souleoprovencepottery.com
Salad plates – Souleo Provence – souleoprovencepottery.com
Small and large serving tray, large handle serving bowl, and deep bowl
- Souleo Provence – souleoprovencepottery.com

Glassware
Wine glasses – Crate and Barrel – crateandbarrel.com
Water glasses – Crate and Barrel – crateandbarrel.com
Silverware – World Market – worldmarket.com
Hanging lanterns - Target – target.com
Candles – Bed Bath and Beyond – bedbathandbeyond.com

Music
itunes - apple.com/itunes - Barns and Nobel – barnsandnobel.com.
Amazon - amazon.com

Accessories
Large, oval galvanized tub (Cattle feeding trough) Ace Hardware –
acehardware.com
Large, round wicker basket – World Market – worldmarket.com
Throw pillows – Home Depot – homedepot.com
Outdoor, iron rack – Wisteria – wisteria.com
Over-sized wicker chair – Pottery Barn – potterybarn.com
Towels, soap and back scrubber – Target – target.com
Burlap sacks – cut-to-fit – JoAnn Fabric – joannfarbric.com
Enamel numbers (reproduction address numbers) local antique store or
eBay – ebay.com
Gold picture frame – Hobby Lobby – hobbylobby.com
Wine tasting kit – Red Envelope – redenvelope.com
Green double lantern – local antique store or eBay – ebay.com
Green head planter – Ballard Designs – ballarddesigns.com
Large rectangular and small square wooden tray – local antique store or
eBay – ebay.com
Vintage wine basket – local antique store or eBay – ebay.com

Takeaway Gifts
Photo drink coasters – Beau-Coup – beau-coup.com

Vary it
Issue of Food and Wine, Wine Spectator or a similar magazine –
Barns and Noble – barnsandnobel.com - magazines.com or
amazon.com/magazines

Simplify it
Custom wine labels – Bottle Your Brand – bottleyourbrand.com

Items not listed belong to the homeowner who graciously allowed us
to use their home.

Formally Frightful

Invitations

    Designed cards by George Stanley

    Chandelier and bat stickers – Hobby Lobby – hobbylobby.com

Vary It

    Card stock paper – Hobby Lobby – hobbylobby.com

    Small tubular vials (or spice tubes) The Container Store –
      containerstore.com

Simplify it

    Grey card stock paper – Hobby Lobby – hobbylobby.com

    White spider webbing and small spiders – Hobby Lobby – hobbylobby.com
    or Target – target.com

Table

    Tablecloth

    Torn deluxe creepy cloth – Oriental Trading Company – orientialtrading.com

Napkins

    Black cotton – World Market – worldmarket.com

Dishware

    Dinner plates – Target – target.com

    Salad plates – Target – target.com

    Soup bowls – Target – target.com

    Large silver serving bowl – Pottery Barn –potterybarn.com

    Small mercury glass bowl – Target – target.com

    Medium glass serving bowl – Crate and Barrel – crateandbarrel.com

Glassware

    Wine glasses – Crate and Barrel – crateandbarrel.com

    Water glasses – Crate and Barrel – crateandbarrel.com

    Science beakers – Carolina Company – carolina.com

    Silverware – World Market – worldmarket.com

    Candles – Pottery Barn –potterybarn.com

    Silver candleholders - Pottery Barn –potterybarn.com

Music

    itunes - apple.com/itunes - Barns and Nobel – barnsandnobel.com.

    Amazon - amazon.com

Accessories

    Styrofoam white pumpkins – Hobby Lobby – hobbylobby.com

    Wooded glitter candelabras – Z Gallerie – zgallerie.com

    Battery operated lanterns – Oriental Trading Company – orientaltrading.com

    Black crows, white owls, and furry rats – Hobby Lobby – hobbylobby.com

    Rubber rats and rubber frogs and spiders– Wizards Chest –
      wizardscrest.com

    Wire candle tree – The Tended Thicket – thetendedthicket.com

    Large cobweb – Pottery Barn Kids – potterybarn.com

    Small plastic bones, moss, twine and faux dried leaves – Hobby Lobby –
      hobbylobby.com

    Large pre-lit wire tress – Gardin Road – gardinroad.com

    Witch 's fortune telling ball - Target – target.com

    Witch's hat and brooms – Wizard's Chest – wizardscrest.com

    Vintage dictionary – eBay – ebay.com

Takeaway Gifts

    Assorted fruit candles, woven basket and filler – World Market –
      worldmarket.com

Vary it

    Haunted history books - local bookstore or Barns and Noble –
      barnsandnobel.com

Simplify it

    Tarot Card – Barns and Noble- barnsandnoble.com or eBay – ebay.com

Items not listed belong to the homeowner who graciously allowed us
to use their home.

Birds of a Feather

Invitations

    Cream-colored card stock paper _ Hobby Lobby –hobbylobby.com

    Petite feather and red ribbon – Hobby Lobby – hobbylobby.com

Vary It

    Cream-colored card stock paper – Hobby Lobby – hobbylobby.com

    Washable finger paint, feathers and plastic eye – Hobby Lobby – hobbylobby.com

    Padded mailing envelope – Container Store – containerstore.com

Simplify it

    Cream-colored card stock paper – Hobby Lobby – hobbylobby.com

    Small bushel of straw and velvet ribbon – Hobby Lobby – hobbylobby.com

    Mailing box or padded envelope – Container Store – containerstore.com

Table

    Tablecloth

    Cream tablecloth – Bed Bath and Beyond – bedbathandbeyond.com

    Red paisley scarf – (homeowners)

    Napkins

    Pottery Barn – potterybarn.com

Dishware

    Dark bronze melamine chargers – Target – target.com

    Dinner plates – Marbleized plates – Pottery Barn – potterybarn.com

    Individual glass pedestals – Z Gallerie – zgallerie.com

    Mini tassels – Hobby Lobby – hobbylobby.com

    Salad plates and bowls – White porcelain – (homeowners)

    Small pewter tray – a local antique store or eBay – ebay.com

    Cream platter - Anthropologie – anthropologie.com

    Large soup bowl – (homeowners)

Glassware

    Wine glasses – Crystal (homeowners)

    Water glasses – Crystal (homeowners)

    Venetian style champagne flutes – City Floral – cityfloralgreenhouse.com
      or Napa Style –napastyle.com

    Silverware – faux bone – Pottery Barn – potterybarn.com

    Candlesticks- silver – Pottery Barn – potterybarn.com

    Candles – Bed Bath and Beyond – bedbathandbeyond.com

    Large feathers – Pottery Barn – potterybarn.com

    Small feathers – Hobby Lobby – hobbylobby.com

    Garden statue – a local antique store or eBay – ebay.com

    Wooded pedestals – Ballard Designs – ballarddesigns.com

    Garland – Pinecone and stick – Smith and Hawken – target.com

    Burlap sacks (hung from chairs) Container Store – containerstore.com

    Stamp, ink and feather clip (on burlap sack) – Hobby Lobby – hobbylobby.com

    Vases –Silver - Two's Company – twoscompany.com

    Moss and twig plant / candle sleeve – Pottery Barn – potterybarn.com

Music

    itunes - apple.com/itunes - Barns and Nobel – barnsandnobel.com.

    Amazon - amazon.com

Accessories

    Copper log holder – local antique store or eBay – ebay.com

    Large iron tree – eBay – ebay.com

    Gift tags, leaves and twine – Hobby Lobby – hobbylobby.com

Gift Wrap

    Burlap – cut-to-fit fabric – JoAnn Fabric – joannfabric.com

    Red, white and gray ribbon, feathers, charms and safety pins – Hobby Lobby – hobbylobby.com

Takeaway Gifts

    The book "One" – Barns and Noble – barnsandnoble.com or Amazon – amazon.com

Vary it

    Luggage tags – Container Store – containerstore.com

Simplify it

    Rum or cider seasoning – William Sonoma – williamsonoma.com

Items not listed belong to the homeowner who graciously allowed us to use their home.